# THE CHURCHES OF GOD

# THE CHURCHES OF GOD

## A TREATISE FOR THE TIMES

*Upon the Constitution, Government, Discipline, and Ministry of the Church of God and the Principles and Practice of Service in the Gospel*

*By*
G. H. LANG

Shoals, Indiana

*The Churches of God*

PUBLISHED BY KINGSLEY PRESS
PO Box 973
Shoals, IN 47581
USA

Tel. (800) 971-7985
www.kingsleypress.com
E-mail: sales@kingsleypress.com

ISBN: 978-1-937428-24-2

Copyright © 1985 by Schoettle Publishing Co., Inc.
First published by C.J. Thynne & Jarvis 1928
Revised edition published by Paternoster Press 1959
First Kingsley Press edition 2012

This first Kingsley Press edition is published under license from Schoettle Publishing Co. Inc., Haysville, North Carolina.

All rights reserved. No part of this book may be reproduced or transmitted in any form or by any means, electronic or mechanical, including photocopying, recording or by any information storage and retrieval system without written permission from the publisher, except for the inclusion of brief quotations in a review.

# Contents

    Foreword ................................................................7
1. Constitution and Order .........................................9
2. The Administrative Independence of Each Local Church .15
3. The History of Church Federation .......................23
4. Divine Reasons for Primitive Church Order ........35
5. Some Evils of Church Federation ........................43
6. Baptism ...............................................................55
7. The Lord's Supper ...............................................67
8. The Institution of The Lord's Supper ..................83
9. Ministry and Oversight .......................................95
10. Excommunication on Doctrinal Grounds .........107
11. Unanimity .........................................................115
12. The Public Ministry of Women ........................137
13. Some Aspects of Gospel Service .......................173
14. Conclusion and Appeal ....................................193
    Index ................................................................219

# Foreword

THIS treatise, first published in 1928, was revised by the author with a view to a second edition not long before his death in 1958.

A number of sections which have lost their relevance with the passage of a generation have been omitted, and others (notably the chapters on Baptism and the Lord's Supper) have been added.

It is a matter of some interest that Chapter 11, on "Unanimity," represents the author's first published work; it was originally composed in 1900 for the guidance of the church at Unity Chapel, Bristol, of which he was then pastor.

The author was an independent thinker, and therefore not all his arguments and conclusions will command general assent among Christians—not even among those with whom he was most closely associated in church fellowship—but they do set forth the principles by which he consistently lived for the last sixty years of his life. How he proved them in his own experience may be read more fully in his autobiography, *An Ordered Life*, issued by the publishers of the present volume.

Chapter 1

# Constitution and Order

THE church of God is a divine institution, conceived in the mind of God (Eph. 1),[1] instituted by the Son of God (Matt. 16:18), energized by the Spirit of God (1 Cor. 12:13). Apostles and prophets, divinely commissioned and guided, laid its foundations (Eph. 2:20); inspired writings became and remain its only standard and rule (2 Tim. 3:14–17; 1 Cor. 14:37; 2 Pet. 3:2, 15, 16; Rev. 22:18-19). Its present purpose and service in this age, and its ultimate glory and service in future ages, have been settled and revealed by God.

As in Israel there was a material temple in which God dwelt, so is the church a spiritual temple for His indwelling (Eph. 2:20–22). As not one detail of that earthly house was left to the invention or introduction of men, not even of the faithful Moses (Heb. 8:5; 1 Chron. 28:19), but all things were to be made according to the patterns shown, so it is with the living temple. Christ gave a positive assurance that His Spirit would guide the apostles into "all the truth" (John 16:13), which must include all truth concerning the church as an institution. Of this truth the New Testament is the only authoritative record. Presumption can scarcely go further than that one should alter the appointments and arrangements of another's house (Rom. 14:4; 1 Cor. 14:36).

Nor is there need, nor can there be hope, of improving upon the Lord's orderings. He knew perfectly the purposes which His church was to serve on earth, and knew fully the conditions amidst which it must work; and He instituted through His apostles the very best arrangements and methods for doing the intended work in the given conditions. To assume otherwise is to impute folly to God.

---

1 References are to the Revised Version.

It is a fallacy that conditions alter essentially, or indeed at all, in relation to the business of the church of God. God changes not; His claims upon and principles of conduct for mankind alter not; the sinfulness and rebellion of the natural man abide undiminished; and, for the purpose in view, racial and religious differences, or a local veneer of mental education or of civilization, matter nothing. The impending wrath of God is an abiding solemnity; the total inability of man to render himself acceptable to the Holy One is a changeless fact; the exact suitability of the work of our Lord Jesus Christ fully to meet the claims of God and the needs of man is an unaltered reality. That the eternal Spirit is as equal as ever to the task of convincing and regenerating the sinner is unquestionable; that faith and prayer still are the sufficient resource of the church, bringing into operation the controlling power of God, is an unimpaired certainty.

As, then, all the essential factors abide as they were in the apostolic times, the apostolic plan of church life and of Christian service will be, and has been, found to be as divinely suited to this age as to that; indeed, Scripturally speaking, it is but one age.

Only when some human purpose has been pursued have other methods been found needful. If the church, in this period of her Lord's absence from and rejection by the world, is to "uplift the masses," to control and purify the State, "to reconstruct society on the basis of brotherhood," and "to transform this modern world into a Christian society," then indeed new machinery, and other power than that of the Spirit of God, must be used, these not being purposes for which He is now on earth. But as long as Christians address themselves only to the God-appointed business of standing as witnesses to the claims of the Lord, whom the world crucified (John 15:26-27; Acts 1:8), and of gathering out from the nations a people for His name (Acts 15:14), in preparation for their serving Him at His return and in His kingdom, for so long the New Testament Church organization and the apostolic lines of service will be found entirely adequate.

For the ecclesiastical doctrine of development, by which it is held that the church has both duty and right to adapt her institutions and alter her methods to suit the times, there is neither spiritual necessity nor Scriptural authority.

An acute writer, contrasting the apostolic work with the more usual modern missionary methods, has said that "we found missions, the apostles founded churches." The distinction is sound and pregnant. The apostles founded churches, *and they founded nothing else*, because for the ends in view nothing else was required or could have been so suitable. In each place where they laboured they formed the converts into a local assembly, with elders—always elders, never *an* elder (Acts 14:23; 15:6, 23; 20:17; Phil. 1:1)—to guide, to rule, to shepherd, men qualified by the Lord and recognized by the saints (1 Cor. 16:15-16; 1 Thess. 5:12-13; 1 Tim. 5:17-19); and with deacons, appointed by the assembly (Acts 6:1-6; Phil. 1:1)—in this contrasted with the elders—to attend to the few but very important temporal affairs, and in particular to the distribution of the funds of the assembly. Apostles and evangelists went hither and thither, acknowledged and supported but not controlled by the assemblies (Acts 13:1-4; Phil. 4:10; 2 John 5-8). It was required that one about to give himself to the work of the Lord should have a good report from the brethren in assemblies where he was well known (Acts 16:2); but as they would know him sufficiently, and as the Spirit of the Lord was with them to guide, no district or other committees were created to approve or disapprove of his going forth. They were sent out at the ordering of the Lord only, and directed by the Holy Spirit (Acts 16:6, 10); and all that these did in the way of organizing was to form the disciples gathered into other such assemblies. No other organization than the local assembly appears in the New Testament, nor do we find even the germ of anything further.

All believers were to be witnesses, and could spread the gospel message as they were guided and used of the Lord (Acts 8:1; 11:19), and thus propagation was simple. The assembly was at once the nursery, home, school, training institute and hospital, where all in the Father's family were developed, and in which each was to exercise his God-given gift for the good of all. Nothing more was requisite than the due working of each several part of this body (1 Cor. 12; Eph. 4:1–16).

It is quite remarkable what a host of earnest persons miss or shun this vital feature of the apostolic service. The highest inventiveness is displayed to organize something else than local churches. These good people will toil to found every conceivable form of organization, and will compass the whole earth to secure funds to maintain these humanly devised agencies. It seems they will labour into death along these lines; in short, they will do anything conceivable except found a local church, or confine themselves to "confirming the souls of the disciples" individually, and "confirming the churches" (Acts 14:22; 15:41).

But further, should the gospel message be so blessed that churches spring up spontaneously through the testimony of evangelists or other believers, then forthwith men will arise whose great business seems to be to federate these local assemblies into Fellowships, Unions, Denominations. God, on the contrary, is working today in exactly the opposite direction, towards a return to His chosen plan as recorded in the New Testament. Groups of godly souls are leaving these federations and forming into congregations where they can be free from evil teachings and worldly practices. To encourage these to follow the New Testament only and fully were a worthy work; but without delay someone organizes a "fellowship of unattached churches," so "attaching" them one to another, a scheme which one fears will simply lead in due time to one more inter-church federation, to develop the same evils they seek to avoid.

We are in no wise challenging motives, but only noting the remarkable and regrettable fact that so many servants of the Lord seem unable to do His work according to His plan and method. With deep searchings of heart and most praiseworthy devotion to the truth numerous godly souls seceded from a great missionary society; but instead of beginning from the beginning with the New Testament and testing every practice thereby, instead of seeking to encourage the apostolic method of individual responsibility and direct faith in God in gospel service, these devout persons at once formed another similar missionary society, which may be expected in the course of time to go the same downward spiritual road as preceding societies.

And when we consider the manner of the work carried on under such auspices, naturally we find the same feature developing in the lands where they labour. There is the same disinclination to follow the apostles in forming local churches and nothing more. Thus after a century of modern missionary work, western denominationalism and new "national churches" are in much evidence in heathen lands, to the serious corruption of the work of the gospel there as everywhere.

It is evident that each local assembly was intended to be self contained. This was essential, especially considering that under ancient conditions of travel and life much and prolonged isolation was often inevitable. The church of God is verily a unity, but its unity is that of an organism rather than an organization. Each Christian was to exhibit this unity by a life of pure love towards each other believer; and the connexion of all with a local assembly afforded a corporate sphere for its manifestation.

I once met in the street a godly and beloved clergyman, a neighbour. He presently said, "I was passing your place on Sunday, and, by the by, to what denomination do you belong?" I replied, "Did you not look at the notice board as you went by?" "Yes," he said, "I did, but I could not see there anything about it." "That," I answered, "indicates to what denomination we belong." Smiling, he said, "I see. But are there no other folk who believe as you do?" "Yes," said I, "I thank God that there are very many such." "Well," he inquired, "why do you not affiliate with them?" "Can you," I asked, "give any Scripture which suggests that it is the mind of God that we should do so?" "Yes," he replied, "the passage, 'giving diligence to keep the unity of the Spirit' (Eph. 4:3)." "But what is the unity of the Spirit?" I next asked. "Well," said he—"Yes, yes; hem! well, how would *you* define it?" And I said, "First of all the unity of the Spirit is a spiritual unity, and not an external organization. You and I meet here in the street; we know and love each other as brethren in Christ; we say a few words to cheer each other on life's way; and that is one example of what I understand by keeping the unity of the Spirit."

Of this holy and heavenly unity the church was to be full. It is its chief present glory and distinction. "By this shall all men know that ye are My disciples, if ye have love one to another" (John 13:35). "See how these Christians love one another!"

Regeneration, upon repentance and faith, accompanied or followed by baptism in the Holy Spirit, afforded entrance to the church spiritually considered (John 3:3; Gal. 3:26-27; 1 Cor. 12:13; Acts 1:5; 2:4; 8:14–17; 10:44–48; 19:1–7; Eph. 1:13-14). Immersion in water was the method appointed by Christ by which one who professed to acknowledge Him as Lord was to make this confession publicly.[1]

Further, every company of saints was visibly organized, simply and almost loosely, after one type; with elders and deacons; with immersion in water as the public acceptance of the Christian standing and the public recognition of the same by others (Acts 2:41); and with partaking of the one loaf and cup as a symbol of communion with Christ and each other (1 Cor. 10:16-17). These features, together with adherence to and teaching of the same body of divinely revealed truth, "the faith once for all delivered to the saints" (Jude 3; Phil. 1:27)—for which purpose the Holy Spirit qualified some as pastors and teachers (Eph. 4:11; 1 Tim. 3:2; Acts 13:1)—sufficiently marked the Christian communities as one circle, meeting locally, but universally one spiritual body. And this oneness was further exhibited by the fact that every member was recognized as already a member of any local assembly to which he might come by reason of life's changing circumstances, no further formal reception being required (Rom. 14:1; 15:7; 16:2; 1 Cor. 16:10, 11; 3 John 5-8).

Of any scheme or form of interlocking of assemblies we see no trace. Neither racial, social, geographical, nor political groupings or divisions were to be found; indeed, any such thought was wholly alien to the mind of the Lord as touching His church.

There were "the saints in the whole of" a province (2 Cor. 1:1), "the church in" a city (1 Cor. 1:2), "the churches of Macedonia" (2 Cor. 8:1) and "of Galatia" (Gal. 1:2), that is, situated in those territories, and we read of "the church throughout all Judea and Galilee and Samaria" (Acts 9:31); but there was no church of Galatia or Judea or Macedonia, no combination of churches in a given area into the church of that area, and thus by organization and locality a body corporate, distinct from the church universal, only a part thereof.

---

1 See Chapter 6.

Chapter 2

# The Administrative Independence of Each Local Church

UPON the fact of the original, administrative independence of each Christian church let us hear some competent witnesses whose ecclesiastical position in such a highly organized and national system as the Church of England makes their testimony the more important.

Dr. Edwin Hatch, in his *Oxford Lectures on The Organisation of the Early Christian Churches*,[1] says:

> For although it is indisputable that our Lord founded a Church, *it is an unproved assumption that the Church is an aggregation of visible and organized societies* (pref. xii)... the theory upon which the public worship of the primitive Churches proceeded was that *each community was complete in itself*, and that in every act of public worship every element of the community was present (p. 79).

He indicates that the combining of churches is not apostolic by saying (pp. 170, 171):

> In the course of the second century the custom of meeting in *representative* assemblies *began* to prevail among the Christian communities... the result of the deliberation of such a conference was expressed sometimes in a resolution, sometimes in a letter addressed to other Churches.... But *so far from such letters having any binding force on other Churches, not even the resolutions of the conference were binding on a dissen-*

---

[1] Sir Robert Anderson described this as "one of the greatest theological books of the age." He remarked that "it appears to be boycotted by High Church and Low Church alike." The reason no doubt was that it shows that *no* federated Church of any complexion is apostolic or even sub-apostolic. (*The Bible and Modern Criticism*, 199, note.)

*tient minority of its members.* Cyprian,[1] in whose days these conferences first became important, and who was at the same time the most vigorous of early preachers of catholic unity—both of which circumstances would have made him a supporter of their authoritative character if such authoritative character had existed—*claims in emphatic and explicit terms an absolute independence for each community.* Within the limits of his own community a bishop has no superior but God. "To each shepherd," he writes, "a portion of the Lord's flock has been assigned, and his account must be rendered to his own Master." The fact that some bishops refused to re-admit to communion those who had committed adultery is *no argument*, he contends, *for the practice of other* bishops; nor is the fact that a number of bishops meeting in council had agreed to admit the lapsed a reason why a bishop who thought otherwise should admit them against his will.[2]

Now, seeing that the marked set of the times was away from independence towards church federation, this "absolute independence" must have been a survival of, not a departure from, the apostolic conditions; and it is specially to be observed that the vital matters of reception to and exclusion from the church are explicitly reserved for settlement in each church, and that the practice of one church has no binding force upon another church. . . . The *paroikia*[3] of early days was neither a parish nor a diocese, but the community of Christians living within a city or district, regarded in relation to the non-Christian population which surrounded it. Every such community seems to have had a complete organisation, and *there is no trace of the dependence of any one community upon any other.*

And so Dr. F. J. A. Hort, in his Cambridge Lectures, *The Christian Ecclesia*, on "The Early History and Early Conceptions of the Ecclesia," speaking of the *dogma* (Greek), the "decree" of the apostles and the church at Jerusalem given in Acts 15, says (pp. 82, 83):

> The New Testament is not poor of words expressive of command, *entellomai, epitasso, prostasso, diatasso, diastellomai*. . . and their derivatives, to say nothing of *keleuo* and *parangello*: yet none of them is used. . . . *The independence of the Ecclesia of Antioch had to be respected*, and yet

---

1 Bishop of Carthage, N. Africa, martyred A.D. 258.
2 Before this the disastrous departure had taken place of a single "bishop" superseding the apostolic plurality of elders in the rule of the local church.
3 *Paroikia*, sojourners; used in Acts 13: 17; 1 Pet. 1: 17.

not in such a way as to encourage disregard either of the great mother Ecclesia, or of the Lord's own Apostles, or of the unity of the whole Christian body. Accordingly we do not find a word of a hint that the Antiochians would have done better to get sanction from Jerusalem before plunging into such grave responsibilities [that is, of settling for themselves a matter *thoroughly fundamental to the gospel*]. But along with the cordial concurrence in the release of Gentile converts from legal requirements there goes a strong expression of opinion, more than advice and less than a command, respecting certain salutary restraints. A certain authority is thus implicitly claimed. *There is no evidence that it was more than a moral authority*, but that did not make it less real.

It is of the utmost possible importance to remember that the then Jerusalem church having passed away, no other church, not even the succeeding generation in that same church, could possibly occupy the same position of being the original Christian community. Nor was the prestige of being such as great as may easily be imagined, for the most momentous fact concerning it was its enduement with the Holy Spirit at Pentecost, and in that enduement every other church shared equally, thus elevating all churches to the one level of spiritual privilege and possibilities. Also, the apostles and first elders having died, no other persons could possibly take their place as having received doctrinal communications and apostolic commission direct from the Lord Jesus in the days of His flesh. Hence, the only way by which Christians since have been able to follow the example of the church at Antioch and to "go up to Jerusalem unto the apostles and elders" about any question, is to consult their writings. By so doing we obtain exactly the decisions which they gave, and would still give, for men divinely inspired will not hold variable opinions. The absolutely irreconcilable controversy is between, on the one hand, the sufficiency and finality of Holy Scripture, and, on the other hand, either the figment of apostolic succession, and the falsehood of there being an unwritten apostolic tradition, or the assertion of the continuous inspiration of the Spirit being granted. This last is denied by the Lord's promise that the apostles should be taught all things, be guided into all the truth, and be taught the things of even the distant future (John 15:26; 16:13). This having been duly fulfilled, there necessarily can be no more truth that God has to reveal to men, nor in fact, has there been any subsequent utterance that the spiritual will for a moment rank with Holy Scripture.

The common declaration of nearly all communities that aim at opposing modernism is signally, crucially faulty. The usual assertion is that Holy Scripture is the supreme authority, which allows that creeds, synods, councils, prayer books, confessions have some authority, though lesser. The only true and safe position is that the Word of God is the sole authority—the alternatives being, as above, tradition or continuous inspiration, and these may as well vest in the Pope of Rome as in anybody else.

Again, Dr. Hort, after detailing by what moral considerations the spiritual oneness of the churches was to be maintained, says:

> By itself each of these details may seem trivial enough; but together they help to show how *St. Paul's recognition of the individual responsibility and substantial independence of single city Ecclesiæ* was brought into harmony with his sense of the unity of the body of Christ, as a whole, by this watchful care to seize every opportunity of kindling and keeping alive in each society a consciousness of its share in the life of the great Ecclesia of God (122).

So that the "unity of the body" was of a spiritual nature only, maintained by moral measures, and was not a visible inter-church organization maintained by ecclesiastical measures. This is fundamental and vital to the true working of the church of God. For administrative purposes each assembly was autonomous, that is, self-governed.

Dr. Hort declares this explicitly in the following comments on the Epistle to the Ephesians:

> ... it is important to notice that *not a word in the Epistle exhibits the one Ecclesia as made up of many Ecclesiæ*. To each local Ecclesia St. Paul has ascribed a corresponding unity of its own; each is a body of Christ and a sanctuary of God: but *there is no grouping of them into partial wholes*—[that is, into a church of a province or a country]—or into one great whole [a universal organisation]. *The members which make up the One Ecclesia are not communities, but individual men.* The One Ecclesia includes all members of all partial Ecclesiæ; but its relations to them all are direct, not mediate [that is, the believer is a member of the church universal, the body of Christ, by virtue of his relation to Christ, by faith, through the indwelling Spirit, not by virtue of membership in a local

## The Administrative Independence of Each Local Church

church.] It is true that, as we have seen, St. Paul anxiously promoted friendly intercourse and sympathy between the scattered Ecclesiæ; but *the unity of the universal Ecclesia as he contemplated it does not belong to this region*: it is a truth of theology and of religion, *not a fact of what we call Ecclesiastical politics* (168).[1]

These university historians and theologians are cited, not only for the truth of their interpretation of the New Testament, but also that it may be seen that the administrative independence of each assembly is not a peculiar notion of a few unscholarly folk, but has been taught by men of the highest scholarship, whose own ecclesiastical position was denied any basis in the Word of God by their honest dealing with the New Testament. By faithful exegesis they reached the truth indicated symbolically by the churches being shown as seven separate lamp stands (Rev. 1:12), in contrast to Israel, which, being a visible national unity, had in its temple but a single lamp stand with seven branches conjoined.

Two other unlikely testimonies to the same effect may be cited.

Speaking at the Old Catholic Congress, Berne, 1925, upon Anglican and Old Catholic Problems, the Rev. J. A. F. Ozanne, Rector of St. Pierre du Bois, Guernsey, said:

> ... if one gazes back through the vista of the ages it is of more than passing interest to observe the state of Christendom during the fifth and sixth centuries. One notes that at that period Catholic Christendom was divided into three groups, that is to say, the church of the East, whose centre was at Constantinople; the church of the West, whose centre was at Rome; and the church of the North-west, whose centre was in Ireland. The churches of the East and of the North-west had this in common, namely, each church was, as it were, composed of a group or body of local churches, each local church autonomous in itself but in intercommunion with the others....
>
> One submits that these principles of autonomy and intercommunion are not only of apostolic origin but that their observance persisted throughout the sub-apostolic age and only waned as the power of the papacy increased. (From the official Congress Report, 51, 53.)

---

1  The italics in all these quotations are mine.

Cardinal Newman's *History of My Religious Opinions*, in his *Apologia*, has this significant passage. Writing in 1864 of his Oxford studies, and of his opinions and writings in 1839, six years before he joined the Church of Rome, he says (ch. V):

> I contended that the Roman idea of Catholicity was not ancient and apostolic. It was, in my judgment, at the utmost only natural, becoming, expedient, that the whole of Christendom should be united in one visible body; while such a unity might be, on the other hand, a mere heartless and political combination. For myself, I held with the Anglican divines, that, in the Primitive Church, there was a very real mutual independence between its separate parts, though, from a dictate of charity, there was in fact a close union between them. I considered that each see and diocese might be compared to a crystal, and that each was similar to the rest, and that the sum total of them all was only a collection of crystals. The unity of the Church lay, not in its being a polity, but in its being a family, a race, coming down by apostolic descent from its first founders and bishops. And I considered this truth brought out, beyond the possibility of dispute, in the Epistles of St. Ignatius, in which the bishop is represented as the one supreme authority in the Church, that is, in his own place, with no one above him, except as, for the sake of ecclesiastical order and expedience, arrangements had been made by which one was put over or under another.

So that even in sub-apostolic times there was no visible universal Christian Church, and how much less in the days of the apostles. In the period of which Newman speaks, that of the Primitive (not Apostolic) Church, change and corruption had set in strongly. The dominance of the local church by a single bishop, and the combining of several local churches into a see or diocese under a single bishop, is indicated by him. Thus no appeal to church fathers or councils can lead to any certain knowledge of the mind of God for His church. They can only show us the facts and opinions of their times.

The whole ruinous controversy in the Church of England initiated by Newman turns largely upon the question whether Romanism or Anglicanism represents today the original, visible, universal (catholic) church, outside of which (they say) man cannot be saved. This whole controversy, and many such preceding it, and more, it is to be feared, to follow, never would have defiled the church of God with the din and dust of battle if the apostolic separateness of each local church had continued. Controversy on this point between such church corporations is as if two negroes should contend as to which of them represents the original white race of mankind.

When it is asked by what means, in spite of the known fact of the apostolic distinctness of churches, it is sought to justify the existence of visible church corporations, the answer is by the doctrine of Development. By this specious plea any man or any system can justify any desired reversal of New Testament principle and practice. Newman himself was finally carried by it to Rome. He says: "All this time I was hard at my essay on Doctrinal Development. As I advanced my view so cleared that instead of speaking any more of the 'Roman Catholics,' I boldly called them 'Catholics.' Before I got to the end I resolved to be received" (that is, into the Roman Church).

There is no safe standing save in a *thorough* and *practical* submission to Holy Scripture as the ONLY authoritative utterance of the will of God today; which means denying *authority* to *any* other statement, Protestant equally with others. In this matter the Church of England is faulty. As to what is necessary to salvation it indeed makes Holy Scripture the only authority (Article VI), but as to church rites, ceremonies and traditions, it puts these definitely upon the basis that man has *authority* therein, so long as he ordains nothing actually contrary to the Word of God. Thus these may rightly be increased, varied, or abolished by any particular or national church, leading to endless variety and controversy. In these matters it refuses any private liberty, thus going so far as to attach legislative and penal authority to human rules, almost inviting schism by intolerance (Articles XX and XXXIV). The result in theory is that in church order and worship human tradition and preference have equal authority with Holy Scripture, while in practice they displace it. Might not the Son of God say: "But in vain do they worship Me, teaching as their teachings the precepts of men"? (Matt. 15:9).

Chapter 3

# The History of Church Federation

SINCE Dr. Hatch was an ecclesiastical historian of acknowledged accuracy, it will be profitable to give his account of the process by which the churches degenerated from their original apostolic independence into the vast confederation which, in due time, persecuted the true saints of God. We can thereby discern how utterly worldly were the influences and considerations that operated, and how complete and withering was the spiritual bondage that enslaved the church. Herein is illumination and warning for ourselves as churches and individuals.

Speaking further of those representative assemblies which only began, be it well remembered, *after* the apostles had died, and which therefore, by this fact alone, are unwarranted and suspect for such as hold to the finality of the Book of God, Dr. Hatch continues (pp. 170–173):[1]

> In the course of the second century the custom of meeting in representative assemblies began to prevail among the Christian communities. There were points of practice—for example, the keeping of Easter—on which it was desirable to adopt a common line of action: there were questions as to Christian teaching—for example, those which grew out of Montanism—on which individual Churches were divided, and on which they consequently desired to consult with their neighbours: there were questions of discipline which affected more than one community—especially the question, which for a time assumed a great importance, as to the terms upon which those who had renounced Christianity under pressure of persecution should be received back again.

---

1 A few single words, marked with an asterisk, are italicized by Dr. Hatch; other italics are mine. I have inserted in brackets a few dates, and have added one or two explanatory notes.

*At first these assemblies were more or less informal.* Some prominent and influential bishop invited a few neighbouring communities to confer with his own: the result of the deliberations of such a conference was expressed sometimes in a resolution, sometimes in a letter addressed to other Churches. It was the rule for such letters to be received with respect: for the sense of brotherhood was strong, and the causes of alienation were few. *But so far from such letters having any binding force on other Churches, not even the resolutions of the conference were binding on a dissentient minority of its members.* Cyprian (martyred A.D. 258), in whose days these conferences first became important, and who was at the same time the most vigorous of early preachers of catholic unity—both of which circumstances would have made him a supporter of their authoritative character if such authoritative character had existed—*claims in emphatic and explicit terms an absolute independence for each community.* Within the limits of his own community a bishop has no superior but God. "To each shepherd," he writes, "a portion of the Lord's flock has been assigned, and his account must be rendered to his own Master." The fact that some bishops refused to re-admit to communion those who had committed adultery is no argument, he contends, for the practice of other bishops; nor is the fact that a number of bishops meeting in council had agreed to admit the lapsed a reason why a bishop who thought otherwise should admit them against his will.

*But no sooner had Christianity been recognized by the State* (A.D. 313) *than such conferences tended to multiply, to become not occasional but ordinary, and to pass resolutions which were regarded as binding upon the Churches within the district from which representatives had come, and the acceptance of which was regarded as a condition of intercommunion with the Churches of other provinces.* There were strong reasons of imperial policy for fostering this tendency. It was clearly advisable that the institutions to which a new status had been given should be homogeneous. It was clearly contrary to public policy that not only status but also funds should be given to a number of communities which had no other principle of cohesion than that of a *more or less undefined unity of belief.* Consequently, when the vexed question of the ordination of Cæcilian threatened to divide the African Churches, Constantine summoned all the bishops of Christendom—each with representative presbyters from his Church—to a conference or council at Arles (A.D. 314). It was an obvious condition of such a conference that its decisions should be binding on those who so far took part in it as to subscribe to its acts.

And *since those who did so take part in it were the most important bishops in Christendom, a \*confederation was thereby established; which placed dissentients at a great disadvantage.* The main points of agreement which were arrived at in this conference have constituted the basis of the confederation of Christian Churches ever since. It was resolved that *those who had been appointed to minister in any place should remain in that place* and not wander from one place to another; that a deacon should not offer the Eucharistic sacrifice; that bishops should be appointed ordinarily by eight, but at least by three bishops, and that one bishop should not have the right of appointing another by himself alone.

Henceforward there were two kinds of meetings or councils. For matters which affected the whole body of Christian Churches there were general assemblies of the bishops and other representative members of all the Churches of the world: for minor matters, such as a controversy between one Church and another, or between the majority of the members of a Church and one of its officers, there were provincial assemblies. These latter were held upon a strictly local basis; *they followed the lines of the civil assemblies* whose ordinary designation they appropriated. They followed them also in meeting in the metropolis of the province. The bishop of that metropolis was their ordinary president; in this respect there was a difference between the civil and the ecclesiastical assemblies, for in the former the president was elected from year to year. *In this way the bishop of the metropolis came to have a pre-eminence over the other bishops of a province.* By a natural process, just as the vote and sanction of a bishop had become necessary to the validity of the election of a presbyter, so the vote and sanction of a metropolitan became necessary to the validity of the election of a bishop. In time a further advance was made. Just as civil provinces were grouped into dioceses, and the governors of a "province" were subordinated to the governor of a "diocese," so a gradation was recognized between the bishop of the chief city of a province and the bishop of the chief city of a diocese. *In both cases the civil names were retained*: the former were called metropolitans, the latter exarchs or patriarchs.

*It was by these gradual steps that the Christian Churches passed from their original state of independence into a great confederation.*

It is important to observe not only the closeness with which that confederation followed the lines of the imperial government, but also the wholly *\*voluntary* nature of the process by which it was formed. There was no attempt at coercion. The cause which operated to change its voluntary character is one which flows from the very nature of association, and which existed in the individual communities before confederation began. For it is of the essence of an association that it should have power to frame regulations, not only for the admission, but also for the exclusion, of its members. In the Christian as in the Jewish communities an offending member was liable to be expelled. But the utility of excommunication as a deterrent in the primitive Churches had been weakened by the fact that *its operation did not necessarily extend beyond the particular Church of which a man had been a member*. If he had been expelled for a moral offence, no doubt the causes which led to his expulsion by one community would prevent his reception into another. But where the ground of expulsion had been *the holding of peculiar opinions*, or the breach of a local by-law, it might be possible to find some other community which would ignore the one or condone the other. *When the Churches* of a province, and still more when the Churches of the greater part of the Empire, *were linked together by the ties of a confederation*, meeting in common assembly, and agreeing upon a common plan of action, *exclusion by a single Church came to mean exclusion from all the confederated Churches*. This rule was recognized by the Council of Nicæa (A.D. 325), which at the same time made provision against an arbitrary exercise of the power of excommunication. But as no penalty was attached to a violation of the rule, it was probably disregarded, *for the Council of Antioch*, about twenty years later, found it necessary *to enact that a Church officer who admitted to communion one whom another Church had excluded should himself be cut off from communion*. This later form of the enactment was repeated in the code which is known as the Apostolic Canons (fifth century); and ultimately became the standing rule in both East and West. The observance of the rule was fenced round by the *further enactment that no one should be received into another Church without a letter from the bishop of the Church to which he belonged. In primitive days* a Christian who travelled, or who changed his residence from one town to another, *was received into communion with but little question*: but the interests of social order, no less than of faith, compelled a change. *Henceforth, anyone who was formally expelled from his Church was cut off also from all the Churches of the association.* Nor was he cut off only from public worship and from participation in the Church offerings. He was denied social intercourse with those who remained faithful: the rigorous command of the Apostle was applied to him, "with such an one no not to eat."

Now as long as Christians were in a great minority, a man might be cut off from social intercourse with them without sustaining any serious social loss. But when Christians began to be a majority in all the great centres of population, *excommunication became* a real deterrent, and consequently *a powerful instrument in the hands of those who were desirous of tightening the bonds of association.*

And yet it is doubtful whether it would have been a sufficiently powerful instrument to produce the uniformity which ultimately prevailed, *if the State had not interfered.* The associated Churches might have been strong enough to crush isolated individuals, but it may be questioned whether they could have held their ground, without State interference, against whole Churches or a combination of Churches. It might happen that not an individual but a whole community—bishops, presbyters, deacons, and people—declined to accept the resolutions of a provincial council, and that they were consequently cut off from the association. There was nothing to prevent their continuing to be and to do what they had been and done before. Even before Christianity had been recognized by the State, when Paul of Samosata refused to give up possession of the church buildings at Antioch, and claimed still to be the bishop of the Church, there were no means of ejecting him except that of an appeal to the Emperor Aurelian. A number of such Churches might join together and form a rival association. In one important case this was actually done. A number of Churches in Africa held that the associated Churches were too lax in their terms of communion. How far they were right in the particular points which they urged cannot now be told. But the contention was for purity. The seceding Churches were rigorists. Their soundness in the faith was unquestionable. They resolved to meet together as a separate confederation, the basis of which should be a greater purity of life; and *but for the interference of the State* they might have lasted as a separate confederation to the present day. The interference of the State was not so much a favour shown to the bishops who asked for it as a necessary continuation of the policy which Constantine had begun. For as, on the one hand, it was necessary to draw a strict line of demarcation round the persons by whom the privileges of Christians could be claimed, so, on the other hand, it was impossible for the State to assume the office of determining for itself what was and what was not Christian doctrine. *It was enough for the State that a great confederation of Christian societies existed. With that confederation, and it alone, the State found it expedient to deal.* The terms of membership of the confederation must be left to the confederation itself. *Those who were within it, and those only, were Christians and entitled to the privileges of Christians.*

The interposition of the State took three forms:

(1) The State recognized the *decisions of Councils*—i.e. the resolutions of the representative assemblies of the associated Churches—as to questions of doctrine.

(2) The State recognized the validity of sentences of deposition from office, or exclusion from membership of a Church, by a person or body within the Church whose competence was admitted by the associated Churches.

(3) The State discouraged and ultimately prohibited the formation of new associations outside the general confederation. "Let all heresies," says a law of Gratian and Valentinian (A.D. 376), "for ever hold their peace; *if anyone entertains an opinion which the Church has condemned, let him keep it to himself and not communicate it to another.*"

In this way it was that, *by the help of the State*, the Christian Churches were *consolidated into a great confederation*. Whatever weakness there was in the bond of a common faith was compensated for by the strength of *civil coercion*. But that civil coercion was not long needed. For the Church outlived the power which had welded it together. As the forces of the Empire became less and less, the forces of the Church became more and more. The Churches preserved that which had been from the first the secret of Imperial strength. For underneath the Empire which changed and passed, beneath the shifting pageantry of Emperors who moved across the stage and were seen no more, was the abiding empire of law and administration—which changed only as the deep sea changes beneath the wind-swept waves. That inner empire was continued in the Christian Churches. In the years of transition from the ancient to the modern world, when all civilized society seemed to be disintegrated, the confederation of the Christian Churches, by the very fact of its existence *upon the old imperial lines*, was not only the most powerful, but the *\*only* powerful organization in the civilized world. It was so vast, and so powerful, that it seemed to be, and there were few to question its being, the visible realization of that Kingdom of God which our Lord Himself had preached—of that "Church" which He had purchased with His own blood. There seemed to loom out in all its grandeur before the eyes of men the vision of a vast empire, of which, as of the ancient kingdom of David or of Solomon, the boundaries could be told and the members enumerated. The metaphors in which the Jewish Rabbis had spoken of the ancient Israel, and the metaphors which had been consecrated by inspired writers to the service of the new Israel, were applied to it. This confederation, and no other, was the "city of God"; this, and no other, was the "body of Christ"; this, and no other, was the "Holy Catholic Church." In it were fulfilled the ancient types. It was the Paradise in which the regenerated souls of the new creation might walk, as Adam walked, and eat without the threatening of a curse the fruit of the tree of knowledge. It was the ark of Noah, floating with its rescued multitude of holy souls over the moving waters of this world's troubled sea. It was Solomon's temple whose golden roofs glistened with a divine splendour through the dark world's mists and storms, and whose courts were thronged with the new priests and people of God holding sacred converse, and offering spiritual sacrifices upon its altars. It was the new Jerusalem into which "the sons of them that had afflicted her" came bending, and whose "sun could no more go down." It was the "fenced garden" of Solomon's Song, and in its midst was a well of living water, of which all who drank were healed of sin. It was like the widow of Sarepta, whose cruse of oil never failed. It was like the Queen of Sheba, always gathering some new knowledge, and marvelling at some new wonder, among the treasures of the distant Lord. There was hardly a hero of Hebrew story whose life did not seem to prefigure the fortunes and the oneness and the glory of *this vast organized aggregate of believing souls.*

It is impossible not to sympathize with the poetry and with the hope.

But if we look more closely at the assumption upon which all this is founded—the assumption that the metaphors in which the Church of Christ is described in Scripture are applicable only to *this confederation which the State had recognized and consolidated*, that whatever is predicated in the New Testament of the Church of Christ is predicated of it, and it only, that this confederation, and no other, is the Church of Christ in its visible and earthly form—*we shall find that assumption attended with difficulties which do not readily admit of solution.*

(1) In the first place, there is no proof that the confederation was ever complete in the sense of embracing all the communities to which by common consent the name Christian was in its fullest sense applicable. For the most part the *Christian Churches associated themselves together upon the lines of the Roman Empire*: and, so far, just as there were gradations of dioceses, provinces, and municipalities, in the one, so there

were gradations of esarchs or patriarchs, metropolitans, and bishops in the other. But some Churches remained independent. They were not subordinate to any other Church. Their bishops had no superior. They were what the *Notitiae, or *lists of orthodox* Churches, call *autokephaloi*.[1] They were in the position which Cyprian had in earlier times asserted to be the true position of all bishops: their responsibility was to God alone.

(2) In the second place, there is no proof that the terms of confederation were ever settled. The fact that the State did not tolerate any Churches which were not recognized by the confederation is not pertinent to the purely ecclesiastical question. There is no proof that it was not possible for any Church to refuse to admit to communion the members of other Churches, with as little formality as it had accepted them. There is no proof that intercommunion ever changed its original character of a voluntary contract—a corollary of the goodwill and amity which one Christian community should have towards another—so as to become an indissoluble bond. *It would be a strong assertion to say that God is always on the side of the majority*; and that, when the confederation was once formed, whatever the majority of its members resolved upon was binding *de jure divino*[2] upon the minority. But this is the only tenable position if it be asserted, as it sometimes is asserted, that individual Churches which at any one time sent deputies to the general council of the confederation, or admitted an appeal to such an assembly, or admitted the other constituent members of such an assembly to Church privileges, thereby forfeited for all time to come their original right to independent action.

(3) In the third place, *there is no proof that the words of Holy Scripture in which the unity of the Church is expressed or implied refer exclusively, or at all, to unity of organization*. There is, on the other hand, clear proof that they were in early times applied to another kind of unity.

There have been in fact three forms which the conception of unity has taken.

*In the earliest period the basis of Christian fellowship was a changed life*—"repentance toward God and faith toward our Lord Jesus Christ." It was the unity of a common relation to a common ideal and a common hope. The contention of those who looked upon Christians as a whole was that they were "not under the law but under grace"—that

---

1 Lit., self-headed; i.e. with no ruler *external* to the local church.
2 i.e., as a divine law.

they were, as one of the earliest Christian writings phrases it, a *triton genos*,[1] neither Jews nor Gentiles, but a class apart. The word "Church" is used for the aggregate of Christians, "the general assembly of the firstborn"; *but the hypothesis of its use for that aggregate conceived as a mass of organizations seems to be excluded by its having been said to have existed before the world*, and to have been "manifested in the body of Christ."

In the second period, the idea of *definite belief* as a basis of union dominated over that of *a holy life*. The meshes of the net were found to be too wide. The simple creed of primitive days tended to evaporate into the mists of a speculative theology. It became necessary to define more closely the circle of admissible beliefs. The contention of those who looked upon Christians as a whole was that they were held together by their possession of a true, and the only true, *tradition of Christian teaching*. "There is one body of Christ," says Origen (died about A.D. 254), "but it has many members; and those members are individual believers." Not until the dispute between Cyprian and Novatian (A.D. 250) does the question appear to have been raised whether those who held the Catholic faith were bound to be members of particular associations, or whether they had the right to form associations for themselves.

In the third period, insistence on Catholic faith had led to the *insistence on Catholic order*—for without order dogma has no guarantee of permanence. Consequently *the idea of unity of organization was superimposed upon that of unity of belief. It was held not to be enough for a man to be living a good life, and to hold the Catholic faith*, and to belong to a Christian association: *that association must be part of a larger confederation*, and the *sum of such confederations* constituted the Catholic Church.

This last is the form which the conception of unity took *in the fourth century*, and which to a great extent has been permanent ever since.

But both in the fourth century, and, afterwards, it did not gain its position of dominance without a struggle. The same difficulty presented itself in early times which has presented itself again and again in modern times. How can an organization be said to be identical with the Church of Christ when some of both its members and its officers are in reality living unholy lives? The difficulty first took form in the time of Cyprian, when the Puritan party in the Church of Rome declined to recognize the election of Cornelius. It was renewed with a longer and more important struggle in the fourth century by the great section of the African Churches of which I have already spo-

---

1 i.e., a third race.

ken, and who were known as Donatists.[1] "Above all things," said the Donatists, "the Church of Christ should be pure, and we defend its purity." Their opponents, chiefly St. Augustine, pointed to the parable of the wheat and the tares. "The field is the world," they said, "and the good and the bad grow together until the harvest." "The field is the *world*," replied the Donatists, "and not the Church: it is in the world and not in the Church that the good and the bad are to grow together." "*Your* Catholic Church," they said to their opponents, "is a *geographical* expression: it means *the union of so many societies in so many provinces* or in so many *nations*: *our* Catholic Church is the union of all those who are Christians in deed as well as in word: it depends not upon intercommunion, but upon the observance of all the divine commands and Sacraments: it is perfect, and it is immaculate."

The Donatists were crushed: but they were *crushed by the State*. They had *resisted State interference*: *Quid Imperatori cum ecclesia?*[2] they asked. But the Catholic party had already begun its invocation of the secular power; and the *secular power made ecclesiastical puritanism a capital crime*.

The fame of the great theologian who, with somewhat less of Christian charity than might have been expected from so good a man, opposed the Donatists, and the fact that as a matter of history they ultimately passed out of existence, have caused the name of schism which was given by their opponents to their movement to be unquestioned by most historians. But though they were crushed the question which they raised was not thereby solved—At what point did voluntary intercommunion become an indissoluble bond? In other words, assuming that, in the opinion of a Church or a group of Churches, the dominant majority of an association to which that Church or group of Churches has hitherto been attached are lax in discipline or unsound in faith, do the dissentients cease to be Catholic, or cease to be Christian, when they decline any longer to be bound by the resolutions of the association?

And there are some no doubt who will think that even this is but part of a larger question, and that *the real point at issue is not so much the terms* of association as its *necessity*. There are some who will look back with lingering eyes at *that earlier time in which there was no formal association of Churches*, but only what Tertullian calls the "communication of peace, the appellation of brotherhood, the token of hospitality, and the tradition of a single creed." There are some who will think that the effect of

---

1 See F. F. Bruce, *The Spreading Flame*, pp. 296 ff., 337 f.
2 i.e., What has the Emperor to do with the Church?

the enormous power which the Roman Empire in the first instance, and the fall of the Roman Empire in the second instance, gave to the association has been to exaggerate its importance, and to make men forget that there is a deeper unity than that of external form.

For the true communion of Christian men—the "communion of saints" upon which all Churches are built—is not the common performance of external acts, but a communion of soul with soul and of the soul with Christ. It is a consequence of the nature which God has given us that an external organization should help our communion with one another: it is a consequence both of our two-fold nature, and of Christ's appointment that external acts should help our communion with Him. But subtler, deeper, diviner, than anything of which external things can be either the symbol or the bond, is that inner reality of essence of union—that interpenetrating community of thought and character—which St. Paul speaks of as the "unity of the Spirit," and which in the sublimest of sublime books, in the most sacred of sacred words, is likened to the oneness of the Son with the Father, and of the Father with the Son.

Chapter 4

# Divine Reasons for Primitive Church Order

EXTERNAL and inter-church organization, therefore, was conspicuously absent from the apostolic churches.

It is remarkable to what extent this indefiniteness of outward ordering was carried. It is specially observable in the sphere of public worship. Believers assembled when and where they found suitable. The first day of the week, as connected with the Lord's resurrection, appears to have been preferred (Acts 20:7), but any hour and any place were proper. Houses or catacombs were equally sanctified. And when they had gathered, no visible leader was in evidence, nor was a pre-arranged programme followed. Two or even three prophets might address the assembly; psalms, prayers, and other exercises were introduced spontaneously (1 Cor. 14).

Great emphasis is laid on this as being the divine intention by the fact that upon gross disorders arising, and the gatherings becoming unseemly and unprofitable (1 Cor. 11, 14), the apostle by no means suggests any other form of service, but only lays down general principles, the application of which would prevent disorder and promote edification, the method of worship continuing essentially as before. There was indeed a duty to restrain vain and deceitful talking (1 Tim. 1:3; Titus 1:10–16); but there was no legislative or coercive power; the authority of the elders was purely moral; how then was it to be maintained and enforced? Let the question be pondered and the New Testament be scrutinized, and much will then come to light as to the proper spirit and method and control of the church of God (Matt. 18:18; Acts 5:1–11; 1 Cor. 5:3–5; 1 Tim. 4:11, 12; 5:20, etc.).

All this is highly noteworthy, because it is unusual and unpromising. Surely so inarticulate a society will suffer speedy disintegration.

So flimsy a structure will scarcely support its own weight, and still less will it withstand the strain of outward tempests. What else but disorders can be expected in public assemblies in which apparently every man may do what is right in his own eyes?

And yet we say that the church is a divinely ordered institution, and that very plainly these are methods and features that marked it in its earliest and palmiest days. Then upon what principles did the Head of the church proceed? and why did He ordain such conditions?

The answer is not difficult to discover, and is found in four main considerations.

I. Universality. The church is a society to be gathered out from "all the world," and is to include "men of every tribe and tongue and people and nation" (Mark 16:15; Rev. 5:9-10). Therefore its construction and methods must be easily capable of universal application. Methods and forms which have only local or racial or class suitability are contrary to the genius and the need of the church. The simple apostolic institutions have been found as workable today as in the first century, amongst converted savages and cultured Europeans, for every race and in every country. Of no other form of organization can this be unreservedly said.

Christendom, upon becoming the State religion, modelled its institutions in the elaborate and rigid iron mould of the Roman Empire. From this plan and type Western Christianity has seldom wholly escaped, not even in the Reformed Churches; much of the weakness of modern missionary work is to be traced to the hopeless and unapostolic attempt to impose this worldly, western, artificial, imperial, not to say hierarchical and sacerdotal, organization upon communities to which it is essentially foreign and necessarily irksome. If we will force loosely robed Easterners and scarcely dressed aborigines to don stiff Western clothes, we must long expect them to look ungainly and walk awkwardly. When Christ's Davids of today have boldly put off this Saul's armour, and have returned to the unarmed simplicity of apostolic slings and stones, they have seen again and again that Jehovah of hosts is with His people to give victory, liberty, and peace.

The principle of universality applies to many questions, e.g. church discipline. Believers have often been excommunicated for divergence of doctrine. How far does the Word of God justify this? We shall discuss this question more fully in chapter 10, but, for the moment let the rule of universality be applied. Converts from paganism or Islam constantly bring over into their converted life many wholly erroneous notions, and it is oft-times long ere these are banished from their minds. If discipline were exercised until those only were left who were presumed not to differ from any orthodox dogma the most alarming and cruel havoc would be made in the assemblies in mission spheres.

For ourselves we hope that we are wholly and strenuously orthodox on all fundamental doctrines; it is our desire to "contend earnestly for the faith," nor would we countenance the teaching of error in the assemblies; here it is only a question of what is the Scriptural attitude towards those who do differ in belief, while true to the Lord Jesus as the Son of God and the only Redeemer. It seems to us that any rule which was not applied in apostolic times and assemblies, and which could not be applied profitably in all assemblies, is not warranted in any assembly.

To this rule of universality the Apostle refers in 1 Corinthians 7:17 and 11:16, applying it to aid the settlement of two vexed questions; and again in ch. 14:33, where the Nestlé Greek text puts the period after "peace": "God is not the author of confusion but of peace," and then commences a new sentence: "As in all the assemblies of the saints, let your women keep silence in the assemblies, etc." (Upon this last passage see chapter 12).

II. EXPANSION. A second reason for the primitive type of church life was that the Lord and the apostles contemplated the rapid dissemination of the gospel and expansion of the church; and this was seen. Diffusion, not concentration, is the law of Christian activity. "GO" is our Master's key word as to method (Matt. 10:5-7; 28:19). The church was to be a mobile force. Such a force dispenses with all possible *impedimenta*. Complex machinery takes much time to construct and erect; it is long before it can be in running order. This forbids rapid extension, and speedy removal. The work in hand needed a form of institution which could be quickly planted, would rapidly take root, and from the first flourish in every soil and clime. The simplicity of the apostolic assembly met this necessity. Forms of church life which converts can only slowly and dimly comprehend, which take long to institute, and remain to the end cumbersome and complicated, are neither suitable nor Scriptural.

III. PERSECUTION. Statesmen have ever to bear in mind the possibility of war, and to order the State accordingly, even in times of peace. Similarly, the Lord knew that His church must be so constructed as best to endure the severe strain of extended periods of persecution.

An interesting hint of this is the very small place that is given in the epistles to singing, which is in very marked contrast to the general modern Western practice. In the worship of Israel, settled in their land and prosperous, singing had a large and noble sphere, as indeed it has in the heavenly regions (Heb. 2:12; Psa. 22:22; Rom. 15:9; Psa. 18:49). In the Epistles there are but three brief references to singing in the assembly (1 Cor. 14:15; Eph. 5:19; Col. 3:16), and one to private singing (Jas. 5:13); while in the whole history of the apostolic days and churches there is but one reference to this exercise, that to Paul and Silas singing in prison (Acts 16:25). Its use as an "attraction" is not of the Lord or His ways, but it is certainly allowable as a means of edification. Yet the ease with which persecutors could thereby trace the place of meeting obviously often rendered it an inadvisable exercise. It should not be thought indispensable, nor be given primary place.

The extreme simplicity of assembly organization was admirably suited to periods of oppression. Fearless elders could persevere in tending the sheep, and devoted deacons in caring for the poor. Assembly worship could proceed, and the holy ordinances be observed, wherever two or three could meet in His name. This machine could keep running when an elaborate mechanism would collapse. The forest dweller hides till the cruel raider has passed, and then easily replaces his simple tools and returns to his simple life, whereas the highly complex and artificial affairs of civilization are long in recovering from war. The more imposing the edifice the more easily it is found by the gunner. The more obvious and obtrusive an organization the more readily it is attacked and ruined, and all shattered that depended upon it as a structure.

This consideration will never be obsolete in the experience of the people of God in this age (Luke 21:12; 1 Pet. 4:12–19), and least of all as its end approaches. Satan will then become the more wrathful as his time of liberty nears its close (Rev. 12:12). The wise lay plans and adopt methods today, which will bear the strain of tomorrow. He is the worst prepared who is least prepared for the worst.

IV. SPIRITUALITY. By this is meant a state of heart dominated by the realities of heaven, the spirit world. Such a heart therefore is characterized by a supreme regard to things immaterial and invisible. It serves the Creator rather than the creature, and counts upon Him for energy and order; it is more concerned with moral quality than material circumstances; it lives in the present in the light of eternity.

In the sphere of the assembly of God the spiritual man has regard first and always to a momentous but physically undiscoverable fact, even that the Lord the Spirit is personally present (1 Cor. 3:16), and, as reverence requires, is to be habitually owned, deferred to, and depended upon. His will concerning the house of God is set forth in His writings (1 Cor. 2:13); behaviour in that house is to be as befits His presence (1 Tim. 3:14, 15); the exercises of public worship are to be directly controlled by Himself; He moving each heart (1 Cor. 12:7–11); offences in the house are committed against Him (Acts 5:1–11); and He it is Who orders and makes effective the labours of the Lord's servants who go forth from the house to constrain others to come in.

Here is a primary clue to God's methods. As is the power so is the machinery. The church of God in all its parts and working is intended for the manifesting of His invisible presence (1 Cor. 12:7). With intention it is so constructed as to be unworkable save as He is present, and is free to maintain and employ it. Evangelistic labour is not intended to be fruitful save as the Spirit of God is its power; public worship is meant to be a fiasco apart from His immediate impelling and restraining. It is notable how promptly forms and routine of worship are broken up in a time of genuinely Spirit-wrought revival, and how immediately the apostolic type of gathering revives. Nothing is so wholly edifying as such worship, nothing more profitless than the form without the life.

But when the Holy Spirit is grieved, when failure appears and edification is ceasing, it is the changeless tendency of the human heart to resort to visible, material and mechanical measures in order to maintain a semblance of the real. It is not till subapostolic literature that we first read of a person unknown to the New Testament, a presiding officer at public worship. That Paul as an evangelist should have a preaching station (Acts 19:9) where he habitually taught truth that he alone in that place knew is one thing, and it may be held to justify gatherings specially for the ministry of the Word by acknowledged teachers and preachers; that on the occasion of a rare and farewell visit (Acts 20:7, 11) the apostle, in assembly, might occupy almost the whole time with priceless exposition is fully comprehensible;[1] but never did even an apostle regularly "conduct" and monopolize the exercises of the assembly of saints as if the Lord were absent and His Spirit not there to lead as He saw fit. This was a device resorted to as the Spirit's power was withheld on account of tolerated evil and waning faith.

But the Spirit of holiness being resisted, rules of conduct will not conserve spirituality, or even morality, for long; the Spirit of truth being rejected, creeds will not preserve the faith inviolate; the Spirit of God being restrained, forms of service will not compensate; "the body without the Spirit is dead"; the organism is now but an organization. If the coherent power of life is gone, the frame may be bound and moved by wires, but it is but a skeleton, however finely dressed.

By this process the church steadily ceased to be a testimony to the existence, presence, and working of the living and true God. Less and less often did unbelievers coming into the assembly, and beholding in the spirit and unity and conscience-searching power of the

---

[1] It is to be noted that on that occasion ministry of the Word both preceded and followed the breaking of bread. Both are in order, as the Spirit leads, to lay down rules is to restrain HIM.

worship, the evidences of His presence and control, exclaim: "God is among you indeed" (1 Cor. 14:24-25). God was worshipped, but as absent; and presently the beauteous divine simplicity of the first days had been materialized into the lifeless magnificence of Roman ritual.

The true remedy for decline is repentance for sin, shown by humiliation and fasting before the Lord, with steadfast and expectant trust in His mercy; beseeching that He will again take His own place in the assembly, and again reveal His own sufficiency along the line of His own appointed methods. To resort to non-apostolic organization is but to sin more deeply against Him, to depart more thoroughly from His ways, and so more surely to confirm the unspirituality and ineffectiveness of the church. For the more subtle the force operating, the more it is retarded by apparatus.

If the due recognition of the invisible Lord as present to control His church is a first mark of the spiritual man, very surely is it a second sign that the impotency, the nothingness, of man in himself is acknowledged (John 15:4-5). Spirituality implies humility; humility involves dependence. Elihu truly remarked that one clue to God's ways with men is that He wishes to withdraw man from his own self-chosen purpose, and hide pride from man, that He may keep back his soul from the pit, towards which all man's progress takes him (Job 33:17, 18).

Because distrust of God is the very root sin, therefore salvation must of necessity be by faith in God; because pride is the very climax of wickedness, therefore all God's methods must tend to humble man. Lest man should be confirmed in conceit of intellect God will not allow the world by the wisdom of its own philosophizing to discover Him (1 Cor. 1:21). Lest there should be boasting in birth or wealth or power, and so we be hardened in the pride that ruins, God has commonly chosen for His purposes persons that are accounted poor and base and weak (1 Cor. 1:26–29). So that man shall of necessity be delivered from self-esteem, salvation reaches him through one whom men crucified as a malefactor (1 Cor. 2:2); and so that no credit for the work should attach to the servant, but all glory ascend to the Lord, the mighty miracle of changing and cleansing the foul heart of man is wrought by so unlikely a means as a mere human testimony concerning that Saviour who was crucified through weakness.

This principle is as needful in the life and work of the assembly as in evangelistic labours. It is fatally easy for Christians to depend upon and boast in the carefully planned and splendidly equipped organization of their own devising. In the executive officers of a great society there easily arises the spirit that says, "Is not this great Babylon that I have built?" (Dan. 4:30). The last stages of moral degeneracy are these: "I am rich, and have gotten riches, and have need of nothing"; "I sit a queen, and am no widow, and shall in no wise see mourning" (Rev. 3:17; 18:7).

In apostolic times the entire absence of inter-assembly organization effectually delivered from this danger. Conscious weakness both saves from the deadly peril of self-confidence and makes room for the mighty power of God. My strength, said Christ to Paul, reaches perfect display in your weakness: then, declares the true servant, Most gladly I glory in weaknesses, for when I am weak, then am I truly strong, and thus is served the whole end of my life, the full and final desire of my heart, even that Christ be magnified (2 Cor. 12:9-10).

Chapter 5

# Some Evils of Church Federation

WITH these principles in mind it is easy to see why the apostles, being in their Lord's secret, founded local assemblies and nothing more, and assemblies of so simple a type. The Head of the church contemplated and prepared for universality, expansion, persecution and spirituality, as essential, abiding conditions.

The evils that have resulted from departure from the apostolic pattern cannot be exaggerated.

A Welsh itinerant used to say that, as he traversed the countryside preaching, sometimes he was lodged like an apostle and sometimes like a bishop: as the former when a goatherd gave him a litter of straw at night and black bread and water for breakfast; as the latter when at the squire's he fared sumptuously and reposed on a feather bed. It shall be freely conceded that not all bishops have incurred this humorous reproach. Some, for Christ's sake, have endured the hardships of the pioneer missionary, some have lain in cold prison cells, and some have sustained the fiery ordeal of death at the stake. But taking the long centuries through, and viewing all countries, it cannot be denied that the satire is all too well deserved.

And how came it that the lowly, despised elder of the apostolic days, a man set forth as a spectacle of reproach, accounted the offscouring of all things, degenerated into the lordly hierarch? Merely as a psychological phenomenon the matter is of interest.

Dr. Hatch has offered this explanation. He remarks that the aforementioned presiding elder was already in sub-apostolic times the almoner of the gifts of the faithful for the poor. "He thus became the centre round whom the vast system of Christian charity revolved. ... Of this vast system of ecclesiastical administration the *episkopos* [=overseer, bishop] was the pivot and the centre. His functions in reference to it were of primary importance.[1] How wide a circle was involved may be gauged by the fact that alms were distributed not only to the general poor, itself a large class in those disordered times, but to orphans, widows, travellers, and the ever increasing army of ecclesiastical officials and servants. Thus the needy were a considerable section of the Christian community, and they became dependent upon the goodwill of the president; and the power of the purse being a most ready instrument by which a Diotrephes could gain the pre-eminence he coveted, more and more the financial and administrative influence was gathered into the hands of the bishop; thus it was from so seemingly innocent a beginning that the upas tree started to grow, to be aided later by other influences that further centred authority in the bishop.

But how startling is this as evidence that every departure from apostolic details is pregnant with calamities. That one elder should become the presiding official was one change; that an elder should handle assembly funds was another.

This latter was what the apostles themselves had expressly refused to do (Acts 6:2-3). Financial power was advisedly relegated to those who had no spiritual rule over the assembly. What divine wisdom was here; for thus the authority of the spiritual guides remained purely moral and morally pure.

And yet how easily could such alterations be justified! Was it not seemly that one whom God had been pleased to endow with special administrative ability should be the acknowledged leader, particularly as thereby unqualified men were hindered from obtruding themselves in public? Then perhaps the deacon was a very busy person, and why should not the elder do the work quite as well? Indeed, was not the latter the more likely to be visiting from house to house? and is not economy of time and labour a virtue? Yet the sequel has shown that the foolishness of God is wiser than men.

Similarly, if in the observance of the Lord's Supper there be preserved the essential features of an eastern social meal, the guests gathered around the board, and the bread and the cup passing from hand to hand, it is all but impossible that the office of the Mass,

---

1 *The Organisation of the Early Christian Church* (Lec. III. 39–48).

## Some Evils of Church Federation 45

with its dogma of transubstantiation, should be attached to the ordinance. For in such simple, artless, yet solemn, observance there is obviously no room for an altar with worshippers kneeling before it, and a consecrating celebrant with gorgeous symbolic vestments. The external simplicity protects the internal essence. Yet how few churches exclude every possibility and appearance of priest and altar by the simple plan of placing the table of the Lord in the centre and arranging the seats of the worshippers around it.

In like manner evils manifold and great would have been avoided had the unaffiliated intercourse of apostolic assemblies been retained.

It will be well to consider a few of these evils carefully.

1. Some have been mentioned, such as the danger of humility and God-dependence being lost in pride of organization and confidence therein. Again, dependence upon the visible and material diminishes spirituality of heart. Of this we have before spoken. Merely as an example of the small details through which danger may enter, and over which therefore a spiritual watch should be kept, we mention this case. At a conference of a certain movement it pleased God to give marked blessing. In consequence, gatherings were held in other centres, it being explained that the desire was that the "conference message" should be spread. Such a brief term is certainly convenient; yet lurks there not in it a danger of drawing too much attention to the Conference, to the channel of the truth rather than to the author thereof? If we mistake not, it is the never absent peril of an organization obtruding itself, and drawing the hearer to itself. It is a very fine edged rail that sidetracks the train.

2. Organization begets a man a sense of power eminently perilous to the work of God. "Uzziah waxed exceeding strong... he built towers and fortified them... he had an army... mighty men of valour... that made war with mighty power.... And his name spread far abroad; for he was marvellously helped, *till he was strong*. But when he was strong, his heart was lifted up, so that he did corruptly" (2 Chron. 26). By contrast, Paul, when being most mightily used of God in pagan Corinth, is there "in weakness and in fear and in much trembling"; and thus Hudson Taylor said that when God decided to

open inland China to the gospel He looked round to find a man who was weak enough for the purpose.

When in each early church a presiding bishop had usurped authority, it naturally followed that these should meet together to further common interests. It further followed naturally enough that the bishop who was head of the largest and richest congregation in a district, should have most influence in such a council, especially as usually only a powerful personality would reach such a position. And because the church in a chief district-city or the capital of a province was pretty certain to be the largest and richest, it inevitably followed, from this amongst other causes, that the city bishop became in time the metropolitan of the province. And by that time Christianity had become the State religion and unregenerate members had multiplied exceedingly; and with such a backing and with such resources how powerful was the influence the metropolitan could exert, and how destructive of spirituality was the possession of such power!

Let there be remembered the faithful picture that Kingsley gives in *Hypatia* of Cyril of Alexandria, early in the fifth century, a picture painfully true of what Christendom in general had then and thus become. Cyril can marshal his hordes of baptized heathen and let them loose to loot the Jewish quarter, and the Prefect dare not interfere. Cyril's subordinates barbarously and indecently murder Hypatia in the crowded basilica itself, and the Bishop will haughtily refuse the Prefect's demand that he surrender the chief criminal for due punishment. Such lawless doings and such ungodly resistance of civil authority had been wholly impossible had not affiliation of churches superseded the Lord's institution.

But further: as local bishops came together under their metropolitan, so in turn these chief bishops would presently confer upon universal matters; and as the capital of each province gave prestige to its bishop, so the bishop of the imperial city first claimed, and presently received, primacy over all bishops. The papacy had never ruled in the House of God had affiliation of churches not prepared the way.

And what has the Free Church Council in England been if not principally a machine by which Nonconformist pressure can be brought to bear upon matters public and on authorities? Its fundamental power as an organization used to be its influence upon votes at elections.

How utterly all this is at variance with the apostolic spirit and practice needs not to be demonstrated to the spiritually minded student of the New Testament.

Probably four chief elements entered into the resort to organization. First, Satan's set purpose to paganize the church, in which he was ably served by certain of the church Fathers; second, lust of power by the ambitious and worldly-minded, like that Pope who regarded Christianity as a profitable farce; third, the false, non-apostolic conception that it is the business of the church to "Christianize" the nations, leading to the obliterating of that rigid line of demarcation between those regenerate by personal faith in Christ and those not; and fourth, the desire to frustrate persecution, and so to avoid suffering for Christ's sake. None of these ends could have been so well and easily served without inter-church organization.

3. Another chief peril to be pondered is the undue influence that church affiliation puts into the hands of a few masterful men.

The domination by the Jesuits of the hundreds of millions of Romanists is the chief modern example. But all the established churches illustrate the point.

The Nonconformist bodies reveal the same dangerous feature. At the first, truth-loving disciples formed into congregations for the godly end of upholding and spreading the faith of the gospel, and then it was well indeed. Persecuted and reproached they flourished spiritually, and the work of God prospered. Presently delegates from such churches met for conference and business; inter-church organization resulted, and now, as in earlier times, was the great Enemy's opportunity. For stealthily and steadily there have been introduced into chief places men of capacity and learning, but not devoted to the Lord and His truth; and today few are the Nonconformist bodies that as such are faithful to God and His Word, save perhaps in the formal retention of a disregarded or misexplained creed!

Under the apostolic arrangement a designing leader or a false teacher must have visited, either personally or by delegates, each assembly separately, so as to gain its adherence to his cause or doctrines. Even under these hampering conditions danger was not wholly avoidable (Gal.; 2 Tim. 1:15); but at least landslides so rapid and extensive as have been seen today were all but impossible. The fatal instrument has been church affiliation, with the resulting central organization, from which streams of thought, suggestion, and personal influence flow out at once to all parts of the affiliated body.

Even in so seemingly unorganized a community as the Exclusive Brethren the same principle has worked disaster. For an organization exists in men's minds before and independently of a written constitution, and indeed its principles may be quite effectively worked without ever being reduced to formal propositions.

The apostolic conception was that each regenerate person, indwelt by the Spirit of life, was a member of a living, universal, invisible society, having no universal, visible, organized exhibition, but was also a member of such local, visible assembly as existed where he might be. Consequently a local assembly could shut out the individual from its fellowship; and if it did so on divinely warranted grounds, that decision would be ratified in heaven (Matt. 18:18), and should, of course, be accepted by all other assemblies fully aware of the facts. But the responsibility of such excommunication was with the local assembly only, and the endorsement thereof was by each other local assembly separately, if and when the one excommunicated presented himself for fellowship.

But the Exclusive Brethren developed discipline a stage further, so that if assembly B did not ratify the excommunicatory sentence of assembly A, the latter assembly must excommunicate the former assembly as such; thus arose the cutting off by assemblies not only of the individual, which is Scriptural, but of an assembly as a whole, for which practice no example or warrant is found in Scripture.

Now whilst the individual, being in fact a member of the local assembly, could be cut off from that body, out of what body could an assembly as a whole be excised? Something cannot be cut off from nothing; the part implies a whole; and it is obvious that corporate excommunication of this sort involves the conception of all the assemblies being in their aggregate a body corporate, or there would be nothing out of which to remove an assembly. So that the non-Biblical notion of an affiliated, universal, visible church underlies, as a working conception, the unhappy world-wide divisions of these Christians.

This conception being generally adopted, amongst them also it resulted that a few powerful personalities and writers dominated the whole circle of their assemblies.

4. But there is another, though kindred, type of affiliation which needs consideration.

This is not the affiliating of local assemblies as a whole, but of a group of persons in an assembly with similar groups in other assemblies. For example, in a certain local church there was formed an organization for assisting in retaining and developing young Christians. The plan adopted approved itself, and presently was copied by another and another church; and shortly these local groups were affiliated into a society. The result is a society within a society. Within the church of God, as represented by the local churches concerned, there is a sectional circle, a segment of which intersects each and all of those local churches.

Clearly this circle is exposed to all the dangers before noted. But there are other and special perils. Of these one is that the presence of a great visible society tends to hinder, or at least to dim the perception of the majesty of the true invisible church of God. This, be it remarked, is true of all denominationalism and sectional enterprises. Nature loves to have something visible upon which to feast its eyes. But this is unspiritual; it is walking by sight, not by faith. "From the unhappy desire of becoming great, good Lord deliver us."

Then, as such a society becomes greater its claims upon the interest, time, and funds of its members increase. Special literature must be read, and paid for; Society conferences must be attended, and paid for; the Society's social gatherings and its religious and philanthropic efforts receive precedence, or one is deemed negligent of the Society's advancement.

An honest endeavour to negative this peril may be made. Members may be exhorted to remember that the Society is subordinate to the local church, and some older persons may perhaps succeed in maintaining this attitude. But the many, and especially the youthful, will find this difficult. It might have been otherwise if the local church had remained the only connexion of the Society, but the affiliation of all the branches into one organization will result in practice for the many, in the Society, having the preference, in its tending to become for such virtually their church.

We are not theorizing, but testifying that which we have seen in years of close observation.

Nor are we condemning special attention being given to the young. Let each assembly, if it find it profitable, have a gathering for helping the youthful in their special problems, or for fostering missionary enthusiasm, or for furthering evangelistic labours at its doors. Only let such special efforts remain local, no matter in how many assemblies they may exist, and let there be no attempt to affiliate these local meetings or classes into an inter-assembly federation.

5. A further, and by itself all-sufficient reason against inter-church federation is that it is the certain occasion of division. Given the administrative separateness of churches, a cause of strife in one need cause no division in another; but, bind them into a body corporate, and in due time general strife will be inevitable.

To hinder this, a spiritual autocracy will presently arise, seeking to control and hold together the whole organization. It may be a formal bench of bishops, a committee elected by an annual conference, or a "brothers' meeting," as among Exclusive Brethren. But the issue will always be the spiritual bondage of the community to these few leaders and the regulations imposed. Against this there will duly come revolt, and then division.

It was thus that the Wesleyan community was rent.

> In the year 1848 dissatisfaction with the government of Wesleyan Methodism had gathered considerable force. Men felt that the Wesleyan Conference did not fairly represent the churches, that *this Conference exercised unjustly a tyrannous despotism over local churches* in the connexion, and that salvation lay in a democratic extension of local government throughout the whole field of Wesleyan Methodism. "The real question at stake was: Connexionalism or Congregationalism—*the supremacy of the Conference* as the final court of appeal, or the court of the individual Church. . . . A large number of secessions from the

mother church took place. . . . The loss of membership. . . amounted in the course of a few years to not less than a hundred thousand."¹

It was through J. N. Darby and his friends acting upon the same principle of corporate inter-church connexion and responsibility that the Brethren were first divided in that same year, 1848, and that his followers have suffered their many later and deplorable universal divisions. On the other hand, those of the early Brethren who refused this dangerous principle and acted ecclesiastically upon the principle of the administrative distinctness of each local church, have been thereby preserved from general division, and have been able, by the grace of God, to increase in numbers and in gospel labours.

The Exclusive London Central Oversight meeting is an acute example of the danger here in view. The theory of Darby and Wigram was that all believers dwelling in one town or city form one church, no matter in how many centres they may for convenience worship. For administrative purposes, therefore, brethren from each meeting assemble regularly on Saturday, and settle all cases of reception and exclusion for the whole of London, and all other matters connected with the assemblies can be there surveyed. Theoretically, the meeting does not claim jurisdiction, but any gathering not submitting is liable to be cut off.

The unspirituality, the mechanical nature of the scheme is easily seen. It was shown long since by the late Andrew Miller, formerly an Exclusive. Woolwich and Islington are some eight miles apart on opposite sides of the Thames; Woolwich and Plumstead adjoin: but because the two former happened to be in the civil administrative area called London, the believers in those assemblies formed one church, whereas because Plumstead was just outside that arbitrary area, the saints there were not of that church, and not directly subject to the decrees of the Central Oversight.

The practical working of the scheme was, that because in so large a city but few, comparatively, could attend such a meeting, it followed that control passed into a few hands; and, further, that a still

---

1   Begbie's *Life of William Booth*, Vol. 1, ch. IX. Italics mine.

smaller number of earnest, determined persons were the real masters of all the London meetings. And since London is the centre of the English world, it necessarily followed that decisions reached there carried almost universal authority. Thus this Central Oversight was a ready instrument for world-wide despotism, and a certain occasion of world-wide division.

My father was a Christian of fine quality, a slum worker, a soul winner, a builder up of believers and churches. For sixty-five years he maintained an undimmed testimony at the heart of London commercial life. He found assurance of salvation through attending Bible readings in the house of a well-known Exclusive, Dr. Morrish, joined them in 1858, and continued at the centre of Exclusivism till his death, in 1922. For many years he was lessee of the room in Cheapside where this "Saturday Night Brothers' Meeting," or "Case" Meeting met. In 1921 we spoke together of this meeting and its working. My father said: "Since I have been shut away in this room the past twelve months with my Bible, I have seen that the whole thing was a mistake!" I suggested that the plan must have been attended with decided inconveniences. How, for example, could the brethren at Finsbury Park, on the far north, form a right judgment as to a case of discipline at Greenwich, miles away in the south? He replied: "Exactly; and what I have come to see is that the brethren at Finsbury Park *could not 'put away from themselves' a person who never had been amongst them.*" I gave God thanks that my honoured father had advanced so far, even though too late for the change ever to develop in his case its just consequences; but I silently marvelled that so acute a mind as his should have taken sixty years to see something so self-evident.

This tendency to coalesce the meetings of a civic area is a revival of the feature mentioned by Dr. Hatch, as early changing the primitive church, even of churches forming into groups according to civil areas, resulting in the church of a provincial capital dominating all the churches of the province, the bishop of that church becoming metropolitan bishop, with priority over all bishops, and finally, the bishop of the imperial city, Rome, becoming universal bishop. Solomon's metaphor (Prov. 17:14) may be thus applied: The beginning of slavery is as when one letteth out water (at first a mere trickle): therefore leave off centralizing before there be a flood of tyranny and persecution.

   That affiliation affords impetus and momentum is certainly true; but what if the direction be wrong? Of course, the pioneer must by necessity be an enthusiast; and each such will fondly believe that he will sail safely where all before him made shipwreck. There seems no inherent reason why the perils indicated should not be avoided, so let another attempt be made! But the uniform experience of long centuries and colossal experiments is a lighthouse not to be disregarded. There must be some reason why, in the affairs of the church of God, no one has sailed this sea in safety. There must be abundant reason why the infallible Head of the church rejected the plan with its attendant advantages. And if those reasons still seem obscure, this gives greater occasion for caution; the hidden reef is the more dangerous. Let the Lord's servants be wise enough to keep well within the channel shown on His chart.

Chapter 6

# Baptism

IN New Testament times the oath of allegiance sworn by a Roman soldier to the Emperor was termed the *sacramentum*. Hence the ordinances of Christ which His followers kept as a sign of their allegiance to Him soon came to be called "sacraments."

The Roman Catholic Church and some others recognize seven sacraments: baptism, confirmation, penance, the mass, holy orders, marriage and extreme unction. Of these only baptism and marriage are of Divine authority, for the mass is a perversion of the holy supper as instituted by Christ, and the other four sacraments—confirmation, penance, orders and extreme unction—are unknown to Holy Scripture.

There are but two Christian ordinances, baptism and the Lord's Supper; for marriage, though truly of Divine authority, is pre-Christian and intended for all mankind, not only for disciples of Christ. To baptism, then, let us now turn our attention.

The writer once asked a Greek what the Greek word *baptizō* meant. Pointing to a ship, he said: "If that ship were to sink completely beneath the water, we should say that it had been baptized." When he was asked if that word would be used were some drops of water to be sprinkled on the ship, he replied: "No; for that we should use the word *rhantizō*."

This last verb is used in Heb. 9:13, 19, 21, and 10:22, and its noun *rhantismos* at Heb. 12:24 and 1 Pet. 1:2. They are correctly rendered by "sprinkled" and "sprinkling."

This present-day usage of *baptizō* and *rhantizō* is shown in the *Greek-English Dictionary* of I. Kykkotis. The meaning of the root verb *baptō* is given as "to plunge, to dip." The associated meaning of to colour, to dye, as a garment, was because the dyeing was done by dipping the article. This is the invariable meaning in the New

Testament. *Baptizō* signifies to dip, to immerse, as in Luke 16:24, "that he may *dip* the tip of his finger in water"; John 13:26, "I shall give the sop when I have *dipped* it" in the dish; Mark 7:4, "the washing [dipping] of cups and pots and brazen vessels" ("couches" is to be omitted: see R.V.). It is plain that such articles could not be cleansed by the mere sprinkling of a few drops of water.

Therefore of baptism John the Baptist said, "I indeed baptize you in water" (Matt. 3:11); and we read "they were baptized by him in the river Jordan" (Mark 1:5); and thus it is said of Philip and the eunuch (Acts 8:38), "they both went down into the water, both Philip and the eunuch, and he baptized [dipped] him... and when they were come up out of the water...." To what purpose the descent by both men (which is emphasized) into the stream or pool had the need been for only a few drops for sprinkling? One of the eunuch's servants could have brought a cupful. The medieval pictures of John standing in Jordan and pouring water over a candidate standing beside him are fictitious and misleading. No Greek would have described such an action by *baptizō*. Greek had plenty of words for the act of pouring; as *ballō* in John 13:5, "He poureth water into the basin," and *katacheō* in Matt. 26:7, "and poured it on His head."

The matter is indeed so clear that Bishop Handley Moule in his Commentary on Rom. 6:5 speaks of the baptismal "plunge" and "emergence" and owns that at first baptism was by "entire immersion." And thus also Dean Stanley says that "baptism was not only a bath but a plunge, an entire submersion in the deep water" (*Christian Institutions* 8). In the ruins of the great church at Carthage, which dated from the early centuries, I saw a font of such vast size as shows that immersion long continued to be the practice. In fact, the first direction in the Prayer Book of the Church of England is that the child shall be dipped in the font, sprinkling being allowed only if the infant is certified to be too weak to endure dipping. In practice this direction is universally disregarded, which shows how readily religious persons disregard what is well known to be a requirement of God by Holy Scripture and substitute human tradition and preference.

This last habit of mind began directly after the times of the apostles, that is, as regards baptism; for almost the first post-apostolic writing, at the beginning of the second century, if not earlier, *The Teaching of the Apostles* [*Didache*], sanctions pouring in place of dipping. This was where sufficient water for immersion might not be available, which shows that immersion was the earlier and apostolic baptism. It also illustrates the readiness to vary from the apostolic practice. It shows further that one of the first attempts to corrupt Christianity took the form of an attack upon the form of baptism, since to change the form would destroy the doctrine attached to it. To change the forms of the two Divine ordinances and to introduce non-Scriptural ceremonies were two of the earliest efforts against Christianity, and they were much too successful.

Sprinkling is not dipping, and therefore it is not baptism, though called so by men. It is an unwarranted and misleading use of the word. The Anglicized word *baptize* is not a *translation* of the Greek word, but is simply an unworthy *hiding* in English of the meaning of the Greek word. To have *translated* the word the translators must have used dip or immerse, but that would have opened the eyes of the general reader to what scholars already knew, namely, that the ceremony of sprinkling is not the New Testament ordinance of baptism.

Only by means of the true form of the ordinance can its true doctrine be expressed. For baptism is a burial: "We were *buried* [entombed, Moule] therefore with Him through baptism into death: that like as Christ was *raised* from the dead through the glory of the Father, so we also might walk in newness of life." Who would deem a corpse to have been buried if a few grains of earth were sprinkled thereon and it were left on the surface uncovered? Burial is effected according to the words of Abraham: "that I may bury my dead *out of my sight*" (Gen. 23:4).

There is a principle of law, Divine and human, that the act of an agent is the act of the principal he represents. The greatest example is that the death of Christ is deemed to be the death of the believer in Him. In His burial our "old man" is considered to have been put out of the way; in His resurrection the believer is reckoned to have been raised a new creature to live in a new realm. Before God Christ is the Representative or Agent of man. What He did, suffered, experienced we who believe on Him are held to have done.

He died on account of my sin: then I died on account of it, through Him I have paid its last penalty and am free.

He died out of all relationship to my sins which He had in grace assumed. In Him, then, I too died out of all relationship to my sins, and hence the challenge: "We who died to sin, how shall we any longer live therein?" One cannot at the same time be both dead and alive.

Christ rose again in a life beyond the power of death. Death, as to its nature, is that the *spirit*, the principle which animates man's composite being, is recalled by God who gave it and it returns to Him (Ecc. 12:7; Luke 23:46; Acts 7:59). But the spirit is not the man himself. Man is a *soul* (Gen. 2:7, "man became a living soul"). This man, soul, person dwells in a body of flesh, which body can be useful to him only as long as it is energized by the spirit. When the latter is withdrawn the body corrupts and falls to pieces, whereupon the soul, the man ceases to be a *living* soul and becomes dead; still existing and conscious (Luke 16:23; Rev. 6:9–11), but not living, in God's sense of the term.[1] Thus the human spirit of Christ returned at death to God (Luke 23:46: "Father, into Thy hands I commend my spirit"). He Himself, the soul, went to Hades, the realm of the dead in the lower parts of the earth (Ps. 16:10; Acts 2:27; Eph. 4:9). His body was buried in the tomb.

This break-up of man's threefold being, death, the penalty of sin, we rightly call *dissolution*, because the former partnership of these three elements is dissolved. But glorious is the fact that "Christ being raised from the dead dieth no more, death no more hath dominion over Him" (Rom. 6:9). Having paid the full penalty of the sin He had made His own, our sin, the Father released Him therefrom, immediately, entirely, eternally. Resurrection is the reuniting of spirit, soul, and body, and henceforth Christ liveth in "the power of an *indissoluble* life" (Heb. 7:16).

---

1   1 See my *Firstfruits and Harvest*, 46–58.

Into a share in *this* life, beyond the region where sin blights and death blasts, the believer is introduced by vital union with Christ, his Representative. Of this union with Christ in His death, burial, and emergence, with its escape from the former sin-ruined, death-ruled state, baptism is the Divinely appointed symbolic expression.

It is the office of the Holy Spirit to make all this morally effective in the inner experience and outer practice of the man of faith, which He does according to the measure and constancy of faith. Where faith, instructed by the Word, takes hold of the thought of God, claims daily its fulfilment, dedicates itself wholly to God to do only and fully His will, then and so far the union between the man of faith and Christ is made operative, and the believer knows experimentally God's thought as to baptism, even that "we have been buried with Christ in baptism, wherein also we were raised with Him, through faith in the working of God, who raised Him from the dead" (Col. 2:12). This wide range of vital experimental truth, so admirably expressed by immersion, is completely concealed by sprinkling, to the great impoverishment of the soul even if the person be a believer.

Now no person ought to be buried until he has died. No one should be baptized until, by personal faith in Christ, he has associated himself with the death of Christ as his own death to sin, law, and judgment. The mental apprehension of these truths will at first be imperfect, but the faith must be real, and any ceremony before faith is not baptism according to God, though men may call it this. We are not Anabaptists, for we do not demand the second baptism of one baptized; but we do take the inflexible position that a rite performed upon one not having personally exercised faith is not Scriptural baptism at all, even though it be by immersion.

The great champion of the truth that salvation is by faith, Martin Luther, could not but acknowledge the requirement of Scripture that faith ought to precede baptism. To justify still the baptizing of infants he went to the extreme of asserting that the infant must be supposed to have a capacity for faith. But many who will not adopt this desperate expedient adopt another way of meeting their dilemma, and assert that the faith of sponsors will stand instead of the faith of the infant. But Scripture knows nothing of this vicarious faith unto salvation. It is a theological fiction, carrying no experimental power, but serving effectually to hide from many souls the necessity that they must personally trust Christ.

A truly godly clergyman confided to me that forty years before, he went straight from his ordination as a "priest" to the parish in the east end of London where he was to serve. That afternoon there were infants brought to the font. He told me that as he looked into the faces of the parents and godparents, and saw there the evidence that they were heavy drinkers, yet were about to take solemn vows to rear the children in the fear of God though themselves having none of His holy fear upon their hearts, it rushed over his soul what a hypocrisy the whole ceremony was, and he felt that he must go straight away and resign his orders. But, he added sadly, I did not do so, and so here I still am. Thus may a godly man avoid the way of God, and know through a long life that he had missed God's real will for him. And the like situation can as certainly arise where the parties concerned are respectable persons who nevertheless do not live in the fear of God.

But while only the dead should be buried, all the dead ought to be—every believer in Christ should be baptized. This He commanded. The apostles would have had no more right to omit the baptism of a disciple than to fail to teach him to observe all the Lord's other commandments (Matt. 28:19-20). And therefore Peter commanded the baptism of Cornelius and his friends though these had already received the baptism in the Holy Spirit (Acts 10:45, 48). Peter's action stands squarely against the notion that it is the spiritual alone that matters and he who has received the spiritual need not observe its external symbol. For Peter the baptism in the Spirit was reason and ground for baptism in water, not reason for omitting it. But on this matter those devoted men of God, George Fox and William Booth, knew better than Peter!

Others make void the command of the Lord and the example of His apostles by the device that the period of the Acts was an "interim dispensation," that the period of the church had not yet set in, and that baptism and the Supper of the Lord do not apply now that this last age has come. The fact that baptism and the Supper were unvarying ordinances immediately after the apostles shows that this idea was unknown to the churches that the apostles had taught. It is a modern dispensational invention.

How important and urgent was the question of Ananias to the newly-converted Saul: "And now, what art thou going to do? Arise, get thyself immersed!" (Rotherham, *New Testament Critically Emphasized*, Acts 22:16). That is, the responsibility lay upon Saul to act, to be baptized, accepting the name of the Lord he had hitherto rejected, and thus to wash away openly his sins in so opposing Him. Saul's obedience was prompt: "Straightway... he arose and was baptized" (Acts 9:18).

According to Scripture, *blood* was *sprinkled*, washing was always with *water*. All speaking and singing of washing with blood confuses the typology and conceals the truth. (Rev. 1:5 reads "loosed," not "washed"). For Saul baptism in the name of Jesus was the public confession that his whole public life had been utterly wrong, especially in its opposition to Christ, and thereby he washed it all away from before men and commenced a new life, which life was through Christ, in Christ, for Christ. It was as when a schoolboy wipes his slate clean because he finds that the sum has been quite wrongly worked and he must begin all over again. Cf. 1 Pet. 3:21.

The relationship between baptism and reception into the house of God, the church, the body of Christ, is important.

Baptism as a confession that one was dying out of a former circle of life and entering a new and different sphere, was well known in both the Jewish and pagan worlds before New Testament times. The Gentile when professing to become a Jew, religiously speaking, was immersed. And when a candidate was initiated into one of the heathen religious orders, the "Mysteries," he was immersed. The meaning in either case was that he held himself to have died to the former sphere in which he had moved, to have been buried in symbol as one dead, and thereupon to have entered a new association, to the head of which he was thenceforth utterly surrendered, and to the interests of which order he was to be utterly devoted.

In any land or time where this is understood—as among Hindus, Jews, or Moslems—immersion should be insisted upon as a condition precedent to one being acknowledged as a Christian or admitted to the privileges of the house of God. Upon those who are honoured to bring a soul to faith in Christ Jesus as Saviour and Lord lies the responsibility to see that their converts are at once instructed in the meaning and duty of baptism and are required to give this proof of acceptance of Christ as the LORD to be always obeyed. For in one aspect baptism is a token act, a sample of the rule that is to regulate all the future, even obedience to Christ as Lord. It is painfully evident that many modern evangelists do not follow the example of the apostles in regard to this duty.

But there are spheres where, by reason of false instruction, many evidently regenerate persons, whose lives are markedly consecrated to Christ, sincerely believe that they have been baptized according to the Word of God though they have not been immersed after conversion. They honestly think this latter act unnecessary because they were christened in early days. Directions as to how to deal with these devoted but unenlightened souls cannot be found in Acts 2:37-47, and similar passages, for these contemplate not this class but the former, those who do know the true nature of baptism, and are opposers of Christ. And because in those first days all did understand the real force of baptism the New Testament gives no ground for thinking that any person was considered a member of the house of God until he had been baptized.

But instruction how to treat the unenlightened persons in view may be found in Rom. 14:1 to 15:7: "Him that is weak in faith receive ye, yet not for decisions of doubts," not even though that doubt be as to the place and force of a divine ordinance (circumcision: Gal. 6:15, 16; 1 Cor. 7:18-19). "Wherefore receive ye one another, even as Christ also received you, to the glory of God." The following points should be noted:

(1) The right angle of approach—to see how many may be received, not how many ought to be excluded.

(2) Those who are already of the Fellowship ought to be received—"receive ye *one another*." The sole test is the person's attitude to Christ

as LORD, manifested by obedience to what is known of His revealed will, especially baptism, if the person has light on that command. But if there is not that light, but there is other evidence of obedience to all the light yet gained, then we should receive one another, and not penalize a true disciple for want of light on that ordinance. Since we are all blind in measure, no one seeing all truth, want of light would shut us all out of the house of God. But fellowship with God, and therefore with one another, is dependent upon walking in the light, that is, in that measure of light one has—more than this cannot in love be demanded; and then the blood of Jesus is held to atone for involuntary ignorance (1 John 1:7).

(3) The pattern of reception is, "as Christ received you"; and this He graciously did as soon as ever our heart truly bowed to Him as Lord, without waiting to remove all our ignorance upon His perfect will.

(4) The principle that should guide is the securing the glory of God, which is not done by shutting out of His house any whom He has already welcomed, but rather by our receiving them and helping them to walk in holy fellowship with His people.

Thus baptism is an acknowledgment that the baptized owns the lordship of Christ, on which account the church receives him. But it is of the highest importance to recognize that it is not by baptism that a person "joins the church" or enters the house of God or is incorporated into the body of Christ. This basic error is the essence of the sacramentarian teaching that baptism secures salvation. It was laid down by Augustine that no one can be saved who is not incorporated into the body of Christ: that it is by baptism that this takes place; therefore, without baptism no one can be saved, not even newborn infants who die early. Baptism was therefore to be regarded as a church act. It is the church, they say, that administers baptism, and a leading living theologian has laid down that "in principle baptism cannot be celebrated as a private act" but only "within the framework of the public worship of God." It is therefore vital to see that in the New Testament baptism is never connected with a church but was always an individual act.

The baptism of John was his personal call on the people to repent and be immersed. There was no church in existence to concur or object. The same was the fact when the Lord caused His disciples to baptize others (John 4:1-2). On the day of Pentecost Peter did but continue the former individual service by calling men to repent and be immersed. The 120 took no corporate action. When Philip went down to Samaria there was no church there to proclaim the message or to baptize converts. This was Philip's personal work (Acts 8). The same chapter shows Philip on his own responsibility baptizing the eunuch.

He did not respond to the latter's request to be baptized by saying they must return to Jerusalem that the baptism should be "within the Church ... within the framework of the public worship of God." Cornelius and his friends were baptized by the personal direction of Peter (Acts 10:46–48): it was not a "church" act. There was no church at Philippi when Lydia and her household were baptized (Acts 16:15); and still more notable and to our purpose is the fact that, though a church had been gathered by the time the jailer had been converted, Paul did not defer his baptism until the church could be brought into the matter, but "he was baptized, he and all his, immediately" in that night (Acts 16:33). The same features are seen at Ephesus when Paul baptized again the twelve disciples of John (Acts 19). He and they continued in the synagogue, and it was three months before the church was separated from the Jewish community. The manner of Paul's statement in 1 Cor. 1:13ff. shows that it was Paul's personal choice and action that determined which of his converts in that town he baptized and which not.

The Spirit of truth must have had good reason for thus making clear and emphatic that in every case mentioned in His records the baptism was the personal act of individuals, not a church act. The real situation was, and still is, that each individual upon resting his faith on Christ and on being baptized in the Spirit of Christ, is thereby incorporated into the body of Christ before he is, or has time to be, baptized in water. This is distinct in the case of Cornelius and his friends. Thus baptism is not the means or the occasion of that incorporation into Christ and His universal church; and inasmuch as that union with Christ implies that the person is *ipso facto* a member of any local company of Christians he may touch, it follows that there is scripturally no such thing as reception into membership of a local church, whether by baptism or otherwise, for he is already one of that company by belonging to the whole church of God.

The practice of baptism being performed by a representative of the church, clergyman, minister, or another, and usually in a building, church, chapel, or hall, is foreign to the New Testament. It is one result of Christians now owning special buildings for church purposes, a feature utterly unknown for the first two hundred years after Christ. It is part of the false conception of there being a corporate ecclesiastical body which, through its officers, can perform ecclesiastical functions.

On the other hand, let each believer remember that the grandest promises of God, as to spiritual blessings in this age and glory hereafter, are given to "the church of God"; so that one who by refusing baptism, or otherwise, neglects to associate himself with this company, or later dissociates therefrom, he being no longer of the church militant has no right to expect to have part in the church triumphant. One cannot be both in and not in the fellowship of saints, both of and not of this heavenly company. One is not a member of a community if he is not united with it.

Finally: it is clear that, as only those who have already been justified by faith in Christ should be baptized, therefore salvation precedes baptism. The latter therefore cannot effect or affect the former. The doctrine of regeneration by baptism is therefore a colossal lie, false to Scripture and to fact, a fatal deception assuring the blindness and ruin of souls innumerable. And the doctrine that infants and others who die unbaptized are lost eternally is wholly a *non sequitur*, another monstrous falsehood serving only to make salvation to depend upon the "Church" and its ministers who administer its so-called "sacraments." The salvation of persons incapable of faith depends upon the knowledge which God, the righteous Judge, has that redemption was effected for their benefit by the plenary, substitutionary, atoning sacrifice which Christ offered for the whole world (John 3:16; 1 Tim. 2:3-6; 1 John 2:2).

To confuse men as to the true meaning of baptism, and thus to blur the line of separation between those born of God and those not so born again, was almost the earliest endeavour of Satan in the attack upon the church of God and its message. He succeeded all too well and widely. But this is the greater reason why the ordinance should be maintained and practised according to the Word of God. His double wile was to spoil what is of God and to introduce what is not of God. Let us watch and pray and fight against both forms of his attack, so that in doctrine and practice we may abide in Christ and in His word. Then will He say: "thou didst keep My word and didst not deny My name" (Rev. 3:8).

CHAPTER 7

# The Lord's Supper

THE two ordinances of baptism and the Lord's Supper were intended by Christ for perpetual observance by Christians throughout the period of His absence until His return. It was on the occasion when He instituted the Supper that He said: "I come again, and will receive you unto myself" (John 14:3), and Paul adds that by this ordinance we "proclaim the Lord's death *till He come*" (1 Cor. 11:26). The apostles, including Paul, practised both ordinances.

Fairly early in His ministry the Lord had spoken publicly of the necessity that men should eat His flesh and drink His blood if they would have eternal life (John 6:51–58). This had no reference to the Supper, for

(a) The eating and drinking in question were necessary for the sinful men to whom Christ was then speaking; the Supper was instituted much later, in private, for disciples. As the eating and drinking were needful at the time Christ was speaking it could not be dependent on the Supper, for this was not yet instituted and of it no one knew anything.

(b) In any case, that eating and drinking were not of Christ's actual flesh and blood, or of anything else material. His hearers wrongly supposed the Lord to refer to some eating of His physical flesh, saying, "How can this man give us His flesh to eat?" (John 6:52). But Christ replied that even could they do this it would be useless, for, said He, "the flesh profiteth nothing" (v. 63). Now the only flesh of which He or His hearers had spoken was His own physical flesh, so that His words declared that even the eating thereof would profit nothing.

It is falsely asserted that by priestly consecration the bread and the wine are changed into the veritable flesh and blood, soul and divinity of the Lord. But were this miracle a possibility it would be valueless, according to the above explicit statement of the Lord Himself. For the imparting of spiritual life to the spirit of man is a spiritual process, and can be effected only by a spiritual Agent and means, not by anything material: "It is the spirit that giveth life; the flesh profiteth nothing: the *words* that I have spoken unto you are spirit and life." And so Peter said by the Holy Spirit that believers are "begotten again... through the *word* of God" (1 Pet. 1:23).

For preservation from the dangerous errors connected with the mass, that "fond thing vainly invented," it is important thus to know that John 6 does not refer to the Supper of the Lord, but to a purely spiritual reception by faith of Christ to be our spiritual life, by sincerely believing His words.

The Supper has two chief ends. It is a remembrance and a partaking.

It is a remembrance of the Lord Jesus Christ, even as He said at the institution, "this do in remembrance of Me" (Luke 22:19). Things present and visible press ceaselessly upon us and create a perpetual danger that we forget the past and the unseen. Hence Paul's exhortation to Timothy, "Remember Jesus Christ" (2 Tim. 2:8). The Supper is a powerful external aid to this remembering of the Lord. On this account its frequent observance is a benefit, seeing that the influences occasioning forgetfulness operate constantly.

There is, however, no bondage as to the frequency of repetition or the day or hour for observance. At first believers broke bread every day (Acts 2:46): "And day by day, continuing steadfastly with one accord in the temple, and breaking bread at home, they did take their food with gladness and singleness of heart, praising God." Acts 20:7 reads: "Upon the first day of the week, when we were gathered together to break bread, Paul discoursed [dialogued] with them." It is only an assumption that those at Troas used to meet on the first day of every week to do so. It cannot be dogmatically asserted from the passage that they did this regularly on that day, and on that day only, or that all Christians everywhere did so, or only once a week. All that Luke distinctly affirms is that on *that* first day of the week they had gathered for that purpose.

The first passage cited justifies the ordinance on every day of the week, and therefore on any one of the days. The other passage encourages its observance on the first of the week. It was, however, not instituted on the first day of the week, and therefore in the absence of express precept believers are not limited to that day.

It was instituted in the evening and is accordingly termed a supper, and it ever seems most appropriate and congenial when observed in the evening. It was evening when saints gathered at Troas, for the room was lit with many lights. That it is a supper shows how invalid is the ritualists' demand for early morning communion. As C. H. Spurgeon said, no one ever heard of a man taking his supper before his breakfast until these men invented the idea.

But Acts 2:46 quoted speaks of observance "day by day," not specifying any part of the day; and in point of fact, on the occasion of Troas the actual breaking of the bread did not take place on the first day of the week or in the evening, but in the early hours of Monday; for Paul had discoursed till midnight, then came the death and resuscitation of Eutychus, and only thereafter was the ordinance observed.

These details imply liberty as to day and hour; which is in harmony with the non-legal genius of this age of spiritual liberty given to grown-up sons of God, as argued in the Galatian epistle. And it is of practical moment that this liberty should be preserved, for in periods of persecution such as the church of God has often known, knows still in places, and will know yet further, it is not possible to insist on a set time or day. Nor, as is manifest, can there be one special day or hour when only it is right for Christians to remember Christ.

Acts 2:46 shows further that the holy ordinance was observed in private houses, for they were in the habit of "breaking bread at home," as well as daily. We know a region in Europe where the police had prohibited meetings of believers and they had not broken bread for about a year. Yet any "two or three" might have done so in their homes, with this scripture as warrant, and so have enjoyed the benefit of the ordinance. How wise, simple, and gracious are the Lord's measures for meeting the needs of His people.

The same passage shows that the first believers broke bread in connexion with the ordinary family meals: "breaking bread at home they took their food with gladness." The two phrases standing together are thereby distinguished, which shows that the former refers to the holy ordinance.

It was during the social meal connected with the Passover feast that the Lord had introduced the new association of that bread and cup with His own person and work. Likewise does 1 Cor. 11 show that the believers at Corinth observed the Supper in connexion with a social meal of the whole company. This was known as the *agape* or feast of love, and though it had led to abuses at Corinth the apostle does not repudiate the practice but regulates its observance.

It is thus clear that fasting as an indispensable preliminary to communion has no warrant from the Word of God.

It is healthful that this picture rise before the mind. An ordinary house the place; a customary meal the occasion; the Supper quietly and easily conjoined therewith. No ecclesiastical building, no priest or functionary, no altar or sacrifice, no vestments or ornaments, as lights, incense, or crucifixes, no formality. The Supper observed in simplicity; the home dignified thereby, the ordinary meal sanctified and solemnized.

We have written above (p. 44) as follows:

> If in the observance of the Lord's Supper there be preserved the essential features of an eastern social meal, the guests gathered round the board, and the bread and the cup passing familiarly from hand to hand, it is all but impossible that the office of the Mass, with its dogma of transubstantiation, should be attached to the ordinance. For in such simple, artless, yet withal solemn, observance there is obviously no room for an elevated altar with worshippers kneeling before it, and a consecrating celebrant with gorgeous and symbolic vestments. The external simplicity protects the internal essence.

It has been taught of late, and in a quarter where one least expected and most regrets it, that because the Supper is a remembrance of Christ His absence is implied, not His presence. Those so teaching hold also that only such brethren as have attained spiritually to priestly capacity ought either to minister the word or administer the ordinance in Christian gatherings; but that after one of these has broken the bread and blessed the cup then Christ becomes spiritually present.

Spirituality of mind, priestly energy of a spiritual kind, is indeed greatly to be desired in all who serve God publicly in His church. Without it the service can be of little glory to Him or profit to His people. But the teaching above mentioned is scarcely distinguishable from the Lutheran doctrine of consubstantiation. This doctrine denies, indeed, that the bread and wine have by consecration ceased to be what they appear still to be, bread and wine, and have become what they do not appear to be, the person of Christ, which latter view is termed transubstantiation. But consubstantiation means that when a priest has consecrated the elements of the sacrament, then Christ is personally present in the elements of bread and wine, and the believing partaker does receive the literal, though invisible, body and blood of Christ, as well as the bread and wine.

Transubstantiation, consubstantiation, and the first view before mentioned have in common: (a) that the Lord is not present prior to the blessing of the elements; (b) that upon consecration He becomes present in some sense that before was not the case; (c) that only a limited class of men of a priestly standing can effect this wondrous difference.

But against this is to be put the plain statement of the Lord that when any two or three disciples meet in His Name "there am I in the midst" (Matt. 18:19-20). This is so completely independent of the breaking of bread that the promise stands in connexion with prayer on any subject. Suppose therefore that disciples are met to pray concerning any matters, and that before parting they are moved in love to exercise their right and privilege to bread break in remembrance of Christ, it is clear that He cannot be brought into their midst by means of the ordinance, for He has been with them all the time according to this His promise.

There are godly souls here and there who feel it impossible to share in the Supper if leavened bread and fermented wine are used, and some will not receive to the Supper any who would use such elements elsewhere. They feel that, as in Israel leaven was a symbol of evil, it becomes so very wrong to use it in symbols of the sinless Lord as to necessitate refusal of fellowship in the Supper. In argument they seek to impose the blame for this breach of Christian fellowship upon the vast majority, because these will not banish the fermented elements, whereas in fact it is they who would impose their view upon the mass of Christians under penalty of withdrawal of their fellowship.

Personally we should be happy to have unleavened bread and glad to have unfermented wine. The latter is clearly within our Lord's descriptive term "this fruit of the vine." But we can by no means deem it of the Lord to force this as an indispensable condition of communion.

It does not seem certain that the principle of fermentation in liquors is scripturally the same as that of leaven in bread. We understand that authorities are not agreed as to whether in New Testament times passover wine was or was not of necessity unfermented. It is possible that the wine at the Lord's Supper in Corinth was intoxicating, for we read: "another is drunken" (1 Cor. 11:21). Yet the apostle did not command its banishment, though that would have prevented the abuse he condemns. Evidently he did not deem its presence to nullify the virtue or validity of the observance, though the abuse of it did so (v. 20).

With all respect for the conscience of others we feel (a) that the insistence on this detail is at variance with that freedom from legal restrictions and details which characterizes the gospel age as contrasted with the age of law. This freedom is necessary under the conditions of the church of God. In the case in point it can be easily seen that unfermented grape juice is not, and never can be, available in many remote regions of the earth, in many severe climates, to many extremely poor people. To insist upon such wine would simply deprive multitudes of the Supper. This the gospel does not do: it would be contrary to its essential spirit of love.

(b) We feel also that fellowship of heart, divinely generated by the Spirit of love, is too powerful and too precious to be set aside as to its outward manifestation by such a secondary consideration as the invisible quality of the elements.

(c) Seeing that the Lord graciously and blessedly grants His presence at the Supper where fermented elements are used, who are we, His poor servants, to absent ourselves or to refuse others on such a ground? Are we wiser or holier than He?

Yet for ourselves we approve the use of unfermented grape juice, though on practical grounds. Seeing that in many regions the abuse of intoxicants is so dreadful (as in England), we ourselves completely abstain from them so as to be able with sincerity and a good conscience to exhort and to encourage those who are injured thereby. It seems to us regrettable that many young people should first taste these temptations to sin at the feast that tells of redemption from sin and demands abstinence from sin.

We knew personally an esteemed and much used worker who was converted from a life of drunkenness. Shortly thereafter he attended the Supper of the Lord at a hall we know. As soon as the cup reached the end of the seat, he, at the other end, caught the smell, and the demon passion instantly rose in him in fury. He knew, as he told us, that were he to have put that cup to his lips he would have drunk it all and have rushed thence to get more. Falling upon his knees he cried inwardly for salvation until the cup passed him. We regret deeply to add that the brother in charge of the cup, learning afterwards how the case had been, said, "Oh, you are one of those teetotal fanatics." The babe in Christ gave the sweet but severe answer: "Dear brother, do not call me that: call me the 'weak brother,' and I will tell you how our Lord says you should treat me." Were it not far better to remove the risk of such most deplorable happenings, even if they are happily infrequent?

When one brother refuses to break bread with those who would use fermented wine, and when another, at the opposite extreme, refuses to communicate if the wine is unfermented, one can only deplore the state of soul that ranks such a detail higher than public fellowship with saints in the power of heavenly love. We are assured by happy experience through sixty years that the Lord makes Himself known to loving hearts whichever sort of bread and wine is used. Bitterness and contention for either one or the other is not of Him. "Let us follow after things which make for peace, and things whereby we may build up one another." "But thou, why dost thou judge thy brother? or thou again, why dost thou set at nought thy brother? for we shall all stand before the judgment seat of God." "It is good not to eat flesh, nor to drink wine, nor to do anything whereby thy brother stumbleth" (Rom. 14:19, 10, 21).

Others again agitate for individual cups instead of all drinking from one. It seems to us greatly to reduce the sense of fellowship, of joint participation. We read that at the institution of the ordinance Jesus "took a cup, and having given thanks gave to them: and they *all* drank *out of it*," where the last clause gives emphasis to the fact that they all drank out of one and the same cup (Mark 14:23). In 1 Cor. 10:14–22, where communion is the leading truth pressed, it is as much and as clearly one cup that is set forward as one loaf and one table. Consistency might demand many tables and many loaves.

It is a supposed gain in hygiene that is urged by introducers of this novelty. In the West this factor is negligible. But we have been at the Supper in lands where lepers partook, and sufferers from even worse diseases inherited from former evil living. In such cases older brethren lovingly request the sufferers to sit where they will be the last to partake. If there is a contentious person who still wishes to force this matter of individual cups upon a church, is not the suggestion of a leading medical man wise and simple, that the one demanding it should be provided with a separate cup for his own use?

The sixth chapter of John, as before noticed, does not refer to the Supper, and all Eucharistic teaching and practice based upon the contrary supposition are false and mischievous. Yet the Supper when instituted later set forth in symbol the same essential truth as Christ had taught in words on that former occasion under the notion of eating His flesh and drinking His blood.

The truth in question is, that there must be by faith a true and actual inward appropriation of the Son of God for the purpose that He shall be the nourishment and strength of the inward spiritual life.

In finite beings activity involves wear and tear, and tends to exhaustion of energy. It has pleased the Creator to store in bread energy such as man needs for recuperation. When he makes bread his own inwardly by eating it, it becomes part of himself, whereupon the stored energy is liberated and becomes his energy, by which he lives and labours afresh.

It is thus in the spirit realm also of man's being. Through trespasses and sins this nature in man is devoid of divine life, for these separate between God and man, and the sinner is thereby dead towards God.

Christ, by death for our sins and by resurrection life, is to the spiritual nature the bread of God come down from heaven to give life unto the world. To eat His flesh and to drink his blood means that one appropriates to one's own case and need the atoning sacrifice which Christ offered for the putting away of sin. He "bare our sins in His body on the tree" (1 Pet. 2:24): He shed His life-blood, He poured out His soul unto death, to discharge the appointed penalty of our sins.

To accept this sacrifice for one's personal salvation from sin and judgment is, as the figurative language expresses it, to eat His flesh and to drink His blood. This we do by believing His words on the subject, so appropriating them personally and receiving as our life Him of Whom the words speak.

We knew in India an Englishman of low life and violent temper, a drunkard, curser, wife-beater, and blasphemer. He had threatened to kill his wife if she read the Bible to the children. He was by religious profession Unitarian. Reading secretly in John 6 the words "I am the living bread which came down out of heaven" (ver. 51) the Spirit of truth caused his mind to move at last correctly. He said to himself: "I always allowed that Jesus was a good man; but if He was a good man I ought to believe what He says, for good men do not tell lies. So as He says He came down out of heaven I ought to believe it." As he said to us after: "I ate of that Bread." The immediate result was a simply brilliant manifestation that he had indeed received a new life and was a new creature in Christ Jesus.

Until one has thus received the Son of God he has no life in himself (John 6:53); but, on the other hand, the Lord said: "he that eateth Me shall live because of Me" (ver. 57), that is, because of what I will become to him as the inward vital energy of his nature. For according to the quality of the bread so is the energy of the eater. Because Christ is nothing less than that eternal life itself, which was with the Father, and was presently manifested in this world, therefore it is the energy of that divine, eternal life which is liberated to work actively in the one who by faith receives Christ to be his indwelling life.

This exalted and encouraging truth is set forth symbolically in the Supper. For we not only look upon the bread and the cup that would suffice to remind us that the Son of God loves us and gave Himself up to justice for us; and were no more than remembrance intended by the ordinance nothing more were needful than to look and to ponder. But we are to eat the bread, as well as to look upon it, which signifies that faith is to appropriate inwardly, for our inward invigoration, all that Christ is as the true life of the believer.

The frequent repetition of the ordinance reminds us that faith must be continually appropriating Christ, that He may be ever renewing our spirit for the ceaseless battle and service of the Christian course. He said not: He that once ate of Me shall live because of Me; but "he that *eateth* Me shall live because of Me."

The actual conscious experience of this renewing may be most blessedly known by the heart through faith as the bread is eaten and the cup drunk; for these actions are symbolic of the interior activity of faith in appropriating Christ afresh to meet the constantly recurring strain that life puts upon the spirit. When thus enjoyed, how very far is the feast from being a formality: then truly does the soul sit at the table of the Lord and feast upon Himself as its heavenly food.

Further, the eating of the bread is external and symbolic: the internal reality is the appropriating of the words of God by or concerning His Son. Hence it is harmonious with the ordinance, and helpful to faith, that ministry of the Word should accompany the observance. This will be dealt with more fully in the next chapter.

When given in the power of the Spirit of truth, and received into the heart with faith and obedience, such ministry as occupies the heart with Christ will enable the soul most profitably to eat of the bread and drink of the cup, for it will aid that spiritual feeding upon Christ which is the reality that visualizes the symbolic eating in the ordinance. And *all* opening of the Scripture does this, for Christ is the ultimate subject of *all* truth.

The broken bread and the poured out cup draw particular attention to the body and blood of Christ sacrificed for our sins. Yet Christ in His death is not the whole Christ presented to our hearts by God in His Word, nor does it meet our whole need. Therefore at that institution of the Supper the Lord gave instruction upon many other aspects of Himself and His work, as upon prayer, the person and coming ministry of His Spirit, and His own return and glory. Nor can it be supposed that the cross and passion of the Lord was the only topic that long night at Troas. To confine the mind to one theme alone is to impoverish the soul. The Spirit presents all truth as He sees needful.

There are those who formally reject the Supper of the Lord as being a mere external ceremony, not necessary or useful to the spiritually advanced. There are also such as neglect the ordinance, and still others who partake in a formal manner out of custom. These attitudes are all to be deplored and avoided, together with the false, superstitious, magical conceptions of the Romanist or other ritualist.

To the humble, reverent, believing soul there is a reality and virtue in the ordinance not to be forgone. There is also a corresponding solemnity not to be forgotten or abused.

Though there is no magical change of the elements into the person of Christ, as declared in transubstantiation, nor mystical conjoining of the two as in consubstantiation, yet, as God sees and declares, there is a real spiritual association of the two, so intimate and practical that he who eats and drinks of the symbols in a sinful state of heart and life is guilty of profaning the body and blood of the Lord (1 Cor. 11:27). It is as if he laid violent hands on that holy Person and wantonly shed His sacred blood.

One who partakes in this unholy spirit does not discern that by partaking of this bread he is approaching to the body of the Lord and dealing therewith. He does not discern that body as connected with the bread. To his dulled apprehension this bread is no more than any other piece of bread.

Such partaking is not merely profitless but positively dangerous, as many in the church at Corinth had found, being dealt with by God in judgment. They dishonoured the Lord's body, and God in recompense chastened them in their bodies. "For this cause many among you are weak and sickly, and not a few sleep," that is, in premature death (1 Cor. 11:30).

As was well known to the Corinthian Christians, the heathen world was interpenetrated with numerous secret religious societies, known as the "mysteries," because their proceedings were kept profoundly secret. Each society was presided over and devoted to one of the principal demon gods.

Upon a candidate being admitted to initiation into one of these orders he was immersed in water, as a token that he held himself cut off as by death from his old outside associations and now deemed the society his real sphere of life. Thereafter, should a conflict arise between the interests of his business, his home, his political, or other spheres, and the interests of the Order, his duty was to the Society at the expense of other claims.

Later in the initiatory rites he was caused to eat of food that had been dedicated to the god of the order, the bread of the god: and if after this act of communion with the god he proved false to his duties and the rights of the order he became liable to condign and perhaps extreme penalties, which were enforced severely.

The solemn declarations of Paul in this chapter (1 Cor. 11) were calculated to make these former heathen to feel that the true and living God was similarly jealous for His just demand for holiness and faithfulness in His people.

That great and holy God had in wondrous love given up to death His own beloved Son for the salvation of sinners, that He might become to them through faith the Bread of Life, the means of holiness and of communion with God. They who had been baptized into a life of association with that Son risen again from the dead, and who had thereupon eaten of that bread of God, must act consistently with this profession and high privilege, and to desecrate the sacred symbols of these holy realities, to prove false to their profession of fellowship with their holy Redeemer, was not to be tolerated by their God and Father.

By so much as the divine reality is honourable is the symbol thereof sacred. A national flag stands forth as the symbol of the empire, and to insult it is to outrage the empire. He who partakes with faith of the true Bread is profited by the symbol thereof; he who reaches not the reality finds the symbol empty; he who by evil ways dishonours the Lord whose name he bears desecrates the symbol of His body, if he dare to handle it while in that moral condition.

Wherefore "let a man prove himself, and so [in this state of self-examination and purging], let him eat of the bread and drink of the cup" (1 Cor. 11:28). Oh, how does this word rebuke the careless, unprepared state of heart in which some come to the Feast. Giving no real care to be present in good time to begin the hour of worship; suffering the mind to roam over needless or even vain topics of talk as they come; indifferent as to whether a brother or sister has rightly somewhat against them—is it any wonder if these enjoy not the Supper or even are injured by partaking?

But it says not of an individual: "Let his *brethren* examine him and so let him *not* eat," but let each examine himself so as to become fit to eat. It is only in extreme and known cases of moral wickedness that the church is commanded to "put away the wicked man from among" themselves (1 Cor. 5:13). Nor is it then merely a question of "putting away from the table," as the phrase runs, though this is included. Such exclusion is to be from all association, private as well as public.

The self-proving is to be personal and with a view to partaking. The heart of Christ still desires earnestly to commune with our hearts. He is the same as when He said: "With [intense] desire I have desired to eat this Passover with you" (Luke 22:15). But our heart can only go forth to His heart, and know His nearness and preciousness, as far as it is holy as His heart is holy.

To the heart that is set on holiness He can reveal His heart, and at His Supper is one place where this is blessedly possible. The very symbols of His person aid us in the remembrance of Himself and His sacrifice of love, so provoking our faith and love to fuller, more satisfying, inward appropriation of Himself as our life.

Let us give heed as He says "This do in remembrance of Me," and in that spirit of unreserved dedication to Him which we once set forth in our baptism in His name, let us fulfil this His dying request. That He appointed only two ordinances is the more reason that His followers should hold both to be sacred, joyful obligations.

It will be sorrowful to meet Him at last and to have to own that we refused, or neglected, or delayed to do His will. Well may we then "shrink in shame from Him at His presence" (1 John 2:28; see Darby, Alford, etc.). But it will be to the joy of His heart and ours, both now and then, to carry out faithfully all His good, well-pleasing, and perfect will.

The fact that all gathered eat of one bread and drink of one cup is a confession by each that he is in communion with all the rest: "We, who are many, are one bread, one body: for we all partake of the one bread" (1 Cor. 10:17). A believer who in heart is at variance with and estranged from any other must of necessity act hypocritically if he eat. By the symbol he testifies to unity with that other, whereas spiritual unity has been interrupted. Oh, that each such would heed his Lord's words in Matt. 5:23-24: "If therefore thou art offering thy gift at the altar, and there rememberest that thy brother hath aught against thee, leave there thy gift before the altar, and go thy way, first be reconciled to thy brother, and then come and offer thy gift." It were wiser, very far better, to refrain from eating the bread until all bitterness and variance were purged from the heart. We have the most vivid recollections of a gathering in south-eastern Europe when eighteen believers met, seventeen of them at serious enmity with the one and he with them all. They had wisely, though sadly, not held the Supper for six months. This morning they had met in the power of solemn truth that had been spoken to them for some weeks; there was frank and true confession by every person present;

they one after another shook hands with the one brother in question; and then the holy feast was held, and perhaps we may never again be privileged to be at a season when so much grace was experienced in so short an hour. God abhors unreality and all hypocritical formality; but oh, how blessedly do hearts feel bound together in holy love as they join sincerely in this ordinance of love and fellowship. An instance is seen in the lines that close this chapter.

———

*Lines written in November 1857, by Miss Paget when her sisters and friends wished her to leave Barnstaple to reside in Exeter.*

> I cannot now return to thee,
> I cannot leave my rest;
> For here God's children comfort me,
> And here I find I'm blest.
> We worship not 'neath fretted dome,
> Or organ's feeling sound,
> Nor where the dim light streams athwart
> The long aisle's sculptured round;
> But simply, as of old they came,
> According to the Word
> They met in Jesus' sacred Name,
> And called upon the Lord.
> No priests adorned with priestly pride,
> No altar railed around,
> No multitude of mixed race
> Are meeting on the ground;
> But worshippers sincere are there,
> And there the wine and bread,
> Mysterious emblems of their Lord
> Who for them groaned and bled.
> Mysterious! for by faith we look
> Beyond the outward sign
> To Him, who now will come again
> In glory all divine;
> To Him, Who said, Take this and eat,
> Drink and remember Me—
> We do it, Lord, for thy dear sake,
> And long thy face to see:

We do it in sweet fellowship,
Communion with each other;
Not as a stranger alien host,
But brother now with brother.
Then, loved one, call me not away
From this dear chosen band;
I've much to learn, here let me stay,
That I may understand
More perfectly the will of God,
The love of God to me,
That love which changed to sunny calm
Life's dark and troubled sea;
That love which drew me nearer Him,
My portion and my stay,
My port in storms, my light in clouds,
My Lord, my life, my way!

Chapter 8

# The Institution of The Lord's Supper

THE wordy warfare with His foes is over. Jesus holds the field: "No one durst ask Him any more questions." Now the Lord retires from the grand and crowded temple to the quiet of an upper room for converse with the inner circle of His own followers, and to observe for the last time the Passover feast. It was during this evening meal that He took of the bread and received a cup and gave to the ancient solemnity a higher meaning and completion, by instituting the breaking of bread and partaking of the cup as a perpetual remembrance of Himself as the sacrifice offered for the remission of sins, the true Passover lamb.

By the first generation of His disciples the original features of this simple and holy ordinance were preserved, but there soon set in a change in conception and practice which thoroughly corrupted the ordinance and changed it into a sacramental ceremony charged with mystical meaning and magical power, the working and efficacy of which could be secured only by its being solemnized by a consecrated priest. Thus that simple remembrance of Himself which the Lord instituted for the mutual upbuilding of all who partake, was perverted by heathen notions and regulations and became a powerful agent for concentrating authority in a human priesthood.

At rare intervals the Lord has stirred godly hearts to return to His original thought and characteristics for His Supper so that the intended grace might be enjoyed. Yet it is but seldom that this return has been thorough and the observance been sufficiently stripped of the false ideas and corrupting features imported by clerisy. The reason for this is largely that the principle of clerisy itself has seldom been completely rejected. It persists in modified forms and degrees in the State Churches of the Reformation and it lingers in the Nonconformist bodies that refused those State Churches; and it subtly survives or revives even in those smaller circles which have at least intended and endeavoured to be quite clear of its poisonous influence. And now, as ever, this spirit of clerisy finds its surest spheres in the only two ordinances sanctioned by Christ, baptism and the Supper.

It is therefore necessary and salutary that the New Testament records of those first days and occasions should from time to time be scrutinized afresh, that the mind of the Lord, and the practice of the apostles He taught, should rise clearly before the eyes of our hearts. Yet this will prove beneficial only as far as there is a resolute purpose and a vigorous courage to return to those first conceptions and practice. Indeed, without this humility and obedience of spirit even a child of God may not see clearly the picture presented in the Word, or seeing it may reject its claim and continue in some human views and ways. Take heed lest the light that is in thee become darkness, for how deep shall be that darkness!

Let it therefore be observed:

First, that the Supper was instituted in a private house and in a small group of familiar friends. This feature continued. Acts 2:46 tells of the first believers at Pentecost that they broke bread at home, and Acts 20:8 shows that the gathering at Troas was in an upper room, as when the Lord first introduced the feast. This excludes any necessity for a consecrated building, a chapel, or a public hall of any type. This feature continued till well into the third century. For two hundred years Roman law did not permit Christians as such to own property: they therefore met where they could, in houses, catacombs, woods, or elsewhere. The importance of this has been constantly recognized in periods of persecution, and will be so again.

When leaders of a Christian assembly object to the Supper being observed in homes, and insist that it is schismatic to hold it elsewhere than in the hall where the assembly meets, they are plainly unscriptural and are asserting the vital principles of clerisy that the ordinance should be observed in a special building and under the control of leaders. This secret desire of prominent men to have affairs under their control is a corrupting cancer. It is that dominating impulse of all clerics, the love of power.

I asked a godly Baptist minister why he presided at the Lord's table. He replied that it was a question of order. But *whose* order was secured, God's or man's?

Observe, *secondly*, that the Supper arose out of and was linked with a social meal. The Passover was a family festival eaten in the various homes of the redeemed. It was during this repast that the Lord introduced the new element, in which was concentrated the essential thought of remembrance. Israelites were to remind themselves of the redemption wrought in Egypt; Christ's disciples are to remind themselves of His work of redemption on the cross. This social feature the early Christians perpetuated: (*a*) "breaking bread at home; (*b*) they took their food" (Acts 2:46). Thus at Corinth also the love feast of the church and the Lord's Supper were associated (1 Cor. 11:20-21, 32–34). This conjunction could produce opposite effects; either the degradation of the Supper by self-indulgence at the social meal, as at Corinth, or the elevation of the common meal by the solemnizing, sanctifying influence of the Supper.

The effect of this association of the meal and the Supper, and of both taking place in the family home and circle, prevented of necessity the arising of a clerical caste and the sacrosanct, magical notion of a mystical rite.

To the Catholic, attendance at mass is the summit of all religion. If he is diligent in attendance there the remaining elements of religion are only insignificant, and his personal conduct in daily life is secondary. To many a "Plymouth Brother" the breaking of bread meeting is all-important, and sufficient. This solemnity is the acme of religion for too many and if they have broken bread little else is of importance, sometimes including moral behaviour. In both extremes there is a *false* sense of sanctity, a notion of virtue inherent in the ceremony irrespective of the state of heart and practice of the partaker. This is paralysing and demoralizing and can bring the partaker under the solemn warning against partaking unworthily and inducing Divine judgment (1 Cor. 11:28–32). Apart from any distinct visitation in bodily sickness or premature death, this state of soul is ever accompanied by spiritual deadness and by formality. This may be unrecognized by the individuals concerned, who may plume themselves upon their devoutness.

Again, *thirdly*, the Supper was not instituted on the first day of the week or on the Sabbath, but on a week-night. Hence every day is proper. The same verse in Acts 2 shows that the first disciples practised daily communion in their houses (46). It was the only possibility for many thousands of Christians in one confined city. There was no place for a vast congregation of disciples to gather and observe a Christian feast.

This is significant as to the view held of the new ordinance and the spirit of observance. They were all Jews, still attending public worship in the temple, and zealous of ancient customs. This new feast had been lately instituted in connexion with the Passover. That was a feast that might be held only at an appointed time of the year, as with all their other ceremonies. Yet from the very start of the Christian Church they were already emancipated from legal restrictions as to this ordinance, and observed it daily as occasion served.

How contrary to this is the practice and the spirit of the Catholic mass, or the sacrament in the State Churches. How different too from the infrequent and well-controlled observance of Presbyterianism, and from the stated occasions in most Dissenting chapels. And I knew the leaders of an Open Brethren assembly who refused any recognition of a new gathering, where God was working blessedly, because they broke bread on the Saturday evenings! Yet there is no Divine command that the proper time is Lord's day morning at 11 o'clock or the proper place the Meeting Room or the Gospel Hall. It is equally against the New Testament that groups of immature disciples, in heathen lands, must not break bread unless the "missionary" is present or a brother he approves. The Corinthians were mostly heathen lately converted, and abuse quickly appeared at the Supper, but the Apostle did not check these by forbidding them to break bread unless he were present or a delegate. This is in principle rank clerisy and sacerdotalism, destructive of gospel liberty and spiritual growth.

All this bears directly on the practice of the reservation of a portion of the bread and wine used at the general sacrament to be taken to the sick or others who could not be present. This obnoxious proceeding attaches a special sanctity to the elements thus used, so that there is special benefit imparted beyond what could be gained by using non-consecrated elements. This, indeed, is the essence of the matter, that priestly consecration imparts special virtue. It is clerisy again in undisguised ugliness. And all this is wholly nugatory, seeing that any few believers can profitably partake at any time, in any place, without a priest or other special leader.

*Fourthly*: The simple and informal nature of the Supper is marked distinctly by the conversational feature of the occasions. That was naturally seen in the Passover feast, it being a family and social event. There was converse between Jesus and the disciples, and among themselves as to who would betray Him. They disputed with one another as to priority, which led the Lord to rebuke and warn them, and prompted Peter to protest that he was ready to die with Christ, causing the Lord to foretell his coming denial of his Master. There was further interchange of thought as to the matter of now taking purses and swords. A brief colloquy arose as to whether Peter's feet should be washed, and another between the Lord and Judas. While Christ was imparting the instruction recorded in John 14, Thomas interposed a remark and Philip added another, to which the other Judas shortly added a question. A little later (John 16:17ff.) the disciples are heard chatting over a difficulty they feel, and the Lord talks to them about it.

The long night at Troas developed this same element. It is not to be supposed that Paul talked and talked the whole night and the rest only listened. The historian tells us that Paul *dialogued* with them (Acts 20:7, 9) and *homilized* (ver. 11), both words implying conversation.

This is vastly different to an elaborate ornate ceremony such as the mass or a choral service, and considerably different to the common "morning meeting" in other quarters. That night the bread was broken in the unexpected interval caused by the death and resuscitation of the youth who fell from the window, which being over, the conversation was resumed. It would be very scriptural to take the holy Supper in the middle of a conversational Bible reading.

This introduces another and very important feature.

*Fifthly*: The Supper was a brief event in the midst of long instruction in the truth of God.

Combined conversation and instruction was an appointed feature of the Passover. At the very institution of the feast it was taken for granted that the natural curiosity of children would prompt them to ask the meaning of these singular doings, such as eating a lamb with unleavened bread and the redemption of the firstborn child; and the father had the duty to recite the history of the festival and its lessons (Ex. 12, 13). Without this instruction the occasion must have soon become a meaningless religious formality, even as the Supper of the Lord is to countless thousands from either lack of instruction or false teaching. The great facts of redemption from death and dedication to God were illustrated and inculcated by the annual Passover.

Similarly the Lord that night taught that His blood, represented by the cup, was to be shed for the remission of sins, to which was added much instruction as to devotion and obedience to Himself. It is important to observe the vast range of powerful truths which He explained and stressed. It included:

1. That the feast then instituted looked forward to the time when the Lord will renew such fellowship with his followers in the kingdom of God.

2. That in His kingdom the humble slave is the chief ruler.

3. That honour and rule in His kingdom are gained by sharing His present trials.

4. The activity of Satan as the accuser and tempter of the disciple, but His own intercession that the attack and testing should be limited. This short statement of the high priestly service of the Son of God is amplified in *Hebrews*.

5. The searching warning that, though their faith in Him had sufficed in the past to enable them to go on His business without purse or protection, yet that night's test would overwhelm them and they would, from want of faith, be cast on their own resources and would fail.

These features are found together in Luke 22:14–38. Why did the Spirit of truth think well to cause a Gentile Christian, a generation later than the events, to group these subjects together and send the account forth to other Gentile Christians? Does this not tell us of our need of such instruction and that the table of the Lord is a right occasion to give it?

Again, why did the same Spirit of truth cause John, at the close of the next following generation, to record the body of teaching given at the Supper as found in chs. 13 to 16 of his Gospel? What a mighty vista of instruction is here! Observe:

1. That a clean walk (washed feet) is simply indispensable to fellowship with Christ—"If I wash thee not thou hast no part with Me!" (13:8).

2. That lowliness of heart is requisite in disciples, that they may serve their brethren (13:14–17).

3. The possibility of having an untroubled heart; of sharing the Lord's own tranquillity and joy (14:1, 27; 15: 11).

4. The life of interior and abiding oneness with Christ and the fruitfulness that results (15:1–16).

5. The Person and working of the Spirit of God as teacher, sanctifier, and co-witness with the believer to Christ, giving knowledge of the oneness of the Father and the Son (14:20).

6. The illimitable resources and irresistible energy of the prayer of faith in the name of Christ.

7. The return of the Lord as the hope and goal of faith.

These are some of the profound and exalted topics with which the Lord Jesus occupied the hearts of His followers as they conversed at the table that memorable night. He was preparing them for the tasks and ordeals that awaited them without the support of His visible presence. No one will or can be equal to these tasks and tests unless these mighty truths are the energy of the soul. Therefore it is a necessity of Satan to prevent the Christian from being saturated with those invigorating truths, and one of his subtlest devices is seen in such suggestions as that "we meet to break bread," "we meet to remember the Lord," *not* to hear addresses; or that there should be no ministry before the bread has been broken; or, at any rate ministry should be occupied only with Calvary. So far have these injurious ideas been pressed that in one circle of Christians no ministry of the Word is permitted at the breaking of bread. The practical result is general starvation, with the resultant spiritual sickness and weakness of the famished. And one of the alarming symptoms is that the under-fed dream they are well nourished, and know not that they manifest to all the ill health of their spirits in feelings and actions sadly unlike Christ.

On the facts presented it is evident that much of the Lord's instruction that night was concerned with the spiritual state of His followers. This is ever a paramount necessity, which can be seen in Paul's dealing with the Corinthians. He had to tell them plainly that they were in such a state of soul that it was not possible to eat the Lord's Supper (1 Cor. 11:20), and he gave such instruction and warning as healed them.

One severe winter I was plainly guided by the Lord to take a toilsome journey of many hundreds of miles from one foreign land to another which I had not before visited. In a remote mountain village there was an assembly of believers in such a poor condition that they had wisely ceased for six months from breaking bread and risking the judgment of the Lord for doing so unworthily. Nor was there found any spiritual energy to deal with the condition. Their need was instruction, and the Spirit so applied the very first talk given as to begin in the heart of a stubborn leader a work which presently developed into general healing (See pp. 80 ff.).

Such is the condition and the need of churches without number. That village church might have met indefinitely, have droned out favourite hymns, have offered routine and empty prayers, and have partaken outwardly and bodily of the bread and wine, but have gone from bad to worse for want of instruction. "The grace of God hath appeared. . . instucting us" (Tit. 2:11-12), and the false and subtle ideas above mentioned are so many devices of the Evil One to curtail the instruction the Lord would still give, as He gave it that night of old.

Acts 20 shows clearly that long hours were occupied with such conversation and instruction before the bread was broken, and that afterward the dialogue continued till dawn, forbidding the idea that ministry ought not to precede. These facts stare at us out of the pages of Scripture, yet in disregard of them believers will give the hour to many hymns, to long pauses, wearisome prayers, a formal partaking of the bread and cup, and they depart as empty of grace as they came. It is feeding that they need; yet in one such assembly where there lived a well-known teacher his brethren complained that he would give at the Lord's table general instruction, and they did not want it. The assembly paid the price by being underfed and weak.

When the Lord and the apostles had concluded the feast, before leaving the upper room they sang a hymn. One hymn in the whole evening! Almost certainly this was the Hallel, Ps. 118. That they sang permits congregational singing.

That night at Troas was spent entirely in intercourse over the truth of God. To think of believers passing a whole night together without singing! The usual Nonconformist service includes three or four hymns. Many a "morning meeting" has five or six hymns in an hour or an hour and a quarter. One wonders how the time would be filled out without the hymn book. The Epistles contain only two brief references to singing among Christians (Eph. 5:19; Col. 3:16). Moreover, this exercise was not for self-pleasing, nor even for "worship"; it was a form of "teaching and admonishing one another." The Lord has His portion not by the outward song but by the melody of the heart. The exhortation "speaking *to one another* in psalms, hymns, and spiritual songs; teaching and admonishing *one another*," requires solo singing—impelled by the Spirit; it is not fulfilled by all singing the same words together. This continued well into the second century. Thus Tertullian (c. A.D. 200), describing a Christian love feast, includes that "everyone is invited to sing, either from holy scripture or from the prompting of his own spirit some song of praise to God for the common edification" (*Apology*, ch. 39).

How greatly later formalism and human ideas have superseded apostolic practice. It is a sign of spiritual weakness that such large place is now given to singing. It shows little appetite for divine knowledge and much love of self-pleasing. If the average modern

Christian could find himself in a meeting of the early church he might wonder where he had strayed.

Further, will anyone suggest that the whole time that night at Troas was used considering only Calvary? They had indeed gathered to break bread, but in those early days they still experienced the leading of the Spirit of Christ and that at the Supper He occupied hearts with the fulness of Christ in all His offices, past, present, and to come, not with the cross only, though that had its due place.

The human notions and rules mentioned are a denial to the Spirit of His divine right in the house of God, and this restricting of the Spirit is grievous in its nature and results. It is both impious and ruinous. *In principle* the imposing of man's wishes at the Supper is exactly the same as imposing a human ceremonial as in the Roman mass; externally there are differences; in essence they are alike; men offer worship guided by their own ideas, not by God's Word and Spirit. Alas, that word may become as sadly true in the church as it was solemnly true in Israel, that "in vain do they worship Me, teaching as their doctrines the precepts of men" (Matt. 15:7–9).

There is more to be learned than can be mentioned here. The passage on the Lord's Supper in 1 Cor. 11 begins with instruction on prophesying and praying. Prophesying was utterance by immediate impulse of the Holy Spirit.[1] At what formal celebration of the sacrament or communion service is room allowed for this?

One thought more. It is written for our admonition that *"when the hour was come*, He sat down, and the apostles with Him" (Luke 22:14). No one of them was late! Neither would any saint today be late unavoidably were the Lord expected in visible presence. Now to faith He is as really present as if He were visibly so. Therefore in this matter of punctuality, and of all behaviour at the Supper, let us be as reverent as if He were to be visibly before our eyes, remembering that we at least are visible to his eye. Being in this spirit we shall find that in His presence there is indeed fulness of joy, and the joyful heart will praise Him with joyful lips, and thus will be served the high and holy, and all-inclusive end of all worship, of all life.

---

1  See pp. 162 ff below.

Is it not clear that there has been great departure from the intentions of the Lord as revealed in His word? In every attempt to restore what is of God we are met by difficulties and we feel our weakness. "The strength of the bearers of burdens is decayed, and there is much rubbish; so that we are not able to build the wall" (Neh. 4:10). Yet God protected and prospered, and they finished the seemingly impossible. The Son of God knows that we have but little power, but those who are resolved to keep His Word will be established (Rev. 3:8).

"Who is wise, that he may understand these things? prudent, that he may know them? For the ways of Jehovah are right, and the righteous shall walk in them: but transgressors shall fall therein" (Hos. 14:9).

CHAPTER 9

# Ministry and Oversight

IN the "Daily Meditations" of that rare saint and scholar, George Bowen, of Bombay, are the following reflections for October 8:
"Let all things be done unto edifying" (1 Cor. 14:26).

On successive Sabbaths, having a definite object in view, we visit various churches. We sit down with the people of God of a certain denomination, hear the sermon that is preached, and observe the worship that is rendered to God. Again, we worship with those of another denomination. We notice many points of difference in their mode of celebrating divine worship and seeking their own edification; but at length we come to a worshipping body whose customs are so fundamentally different from those of the churches previously visited that the differences among the latter appear to be quite trifling in comparison. In the church that we have now stumbled upon in an out-of-the-way place (in the Epistle to the Corinthians) instead of one man officiating for all, while all sit silent save when they sing or make common responses, and where everything is arranged to exclude as much as possible anything like spontaneousness, we find that when the members come together, "everyone hath a psalm, hath a doctrine, hath a tongue, hath a revelation, hath an interpretation." One, two, or three speak in an unknown tongue; and another interprets. Prophets speak, two or three in succession. If anything is revealed to another that sitteth by, the first holds his tongue. May we not learn from this that the Holy Ghost loves a larger liberty than is accorded by our arrangements? We cleave to them as though they had been imposed by the solemn and unalterable decree of the Great Head of the church: and a proposition to depart from them is regarded almost as treason against Christ. It is singular, however, that the apostolic church should be completely defunct to us, as regards the force of its example in these matters. There were some great abuses in those early churches; think you they were the greatest conceivable abuses? Is it not possible that the apostle Paul, coming into one of our staid and orderly churches, would look upon the whole of the decorous and tasteful service as one unmitigated abuse? He would, perhaps, say, Is the Holy Ghost dead, that you make no provision for his manifestation? Is there no communion of the saints in the assemblies of the saints?

"Let the prophets speak by two or three, and let the others discriminate. But if a revelation be made to another sitting by, let the first keep silence. For ye all can prophesy one by one, that all may learn, and all may be comforted" (1 Cor. 14:29–31).

The picture here given of ministry in an apostolic gathering excludes the presiding officer of whom we have read as arising in the second century. It shows (1) that in the church there were several persons known to have been chosen by the Holy Spirit for the ministry of the word of God; (2) that each and all of these had power and right delegated from the Lord to address the assembly; (3) that the control of their utterance was (*a*) by the Holy Spirit direct, who, while one was speaking, might give to another a message for the assembly; (*b*) by the prophet himself, who retained control of his own spirit, even though energized by the Holy Spirit, and could resume silence.

The control of the assembly by one man was thus unknown. The Lord Himself, by His Spirit, was as really present as if He had been visible. Indeed, to faith He was visible; and He Himself being there, what servant could be so irreverent as to take out of His hands the control of the worship and ministry?

But, on the other hand, most certainly it was not the case that *anybody* had liberty to minister. The liberty was for the Holy Spirit to do His will, not for His people to do as they willed. The notion that every believer had an equal right to speak was not allowed. Everyone who was chosen, qualified, and moved thereto by the Lord the Spirit had the right, and no one else had any right. All *rights* in the house of God vest solely in the Son of God.

The post-apostolic church quickly departed from this pattern. It has been seen and adopted only occasionally throughout the centuries, notably in seasons of powerful revival. A hundred and thirty years ago it was rediscovered by the first Brethren, followed for a while with almost apostolic blessedness, and has been, and is being, very considerably forsaken, with great spiritual loss.

The spiritual energy which accompanied Brethren in their first years is little appreciated today. Robert Govett deemed it the mightiest movement of the Holy Spirit since Pentecost, while the writer of the article "Plymouth Brethren" in Blackie's *Popular Encyclopaedia* says that it "seemed at first to be a movement great enough to threaten the whole organization of the Christian church." In the light of Holy Scripture we may with profit study their experience as a practical and modern example, both of encouragement and warning.

Dr. S. P. Tregelles has left precise first-hand information as to the original practice of Brethren in several localities, including Plymouth (the first such assembly in England), Exeter, Bath and London. He united with the Plymouth assembly as early as 1835. In 1849 he wrote:

> "Stated ministry, but not exclusive ministry," has been the principle on which we have acted all along here. . . . By "stated ministry" we mean that such and such persons are looked on as teachers, and one or more of them is expected to minister, and they are responsible for stirring up the gift that is in them; but this is not "exclusive ministry," because there is an open door for others who may from time to time receive any gift, so that they too may exercise their gifts.
>
> This was then the principle acted on in Plymouth before there was any other gathering for communion in England. . . . When such meetings did arise in other places, there was no thought, at least for several years, of setting up liberty of ministry in the sense of unrestrainedness.[1] Liberty of Ministry . . . was intended to signify that all who were fitted by the Holy Ghost might minister; it was as needful for such to *shew* that they had fitness, as it was for those who wished for fellowship to exhibit to their brethren that they were really taking the stand of Believers in the name of the Lord Jesus Christ.[2]

Tregelles continues:

> I am well aware that some years ago there were introduced in London very democratic views of ministry—utterly subversive of all godly order, utterly opposed to subjection to the Lordship of Christ, and contradictory to all Scriptural doctrine of the gifts of the Spirit bestowed on individuals . . . when these democratic views were circulated he (Mr.

---

1 *Three Letters*, 8, 9.
2 *Ibid.* 6, 7.

G. V. Wigram[1]) published a tract (in 1844, I believe), of four pages, entitled, "On Ministry in the Word." I extract two of the questions and answers:

"E.—Do you admit "a *regular ministry*"?

"W.—If by a regular ministry you mean a *stated* ministry (that is, that in every assembly those who are gifted of God to speak to edification will be both limited in number and known to the rest), I do admit it; but if by a regular ministry you mean an *exclusive* ministry, I dissent. By an *exclusive* ministry, I mean the recognizing certain persons as so *exclusively* holding the place of teachers, as that the use of a real gift by anyone else would be irregular. As, for instance, in the Church of England and in most dissenting Chapels, a sermon would be felt to be *irregular* which had been made up by two or three persons really gifted by the Holy Ghost.

"E.—On what do you build this distinction?

"W.—From Acts 13:1, I see that at Antioch there were but five whom the Holy Ghost recognised as teachers—Barnabas, Simeon, Lucius, Manaen, and Saul. Doubtless, at all the meetings it was only these five, one or more of them, as it pleased the Holy Ghost, who were expected by the saints to speak. This was a *stated* ministry. But it was not an *exclusive* ministry; for when Judas and Silas came (15:32), they were pleased to take their places among the others, and then the recognised teachers were more numerous."

These statements [adds Dr. Tregelles] are sufficiently explicit.[2]

Of late there has been considerable departure amongst Brethren from these principles. The democratic idea that everyone has equal right to minister, which is departure in one direction, has necessarily given opportunity for unedifying speaking. Well merited is Spurgeon's keen comment, that where the whole is *mouth* the result is *vacuum*. This, in turn, had led to departure in the opposite direction by a form of control of ministry which directly conforms gatherings to the very conditions around from which the early Brethren broke away to return to the spiritual, apostolic pattern.

As yet, happily, meetings for worship or for prayer continue in form to be apostolic, but other gatherings pass increasingly under

---

1   The principal leader, after Mr. Darby, among the latter's followers.
2   *Three Letters*, 12, 13.

human control. More and more conferences adopt a closed platform, with a chairman in control and ministry restricted to selected speakers. Sometimes these speakers are left free among themselves as to ministering; at other places their order is settled. At one important annual conference the chairman announced explicitly that the brethren on the platform had been selected by the conveners, and that *no one else would be allowed to express himself under any circumstances*, and this was enforced by the suppression by the chairman of any others who commenced to speak. This example at an important centre greatly accelerated this course elsewhere.

Let this be considered narrowly. A statement by a Christian to the brethren is declared to be a statement to the Holy Spirit (Acts 5:3): thus the announcement before us is really, however unintended, an intimation to the Holy Spirit that under no circumstances is *He* at liberty to use any other of His servants to edify the assembly than those the conveners have selected. And this is *tacitly* the situation created by *every* closed platform.

A certain measure of unpleasing and unedifying talking is, no doubt, prevented by such measures, though selected speakers also may be tedious and unprofitable; and a certain superior style of speech can, no doubt, be generally secured which, in itself, is good, but the psychical effect of which is easily mistaken for spiritual unction. Sixty-five years' constant experience has satisfied me that, on the whole the spiritual profit of gatherings is distinctly less than in former days.

I remember a large missionary conference at which the late Mr. E. S. Bowden gave a most powerful, soul-exercising account of the days of revival in India. The whole audience was bowed before God, and had the Lord been free to hold His people under the influence of that moment, had the assembly been allowed to wait upon God, there was every likelihood of an unusual and blessed visitation of the Spirit. But the chairman had a programme! The golden moment was spoiled; the meetings sank again to the ordinary.

If a meeting or meetings be arranged *avowedly* for *ministry* by an announced person or persons, well and good, though the rights of the Holy Spirit should always be acknowledged, and there should be liberty for Him to use any servant He pleases. With this proviso I would see nothing unscriptural in one and the same qualified brother holding preaching and teaching meetings all the year round in the same hall. That general meetings of Christians were held in that building would not affect the principle. These latter should be under the sole leading of the Holy Spirit, as should be every such assembling of saints; those former might rightly be in the hands of one competent minister of the Word. In Acts 19:9 we see a church gathered by Paul at Ephesus. In that church were the apostle (so long as he stayed in the city), prophets, pastors and teachers, and other saints, *every* joint, privately or publicly, supplying something to the growth, strength, usefulness of the body (Eph. 4). Here, *in the assembly*, is the liberty of the Spirit. But, in addition, Paul, as an evangelist and teacher, had a regular place of his own for ministry, "he reasoned daily in the school of Tyrannus." From the immediate connexion of the words, "he separated the disciples, reasoning daily, etc.," it looks as if that school was the meeting place of the church at that time, which suggests the dual picture I have now presented. Yet even so, I take for granted that if, while Paul was speaking, another spiritual person had received a revelation the apostle would have conformed to his own regulation, "if a revelation be made to another sitting by, let the first (speaker) hold his peace" (1 Cor. 14:30).

But what is sorrowful is the solemnly significant feature that gatherings formerly convened for waiting upon God, that His Spirit should lead and should supply ministry, steadily change from this apostolic type to the prevailing human arrangements, and that new conferences tend from their beginning to adopt the lower method. The departure is symptomatic of spiritual decay, and is already promoting further deterioration of the body corporate by hindering soul exercise as to ministry, and therefore the development of fresh ministers of the Word.

Now that the closed platform, with selected speakers, chairman, and programme, has become the regular method of conferences, how shall the rearing of thousands of young people in this method aid the churches of the next generation to depend upon the presence, government, and leading of the Holy Spirit, confessedly the apostolic plan? Referring to 1 Cor. 14:29-30 (which shows how primitive assemblies were ordered), Dr. Rendle Short well said to a large gathering of Sunday School teachers and workers in November, 1924:

> We spoil God's workings, and we starve our souls, if we depart from this principle.
>
> Someone may say, "But will not things get into dreadful confusion if you seek to follow out these practices? In those days they had the Holy Spirit to guide them, and shall not we go wildly astray, and have dull, confused, unprofitable, perhaps even unseemly meetings, unless we get someone to take charge?"
>
> Is not that practically a denial of the Holy Spirit? Do we dare deny that the Holy Spirit is still being given? The Holy Spirit is at work today as much as He was at work in those days, and we may all join in that creed of all the Churches: "I believe in the Holy Ghost."
>
> Please do not think that what is sometimes called the "open meeting" means that the saints are at the mercy of any unprofitable talker who thinks he has something to say, and would like to inflict himself upon them. The open meeting is not a meeting that is open to man. It is a meeting that is open to the Holy Spirit. There are some whose mouths must be stopped. Sometimes they may be stopped by prayer, and sometimes they have to be stopped by the godly admonition of those whom God has set over the assembly. *But because there is failure in carrying out the principle, do not let us give up the principles of God.*[1]

I very gladly quote this re-affirmation of primitive principles, and earnestly invite all conference conveners and speakers courageously and dutifully to re-adopt the practice of the same, with faith in the Spirit of God, giving heed to the above closing exhortation I have italicized.

The divine method just indicated of dealing with unprofitable talking is effective, without departure from the vital principle of the Lord directly prompting ministry. Paul instructed Titus that the mouths of certain teachers "must be stopped" (Tit. 1:10-14). The word is strong, and means to put on a bridle or muzzle, which was to be effected by "reproving them sharply"; no doubt privately when possible, but publicly if necessary, and always graciously. In the first days of Brethren this was practised. Tregelles says:

---

1 *Young Believers and Assembly Life*, 13, 14 (Pickering and Inglis).

Liberty of ministry was recognized amongst those who possessed ability from God; but it was considered that ministry which was not to profit—which did not commend itself to the consciences of others—ought to be repressed.

And this was the sense in which the phrase "liberty of ministry" was used. . . . On one occasion Mr. Newton had in the assembly to stop ministry which was manifestly improper, with Mr. J. N. Darby's and Mr. G. V. Wigram's presence and *full concurrence*: a plain proof that they *then* fully objected to unrestrained ministry. . . there was restraint, not upon edifying teaching, but upon that which was unedifying; advice and exhortation *in private* were generally resorted to, but *when needful* the case was met in a more public manner. . . . I have had pretty much acquaintance with several localities, and I may specify Exeter and London as places in which it was believed to be right to judge whether ministry was to edification, and to put a stop to that which was considered to be not so. In London this was done repeatedly—far oftener to my knowledge, than ever in Plymouth.[1]

One who was present told me that, long years ago, at Salem Chapel, Bristol, an untrained brother announced he would read two chapters; but upon his early making mistakes in reading, George Müller interposed with: "Dear Brother, as it is very important that the Word of God should be read correctly, I will read these chapters for you." And he did so.

I well remember, at a large conference, a good man so mishandled a certain text that the whole assembly was quickly restive. After perhaps ten minutes, W. H. Bennet rose and said, sweetly but decidedly, "Beloved Brother, I think it is the general feeling of the meeting that you have said enough upon this subject." The speaker at once desisted.

But so delicate, invidious a duty requires for its discharge men of *spiritual* wisdom, weight, authority, men to whom, because the unction of the Holy One is upon them, others bow. It is simpler, though unspiritual and worldly, to resort to the pre-arranged platform; but let us clearly understand that not even the germ of it is in the New Testament: it is a departure from the apostolic method; and from

---

1  *Three Letters*, 6, 8, 9.

the ways of the early Brethren; and every departure leads towards a barren "far country."

This directs our thoughts to another departure. In each apostolic church there were elders, men qualified for ruling and caring for the house of God. Who they were in each church was known. They were set in office (*tithemi*) by the Holy Spirit (Acts 20:28); sometimes appointed[1] by those who were used of God to found the local church in question (Acts 14:23); sometimes only recommended to the church without formal appointment (1 Cor. 16:15-16; 1 Thess. 5:12-13): sometimes appointed by one sent by Paul for the purpose. But *there they were*, known and acknowledged, with duty, right and power to rule the house of God for its well-being and for His praise therein.

At the very first Brethren followed this pattern.

> At Plymouth (says Dr. Tregelles), Mr. J. N. Darby requested Mr. Newton to sit where he could conveniently take the oversight of ministry, and that he would hinder that which was manifestly unprofitable and unedifying. Mr. J. N. Darby addressed Mr. Newton by letter, *as an Elder*: I have seen a transcript of such a document made (apparently for circulation here) in the handwriting of Mr. G. V. Wigram; it was written by Mr. J. N. Darby, from Dublin, and it is addressed to *B. Newton, Esq., Elder of the Saints' Meeting in Raleigh Street, Plymouth* (*Three Letters*, 7, note).

But after fifteen or so years, by 1845, "Darby had taken up very strong views against the formal recognition of elders."[2] It was in that year he found himself frustrated by the elders of the Plymouth assembly in his desire to prosecute his war against Newton *within* that assembly. This at once suggests one of the chief reasons for having "elders in every church" (Acts 14:23): they are a garrison to keep out disturbers. Such an arrangement, had it existed everywhere, would have largely thwarted Darby's measures of universal domination of the Brethren assemblies and universal excommunication.

---

1 *cheiratoneo*, Grimm (Lex.): "with the loss of the notion of extending the hand, to elect, appoint, create, *tina* Acts 14: 23."
2 Neatby, *History*, 108.

Here is seen the wisdom of the divine arrangement and the folly of departing therefrom.

The grounds alleged for this disastrous departure were two. First, a theory that the church is so utterly in ruins that restoration of its original order is quite impossible. Darby and Newton came to agree about this at least, and their combined influence gave to the phrase "a day of ruin" a sanction amongst Brethren scarcely less than that of Scripture itself.

But *what* is in ruins? The invisible church, composed of all Spirit-baptized persons, is indefectible, it cannot be ruined; against *it* "the gates of Hades shall not prevail." The local assembly may indeed be sadly ruined; but *it* can be restored, as, by the grace of God, has been seen times without number—at Corinth, for example. The only other institution in question is that agglomeration of sects which is called Christendom. But *that* is unrecognized by the New Testament, is not of God at all, and that *it* is in ruins is no matter for regret. Hence this specious phrase does but cover a very misleading fallacy. Again it was the undefined notion of something universally visible that allowed of the theory that that something was irreparably ruined as to external form. The only visible body known to the New Testament, the local church, *can* be maintained, by the grace of the Holy Spirit.

Upon this vital matter Anthony Norris Groves in 1847 wrote the following decisive sentences, which fix the issue precisely:

> Of this I think I can now feel practically convinced (as I ever have in theory) that recognised pastors and teachers are *essential* to the good order of all assemblies; and as such are required and commanded of God; and though I should not object to unite with those who had them not, if it were the result of the Lord's providence in not *giving* them any, I should feel quite unable to join *personally* those who rejected them as unnecessary or unscriptural. If the question were put to me (as it often has been), do you consider the Spirit unequal to the task of keeping order in the way we desire to follow?[1] my reply is simply this: Show me that the Lord has promised His Spirit to this end, and I at once admit its obligation in the face of all practical and experienced difficulties: but if I see pastorship, eldership, and ministry recognised as a

---

1 That is (presumably) without recognized rulers.

settled fixed service in the Church to this end, I cannot reject God's evidently ordained plan, and set up one of my own, because I think it more spiritual.

D——[1] seems (? feels) justified in rejecting all such helps as the way of obtaining proper subordination in the assembly of God's saints, by saying the "Church is in ruins"; this is his *theory*; but neither in the *word*, nor in my own experience or judgment, do I realise that this state of the Church, even though it existed to the full extent that he declares, was to be met by the overthrow of God's order, and the substitution of one so exceedingly spiritual (if I may so use the term) as it seemed not good to the Holy Spirit to institute, when all things were comparatively in order.[2]

The other opinion by which the assertion that elders cannot now be appointed was supported, was that none but apostles, or apostolic commissioners, such as Timothy or Titus, could make such appointments. The obvious defect in this theory is that it makes more of the first servants of the Lord than of the Lord Himself, it puts *Him* to a permanent limitation for want of *them*; the Holy Spirit indeed abides with the church for ever (John 14:16), but in this matter He is permanently inefficient for lack of certain of His own agents. And it leaves all local assemblies since that first generation under permanent deprivation and danger. It also sets aside apostolic practice as not being for permanent guidance, and nullifies those parts of the New Testament in question. We, on the contrary, maintain that in these matters of church order, as in all others, the New Testament and the apostolic example are of permanent import and value, and ought to be followed.

When, in 1832, the Lord sent George Müller and Henry Craik to Bristol, He used them mightily to the commencing and building up of a church on simple, primitive lines.[3] They were as necessarily the first rulers of that church as any apostolic evangelists were of churches they founded. But as the fellowship multiplied, and they

---

1 Doubtless J. N. Darby.
2 See my *Anthony Norris Groves*, ed, 159. 2 f.
3 I heard Dr. Pierson remark that the Bethesda Church, Bristol, was one of the two truly apostolic churches he knew. The other was the church at Boston, U.S.A., where A. J. Gordon ministered.

saw the Spirit qualifying other brethren for oversight, and moving them to addict themselves thereto of their own will (1 Cor. 16:15; 1 Tim. 3:1), they invited such formally to join them in the eldership, and then announced to the assembly the names of those thus invited, which followed the example of Paul's exhortation regarding Stephanas. Thus there was no *selection* of rulers by the ruled—a principle contrary to the divine order, since all authority is by delegation from God, the Sole Fount of authority, not by conferment from below, from the subjects: but there was *recognition* by the church, with opportunity for stating any valid objection. This method has continued, with real advantage to that assembly. In 1848 it was the spiritual wisdom and energy of that body of elders that saved the Bethesda church from disintegration in the Darby–Newton controversy. They were the sea wall that kept out the tidal wave of Darby's divisive principles and personal influence. There never was any Scriptural reason why this plan should not have been followed in all other cases when brethren were used of God to commence churches. Following the precedent in Acts 6:3, the church at Bethesda has always itself selected deacons to attend to business affairs.

If it be urged that such God-equipped leaders are few, the answer is swift: "Ye have not because ye ask not." The Head of the Church has hands ever full of gifts and a heart most willing to bestow them where they are "earnestly desired" (1 Cor. 14:1). If any assembly, however young or small, is honestly prepared to forswear the democratic spirit of the age, and to submit to God-given rule, He will give the rulers, if believing prayer is offered. There is no reason on the Lord's side why churches should be evermore dependent upon outside ministry. The history of Brethren meetings has itself often afforded proof of this. But it is one more impoverishing departure from the New Testament that it is generally held that the supernatural conferring of gifts is not now the will of God. One elder brother boldly asserted in a large conference: "I ignore the possibility until the return of the Lord"; and only one voice spoke to the contrary.

Chapter 10

# Excommunication on Doctrinal Grounds

ON p. 36 we remarked that believers have often been excommunicated on the ground of divergence of doctrine, and asked if the Word of God justifies this course. It is clear that if one deny the truth of the person of Christ, that He is truly God come in flesh (2 John 9, 10), or the necessity for and sufficiency of His death for reconciling men to God (Gal. 1:6–9), he is not on Christian ground at all, has no place in the church of God, and should not be received, not even to social fellowship, if he is one who professes to be a "brother." Also, one practising moral evil is to be put away (1 Cor. 5:9–13), and those who defy the united judgment of the whole assembly in a matter of wrong doing are to be treated as non-Christians (Matt. 18:17). Further, no company is to be kept with a brother while he refuses the authority in the house of God of the apostles and their writings (2 Thess. 3:14-15), though in the two last instances discipline need not necessarily proceed as far as formal excommunication.

But what Scriptural warrant is there for excommunicating a true disciple for error in doctrine? The shutting of the door of the house against a member of the family, thus forcing him out from the one sphere on earth in which God is known into that outer world-realm of darkness and danger over which Satan rules, is so solemn an act, fraught with such serious consequences in this age and the next;[1] and is withal so sorrowful a reproach upon the whole family, that we ought to have the same clear mandate from the Head of the house for taking this course on the ground of doctrinal error as is given in the case of evil living. In the latter case 1 Cor. 5:13 is explicit:

---

[1] For one excluded by divine warrant from the church is divinely warned that he shall not inherit the Kingdom of God. The will of God done in the earth-realm of the one Kingdom of God is ratified and enforced in the heavenly realm thereof (Matt. 18:17-18; 1 Cor. 5:9–16: 11; Gal. 5:19–21; Eph. 5:5).

"put away the wicked man from among yourselves"; where is the equally plain command for the former case? The instances (Rev. 2) of the Nicolaitans, Balaamites, and Jezebel will not suffice, for in each of these not only teachings but hateful works, as fornication and idolatries, are in question, bringing them under 1 Cor. 5:13. It is thus also in the cases mentioned in 1 Tim. 1:19-20, For those persons had definitely thrust from them (1) faith, as the principle of holy living; (2) a good conscience, so that their works would not be good; and (3) they had gone on to blaspheming. They had ceased from any Christian profession as entirely as a sailor ends his voyage by shipwreck. Indeed, they seem to have gone out, and did not need to be "put away."

The grounds of exclusion from a community are necessarily related to the terms of reception. What are the New Testament conditions of reception into the church of God? He who fulfils these ought to be received: only he who fails to continue to fulfil these ought to be excommunicated.

Dr. Hatch (pp. 30-31) has well indicated three stages of growth in this matter; the Apostolic, the post-Apostolic, and what we will call the Confederated Church practice.

> (1) "In the earliest period the basis of Christian fellowship was a changed life—'repentance toward God and faith toward our Lord Jesus Christ.'"
> 
> (2) "In the second period, the idea of definite belief as a basis of union dominated over that of a holy life."
> 
> (3) "In the third period, insistence on Catholic faith had led to the insistence on Catholic order... It was held not to be enough for a man to be living a good life, and to hold the Catholic faith, and to belong to a Christian association: that association must be part of a larger confederation, and the sum of such confederations constituted the Catholic Church.
> 
> "This last is the form which the conception of unity took in the fourth century, and which to a great extent has been permanent ever since."

Some communities demand the fulfilment of all three conditions. They look for a changed life, they require assent to what are deemed by them fundamental truths, they refuse church standing unless one consents to belong to that circle of meetings which happens to be acknowledged. Some reject the third condition, but maintain the first and second. One may manifest by a godly life true repentance and genuine faith, but will be rejected unless he avow belief in certain orthodox doctrines as commonly held, or if he become suspected of no longer holding these. The doctrines more particularly and usually in question are the verbal inspiration of the Scriptures and the everlasting conscious existence in punishment of the impenitent.

Now I unhesitatingly avow my full, firm, life-long belief in and constant declaration of both these doctrines; but equally unhesitatingly I challenge proof that the apostles required profession of these or any other such doctrines as a term of communion in the church of God, or, which then amounted to the same thing, as a condition of baptism.

A converted Jew acknowledged, of course, the divine inspiration of every jot and tittle of the Old Testament, but it was not that acknowledgment, but his acknowledgment of Christ as the Son of God, that was the ground of his reception into the Christian circle. A converted heathen usually had not previously accepted those Scriptures, and the New Testament nowhere suggests that it was demanded that he should express, or even form, any opinion upon the mode or measure of their inspiration *as a test for fellowship*. Nor was it demanded that a convert should confess any particular belief as to the future of the wicked, or as to any other such topic, *as a ground of reception*. Christ, and Christ alone, was that ground; Christ, the Son of God, crucified and glorified: the confession being made by the mouth, by baptism, by a godly life. But as such doctrines were not a ground of fellowship, neither could differences upon them be for exclusion; and so Paul, while strongly repudiating and controverting the denial of bodily resurrection, never suggested the casting out of the church of those Corinthians who were teaching it, but acknowledged them as brethren and encouraged them to persevere in the work of the Lord (1 Cor. 15:58).

So that, while it is the emphatic duty of the elders of a church to prohibit the *teaching* of what they deem not to be according to the

Scriptures, there is no warrant therein for *excommunicating* a brother on doctrinal grounds. There are better ways of dealing with such an one.

The basis of baptism, of reception, was such an acknowledgment of the true God and of His Son, Jesus Christ as Lord, as would produce a holy life. Baptism was commonly immediate upon confession with the mouth (Acts 2:41; 8:36, 38; 9:17–19; 10:47, 48; 16:33) unless there was reason to suppose insincerity (Matt. 3:7–9); but the serious risks then attending confession of Christ were a healthy deterrent, and justified speedy baptism. If, however, a godly walk did not develop, or one lapsed into persistent evil practice, he was to be put away (1 Cor. 5).

The baptism in the name of the Lord Jesus supposed an acknowledgment of Him as being God manifest in flesh, very God and very man in one Person, who by His death on the cross offered a propitiation for the sins of the world, so becoming in resurrection the one Saviour of men. One who was not prepared thus to acknowledge Christ could not be counted a Christian. One who had thus owned Him, but afterwards denied these truths, could no longer be counted a Christian. But it is to be observed that neither the refusal of fellowship in the former case nor the withdrawal of it in the latter was the withholding of communion from *a brother*, because such an one could *not* be deemed a brother. Thus the excommunication was not of him as a brother in Christ, but of him as being, by his own denial of Christ as God, no longer a brother, that is, as regards Christians being free to own him as that.

It remains that the only ground for excommunicating one whose standing as a brother in Christ was not questioned was evil conduct. Hence Dr. Hatch rightly says (p. 24) that excommunication in the primitive Churches

> did not necessarily extend beyond the particular Church of which a man had been a member. If he had been expelled for a *moral offence*, no doubt the causes which led to his expulsion by one community would prevent his reception into another. But where the ground of expulsion had been the *holding of peculiar opinions*, or the breach of a local by-law, it might be possible to find some other community which would ignore the one or condone the other.

Now this could not have been, if there had been apostolic rules that "peculiar opinions" were a right ground of exclusion and that the excommunicatory act of one church was binding upon all churches. That the primitive churches did not follow such rules shows that the apostles did not institute such rules. They are post-apostolic, not apostolic; they are a departure; and it is their adoption that has made possible many ruinous general divisions of the people of God. I would fain wrest from the hands of my brethren, and break to pieces, this deadly weapon of excommunication for divergence in doctrine, that further slaughter be prevented, and we be compelled to resort to safer and spiritual measures.

But error upon sundry themes may be so taught as to assail the truth of the Person of Christ, and thus disqualify one from Christian fellowship. Of course, love and justice demand strict inquiry and clear proof that a brother has so taught, and in such wise as to render him liable to excommunication. For it must be ever remembered that one may make a statement which, *if logically developed*, would result in heresy, but which he may *not* develop and the logical implications of which he may not have seen and would repudiate. Unless one has been faced with the deductions, and accepts them, he ought not to be treated as intending the error those deductions reveal. William Kelly wrote that Christ "emptied Himself of His Deity" (*Lectures on Philippians*, p. 50). A more objectionable phrase is scarcely possible. Its obvious deductions are destructive of Christianity and indeed of all Deity. How so competent a theologian made it, and passed it in print, is a mystery. Yet who would think of saddling that most orthodox divine with the fatal heresies reasonably to be drawn from his words, and regarding him as a heretic?

It has been said above that "converts from paganism or Islam constantly bring over into their converted life many wholly erroneous notions, and it is oft-times long ere these are banished from their minds. If discipline were exercised until those only were left who were presumed not to differ from any orthodox dogma the most alarming and cruel havoc would be made in the assemblies in mission spheres."

The New Testament exhibits this feature, and shows how the Holy Spirit through the Apostle Paul dealt with the situation. In the Corinthian assembly were both moral vices and false doctrine. Believers were retaining and spreading the general pagan Greek denial of a resurrection of the dead (1 Cor. 15), involving, of course, the denial of Christ's resurrection. Paul's own stand in relation to this doctrine is beyond question, which makes his attitude on this occasion the more noticeable. He gives positive command that the evil liver shall be excommunicated, but does not so much as hint at this course in the other case, though the doctrine was a fundamental error, fatal to the Christian faith. He argues the question fully, demonstrates the truth, and ends by including those in error amongst his "beloved brethren" and exhorting them, as the others, to persevere in the work of the Lord! And so far was the apostle from refusing to visit the assembly because of such teaching being allowed, and such evils being tolerated, that he was the rather fully proposing to go (1 Cor. 11:34; 2 Cor. 13:1). They were a "church of God" in spite of these conditions (1 Cor. 1:2).

Thus there are measures suited to the case, such as firm but loving remonstrance (1 Cor. 15:12); a full, public exposure of the error (1 Cor. 15:12–19), as to its nature, and its evil connexions and consequences (1 Cor. 15:33-34); plain setting forth of the counteracting truth, together with a definite restraint upon the teaching of the false doctrine. These measures, by the grace of the Holy Spirit, will result either in the happy deliverance of the one in error or in the creating of an atmosphere and situation so intolerable that he will be likely to withdraw. "They went out"—not, were cast out—is said of even "antichrists" (1 John 2:19). Casting out was the method of such as loved the pre-eminence (3 John 10; John 9:34). The long exercise of love and patience will be very good for the assembly, and particularly for the elders; the investigation and exposition required will conduce to general confirmation in the faith; and the risk of friction and disruption will be greatly reduced.

These measures require much spiritual vigour for their successful application, whereas excommunication is too often but the resort to force by those who are officially powerful but morally impotent, and this not by any means in the Church of Rome alone.

The bitterness, strife, and chaos which have been the direct outcome of mutual excommunication challenge the method as being not of the Lord. The misguided brother is seldom recovered; most frequently the evil is aggravated rather than cured, and so other conditions are induced worse than the error itself.

Upon this question we have dwelt at length, because, if we mistake not, it will become increasingly urgent in the future. The present affiliating of denominations is likely to issue finally in a vast corporate religious organization which will fulfil the requirements of Rev. 17, and which will be wholly not of God; it will result in the enlightened and faithful children of God now in the bodies in question being forced out of them in loyalty to Christ. At that time, when Satan will have united thus his own religious forces, he will work untiringly to divide the people of God further by hindering the unity of those who are really Christ's; one of his old and trusted weapons will be mightily employed, namely, persuading saints that agreement in creed is more important than brotherly love, that seeing eye to eye must take precedence over the possession of a common family life and is of greater moment than devotion to Christ and His interests. It deserves to be most widely known, as a fact not open to question, that the requiring acceptance of specified doctrines as a test for Christian fellowship did not obtain until several generations later than the apostles. Dr. Hatch has indicated that the practice was derived from the Greek schools of philosophy,[1] an anti-Christian origin, sufficient to condemn the practice as heathen and human, not Divine and Christian.

---

1  Hibbert Lectures—*The Influence of Greek Ideas and Usages upon the Christian Church* (330 *et seq.*)

CHAPTER 11

# Unanimity

## A Divine Rule of Church Order and Christian Co-operation

A QUESTION of the highest importance is whether the Word of God sanctions the deciding of matters by a majority vote of the believers concerned, or whether the Lord does not rather teach us to defer decision until one undivided judgment is reached.

1. Considering that the church of God occupies the responsible office of visibly representing before the world the kingdom of the Lord Jesus, so that worldly men judge of Him according to that which they see in us, it is manifestly of the utmost importance that, before carrying out any proposed action, we should make as sure as possible that the course proposed is well pleasing unto Him. Experience has abundantly shown that the minority is frequently right, and the majority wrong; and it is therefore manifest that the vote of a majority is at best a very uncertain means of deciding what is the will of God. If this be so in human affairs, with which men may be supposed to have some fair acquaintance, it will be much more so in divine matters affecting the kingdom of God, with which things we have no natural acquaintance whatever.

In these latter concerns we shall be yet more unlikely to arrive at a knowledge of His will by such an uncertain method as voting, if it be the case that, so far from having engaged to make known to the church His wishes by this plan, the Lord has the rather promised to reveal His will by bringing His people to an unanimous judgment.

Considering the vast importance, both for the glorifying of His name and for the blessing of men, that attaches to the doings of His people, and considering also that we cannot be at all sure of doing that which shall glorify Him and be for the good of our fellows unless we have His directions, it would seem very strange had He left no more sure method of receiving His directions than this very uncertain plan of acting according to the view of a majority only.

We are specially likely to make greater errors in things concerning the heavenly kingdom than in things of this world because we are often so very carnally and so little spiritually minded that divine things are but slowly apprehended by us. This is manifestly a great reason for more carefully turning over any matter in our minds, and taking a longer time to consider it than would be needful were we discussing it in a merely secular relationship.

Is it not, amongst other reasons, to guard against the mistakes inevitably arising from haste that the Lord wishes His people to defer decision until unanimity is reached? A method which is as likely to lead to a wrong as it is to guide to a right decision cannot be a divine method, and ought not to be followed by those possessing the divine nature, and therefore capable of having the mind of Christ (2 Pet. 1:4; 1 Cor. 2:16), in whose workings mistakes are unknown.

2. A second and very serious objection is that this plan is eminently calculated to lead to dissension, both secret and public; a truth with which any who have had much experience on the subject must be sadly familiar. Can anything be more likely to cause disaffection than that a section of a church should have their wishes and, possibly, their sincere convictions, rejected by there being another section of the church with no greater advantage than that of being slightly stronger in numbers who have different opinions?

A method at all likely to cause disagreement, and possibly open division, cannot be of that God who is "not a God of confusion, but of peace" (1 Cor. 14:33).

But, when nothing is done till one judgment is reached, everyone is pleased with that which is done; and so discord is averted and concord is strengthened, bringing spiritual blessing to the whole community.

3. Seeing that we pray, "Lead us not into temptation," a method which tends so to lead us cannot be of God, who delivers us from the Evil One. But given a brother possessed of an ardent and hon-

est conviction that the plan he proposes is right and good, does not the method now under discussion present very manifest and severe temptations to him to unseemly conduct? He has every inducement to "pack" the meeting, by secretly urging those who think with him to be present in force, rather than to leave it to the Lord to bring together those whom He knows to be qualified to deal with the matter. He is tempted by vehemence in argument to gain other adherents, rather than by patient reflection to submit his judgment to the Lord. In his eagerness to gain a majority of votes he is more likely to be anxious to persuade others by his reasons than he is to be willing to be persuaded by theirs, even though they may speak with the mind of the Lord.

The fact that such temptations do beset us, and that not infrequently brethren fall under their power as the result of a desire to obtain a majority, at once raises the question whether the method giving rise thereto can be of the Lord.

On the other hand, the first temptation—to "pack" a meeting—is absolutely banished by the necessity for entire accord, and the other two, if not entirely removed, are very much weakened in force; while the desire on the part of all to give up their private views, if needful, and to arrive at the *mind of the Lord*, as the means of reaching an unanimous judgment, is very much increased.

The one method appears likely to lead me to press forward *my* views (possibly honestly believing them to be right and best); the other to necessitate my carefully waiting upon the Lord for His views.

4. In Rom. 12:4–5, 1 Cor. 12:12–27, Eph. 4:11–16, and other scriptures, the relationship of the church to Christ is illustrated by the human body. Of this spiritual body believers are individual members, while the Lord Jesus is the head of the whole body. The more this analogy is prayerfully studied the more it will be seen to be the most perfect comparison the divine wisdom of God has presented to us to illustrate the present working of the church.

Two things mark the human body—(*a*) it is not the members that plan and control; these functions are vested solely in the head, it being the duty and beauty of the members to respond to its directions; (*b*) any lack of unity in the co-operation of the members in doing the will of the head indicates a measure of disease in those members where the failure is found.

When this latter state is reached, the only hopeful course is patiently to resort to such means as will restore the undisputed control of the head; when it is found in the church that there is divergence of opinion, the proper plan is by patience and prayer to wait for the whole body to be brought again under the control of the Lord and into united judgment and action. It is true this is sometimes found impossible in the human body, and means have to be taken to prevent the diseased member from taking any part in the working of the body and from injuriously affecting other members; yet this necessity does not interfere with the *remaining* members still unitedly submitting to the head. So likewise a believer may so far cease to submit to the Lord as to necessitate his being prevented from leading other believers astray either by the Lord's laying him aside by sickness, or removing him by death (1 Cor. 2:30), or by the church, at the direction of the Lord, taking the needful steps to prevent the offender further obstructing the work of the Lord; but here also this does not hinder the remaining members from submitting undividedly to the Lord.

Thus the difficulties in the way of unanimity have their sufficient solution, and afford no ground for the body departing from the law of entire submission to the head and unbroken co-operation of the several members with each other.

For a church to depart from this rule and to act according to the desire of a majority only is as if the actions of a man's body should be decided by the impulses of a certain number of the members, which is a practical denial of the truth that the head alone has the right and power to control. Moreover, it is a sure means of producing confusion and not co-operation, for what would be the case with the human body, if it attempted to move and to work with no surer means of knowing the will of the head than that two legs and feet, one arm and hand, and one eye, being a majority of the active members, manifested certain impulses, as opposed to the other eye and the remaining hand and arm, a minority of the working members?

The violence done to this striking analogy is a sure proof that voting by majority is not a divinely instituted or Scripturally sanctioned practice, however convenient it may appear in worldly societies.

5. Further, by the failure to act in complete unity the church ceases to give one of the most effective possible forms of testimony to the world.

In John 17:20–21, the Lord Jesus, in speaking to the Father, says: "Neither for these only do I pray, but for them also that believe on Me through their word; that they may all be one; even as Thou, Father, art in Me, and I in Thee, that they also may be in Us; that the world may believe that Thou didst send Me. And the glory which Thou hast given Me I have given unto them; that they may be one, even as we are one; I in them, and Thou in Me, that they may be perfected into one; that the world may know that Thou didst send Me, and lovedst them, even as Thou lovedst Me."

It is sufficient to notice three things:

(*a*) The Lord's desire for all His people to be perfected into one;

(*b*) The pattern of that oneness to be the oneness of the Father and the Son;

(*c*) The object of this oneness to be the testimony thereby given to the world.

With regard to (*a*), the prayer of our Lord was in effect that the Holy Spirit might be sent into everyone who should believe on His name, so that by the Spirit of God indwelling each, all might be united into one in God; so that (*b*), the pattern of our unity should be the oneness of the Father and the Son in the communion of the Spirit. But it is to be specially observed that the Father, the Son and the Spirit are not only one in person, but also in *action*—in all their doings there is the most perfect harmonious unity. It would be sheer blasphemy, in fact, logically, the most absolute atheism, to suppose the doings of the Godhead to be regulated by the decision of any two of the persons thereof, the one person being either opposed to the view of the two, or merely submitting to being outvoted.

But this being utterly incompatible with the oneness of the Father and the Son in the unity of the Spirit, how can it be any more in order on the part of those who, being indwelt by the same Spirit, are to be so united as to conform to the pattern of the oneness of God, even as our Lord prayed, "that they may be one *even as We* are one"?

As to our last point (*c*), believers are to manifest a corporate union *publicly*, for the world is to see it. The object of the Lord is that the world may know and believe that He was sent by the Father, and that the believer is a sharer in the love of the Father to the Son. The deliberate departing from oneness of action by adopting the practice of majority voting is undeniably not even attempting to attain such united working, and cannot, therefore, result in that testimony which He taught oneness alone could give.

It is an invariably true principle for the guidance of the children of God that any course of action which tends to mar, though it be but partially, their testimony before the world, is not of the Father, but rather of the world.

6. But how is it possible for unity of judgment to be attained? In divine things the question of "How?" is of comparatively small importance. It is for us at least to endeavour to obey the revealed will of the Lord, and to seek after unanimity; and we may leave to God the question of how it is possible for Him to bring to one mind many persons of different types of character, of different habits of thought, having varying ways of looking at the same subject, and sometimes opposite ways of doing the same thing.

Humanly speaking, unanimity is not possible. To bring together scores, perhaps hundreds, of mere men and women and require them to come to one unanimous decision upon questions of frequently a perplexing and delicate nature is to expect more than fallen human nature can give. Because each human spirit is a separate individuality, possessed of the power and tendency of acting independently of every other being, therefore it is true, "many men, many minds."

But the glorious and all-important fact concerning the children of God is that, in place of being any longer severed spiritually from every other creature, we are indwelt by one and the same Spirit, the Spirit of Christ; and when this fact is *acted upon*, the humanly impossible is divinely possible. The human body is composed of many various substances, and the several members—hand, ears, eyes, etc.—vary vastly in form and use, and yet these manifest differences do not hinder the whole body working together, because each part is under the personal influence of the one spirit inhabiting the body. So the members of the body of Christ differ greatly, but because we are every one indwelt by the one Spirit, the co-operation of all members is *possible*, and should be sought. It may be that with this, as with other Christlike graces, full and eternal harmony will only be attained when the last trace of the rebellious carnal mind shall have been removed at the coming of the Lord; but, on the other hand, with this, as with other fruit of the Spirit, we should aim at perfection and "give diligence to keep the unity of the Spirit" (Eph. 4:3); and then a unanimity can be reached which may astonish us.

Did not the Lord choose this oneness of mind and working as His testimony to the world because the fact of His people acting upon a principle and in a manner that the world has never found continuously possible would make apparent that a divine power was at work amongst them, that the Spirit of God, not the spirit of the world, controlled? This testimony is ruined by the plan of a majority vote settling a question, for this is the very method which worldly men adopt as the only practicable plan known to them. No doubt it was from them that this, like numerous other evil practices, was adopted by the church in days when she had so grieved the Holy Spirit as to forfeit His unifying control.

This testimony from unity in Christian action is the strict counterpart of that from harmony of Christian speech described in 1 Cor. 14:24–25: "But if all prophesy, and there come in one unbelieving or unlearned, he is reproved by all, he is judged by all; the secrets of his heart are made manifest, and so he will fall down on his face and worship God, declaring that God is among you indeed."

Seeing it is one of the functions and rights of the Spirit to control the whole body, for a church arbitrarily to say He shall express His will through a section only of the members of the body present is to assume the office of *dictating* to Him whom it is our duty and wisdom *to obey*, and thus to prevent Him from doing fully that which He would graciously do for our blessing, namely, lead to unanimity. It also forfeits that certainty of knowing what is His will which an undivided judgment alone can give; for while it is certain what is the desire of a man if his whole body works to the one end, it would be by no means so certain were some only of his members to seek that end, and the rest to oppose.

7. *The whole burden of Scripture testimony* is on the side of unanimity. This is the more clearly seen by observing two very remarkable lines of thought—first, that in the Word of God unanimity is associated with spiritual prosperity, and, on the other hand, a divided judgment with lack of spirituality.

For instance, Israel in the wilderness were in a state of unbelief at the time the spies went up to search out the land. Ten of the twelve selected men reflected the condition of the people, dissuading the nation from going forward, and two only, Joshua and Caleb, persuading them to do so. A very striking instance of the minority having the mind of the Lord, but of their being hopelessly outvoted; and by acting on the view of the majority the whole people made a fatal error.

Again, how sad was the state of the kingdom while some of the people followed Saul, and a smaller company helped David: but how significant the statement (1 Chron. 12:40, 38), "there was *joy* in Israel" when "all Israel were of *one heart* to make David king." Once more, what a time of spiritual prosperity was inaugurated when David proposed to seek the Lord once again and to worship before the ark of the Lord: "and *all* the assembly said they would do so: for the thing was right in the eyes of *all* the people" (1 Chron. 13:1–4).

On the other hand, how miserable was the condition of affairs when most of the people worshipped Baal, while 7,000 followed Jehovah (1 Kings 19:18); but what a revival of godliness in Judah is indicated by the words, connected with the proposal to return to the keeping of the Passover feast, "the thing was right in the eyes of the king and of *all* the congregation" (2 Chron. 30:4).

How terrible was the condition of Israel when it could be written (2 Kings 16:21-22): "Then were the people of Israel divided into two parts: half of the people followed Tibni, the son of Ginath, to make him king; and half followed Omri; but the people that followed Omri prevailed against the people that followed Tibni," as compared with the comparative prosperity of Judah and Benjamin in their unbroken submission to the rule of the godly Asa.

It may be said that these examples from the Old Testament have no very direct bearing upon the government of a Christian church; but they were "written for our admonition," and the remarkable frequency with which unanimity and prosperity are connected in these and similar instances, gives an emphatic Scriptural testimony in favour of undivided action by the people of God; and the lesson is yet more impressive when it is seen that the New Testament follows upon the same side, and sets before us under the new covenant the same precept and example.

Take, for example, such exhortations as these:

Rom. 15:5-6: "Now the God of patience and of comfort grant you to be of the same mind one with another according to Christ Jesus: that *with one accord* ye may with *one mouth* glorify the God and Father of our Lord Jesus Christ."

1 Cor. 1:10: "Now I beseech you, brethren, through the name of our Lord Jesus Christ, that *ye all speak the same thing*, and that there be *no divisions* among you; but that ye be perfected together, in the same mind, and *in the same judgment*."

2 Cor. 13:11: "Be perfected; be comforted: *be of the same mind*: live in peace; and the God of love and peace shall be with you."

Galatians: A direct object of this epistle was to bring the saints to oneness of mind upon the question discussed, to exhort them all to walk by the Spirit, and thus to avoid the "strife, factions and divisions," declared to be of the flesh (ch. 5:20).

Eph. 4:3: "Giving diligence to keep the unity of the Spirit in the bond of peace." The "unity of the Spirit," is that unity which is manifested by the Spirit through united action on the party of the body; and therefore in this passage the apostle at once proceeds to a revelation of the inter-working of the whole body in harmony. See verses 3 to 16.

Phil. 1:27: "Only let your manner of life be worthy of the gospel of Christ; that, whether I come and see you or be absent, I may hear of your state, that *ye stand fast in one spirit*, with *one soul striving* for the faith of the gospel."

Phil. 2:2: "Fulfil ye my joy, that ye be of the same mind, having the same love, *being of one accord*, of one mind; doing *nothing* through *faction* or through vainglory."

Phil. 4:2: "I exhort Euodia, and I exhort Syntyche, to be of the same mind in the Lord."

Colossians: When this church met together to discuss the work of the Lord they were met with this injunction, "Whatsoever ye do in word or deed do all in the name of the Lord Jesus, giving thanks to God the Father through Him" (3:17) Now, if a matter had been decided by a majority only, the members of the minority could not have given thanks for the doing of that which they had urged should not be done; therefore the plan of so deciding a matter forces some to take part in doing things for which they cannot give thanks, and which they cannot do in the name of the Lord Jesus. Can a method which forces unscriptural conduct upon some members be itself scriptural? The only alternative is that they continue to show their objections by refraining from the work to which they objected. Can this be considered a scriptural course in the face of the above-quoted exhortation in Phil. 1:27, "with one soul striving"?

1 Thess. 5:13: "Be at peace among yourselves." In section 2 we have seen that dissension is one of the probable and, indeed, frequent results of the plan.

2 Thess. 3:16: "Now the Lord of peace Himself give you peace *at all times* in all ways," which must include business meetings.

1 Tim. 6:3-4; 2 Tim. 2:23; Titus 3:9. In the first passage certain men, and in the second and third certain questions are condemned, and the avoidance thereof exhorted, because they "gender strifes"; that is, not that every time a foolish question is discussed it leads to strife, but that there is a general tendency in such discussion to provoke dissension. So it does not require, before the method stands condemned, that every time a matter is decided by a majority vote it should provoke strife. It is sufficient if it has a tendency that way, if it is not surprising that strife results.

James 1:5: "If any of you lacketh wisdom, let him ask of God, who giveth to all liberally and upbraideth not; and it shall be given him." When a church meets together and some think one course the best, and some another, it is evident that one or both of the parties has not the wisdom of God in the matter. This scripture indicates what should then be done. Not the opinion of the majority to be acted upon, for they may be wrong in their judgment; and for the same reason, not that of the minority: but let all wait on God for wisdom, and it shall be given—in God's time—to those who ask in faith.

Thus saith the Scripture; and in addition to these passages, exhorting to "peace," to "oneness of mind," to "all speaking the same thing," to avoidance of "strife," and "divisions," to being "perfected together in the same mind and in the same judgment," we have the already commented upon words of the Lord Jesus, from John 17, and the scriptural analogy of the body, and also the example of a church transacting affairs in its corporate capacity recorded in Acts 15, which we shall now proceed to consider.

8. As if the Lord foresaw that the precepts and whole tenour of His Word would not be sufficient to preserve His people from adopting almost universally the practice of the world in the matter now in question, He caused to be given a very full narration of the discussion of an important and intricate question by the church at Jerusalem, including the apostles, to whom was specially committed the knowledge of His will, and who were undoubtedly those most likely to know what method was most accordant with the mind of the Spirit. This record is found in the fifteenth chapter of the Acts. When closely studied the story gives not only the decision upon the question actually discussed, but also the principles by which the judgments of believers were influenced, and, further, that which directly bears on our subject, the order of discussion. While this gathering was unique in composition and character, its methods of business abide as our divinely given example.

Before the reader goes further he will do well to read the chapter carefully in the Revised Version, when the following remarks may be the better considered.

To the Gentile church at Antioch there had come from Judea certain men who taught the brethren that, as circumcision had from the time of Abraham been the sign of a person belonging to the visible company of the people of God, they could not be saved unless they were circumcised. Paul and Barnabas dissented from this teaching, and to obtain the opinion of the apostles and elders in the mother church the brethren at Antioch deputed Paul and others to proceed to Jerusalem and there discuss the question; and, we read, "when they were come to Jerusalem, they were received of the church and the apostles and the elders."

The order in which the matter proceeded is then shown as being:

(1) "They rehearsed all that God had done with them," evidently including in their remarks a statement of their having refrained from teaching Gentile believers that they must be circumcised, and also laying before the church the facts concerning the discussion that had gone on at Antioch. That they did this is clear from ver. 24, where the apostles display a knowledge of what had transpired at Antioch.

Thus the matter was laid before the church, and the proposal to enforce circumcision thrown open for discussion; whereupon,

(2) Certain of the Pharisees, not having been yet divested of their sectarian spirit, urged that it was needful that Gentile Christians should be circumcised and enjoined to keep the law of Moses. This imposing of the ceremonial Judaic law upon Gentiles had not been the practice of the early church, as may be seen by the recorded teaching of the apostles and their speeches on this occasion; but the addresses of these Pharisees made clear,

(3) That there was existing a *division of judgment* upon the question. Now, had their method been the more modern plan that we are discussing, it would have been recorded that they ascertained on which side of the question there was a majority, and so settled (?) the matter. But, as opposed to this, when this divergence of view is manifested,

(4) *The meeting is adjourned*, and a fresh gathering of apostles, elders (ver. 6), and the whole multitude of the disciples (ver. 12), constituting the "whole church," (ver. 22), meets to consider the matter.

(5) Upon the subject being again brought forward, there was "much questioning" (ver. 7), showing that those wide and opposed differences of opinion which now manifest themselves were seen then also. Here again we remark that had the apostolic method of reaching a decision been the worldly one, we should expect to find

a record to that effect; but, on the contrary, the questioning and speech-making continued uninterruptedly, Peter, Barnabas, Paul and James all freely expressing their thoughts, until we find the significant record (ver. 22),

(6) "Then it seemed good to the apostles and the elders, *with the whole church,*" to do certain things. This is the essence of the whole question—nothing done until all differences have disappeared in unanimity, then action taken. So that with the approval of the whole church it could be written to the brethren at Antioch, "it seemed good unto us, *having come to one accord*" (ver. 25). And it is of the most momentous importance that we should notice that the church thus "being of one accord" (Phil. 2:2), and having learned "all to speak the same thing" so that there were "no divisions among them" but that they were" perfected together in the same mind and in the same judgment" (1 Cor. 1:10), they are then able calmly and confidently to claim the authority of the Lord Himself for their decision, and say (ver. 28): "it seemed good to the *Holy Spirit* and to us."

Thus does our divine Lord impressively set before His people the method to be followed by the church when considering matters in a corporate capacity, and teach us that when, by patiently waiting before Him, and focusing upon the particular subject in hand the light He has given, the church come to oneness of mind in their decision, we can then claim His authority for that which we do.

This teaching is the underlying basis of the seemingly difficult passage, Matt. 18:15–18. There the Lord says that if my brother sin against me, and I cannot by personal influence lead him to repentance, and thus bury the matter, I am then to take one or two more brethren and see him with them. It is evident that these brethren would not agree to help me unless convinced that I am in the right and my brother is the offender; so that there is thus found a consensus of opinion on the subject. But if the sinning brother will not listen to these further remonstrances, I am then to narrate the circumstances to the church. Once more, it is evident that the church will not side with me unless it deems me to be in the right; but if they—the church, not a section thereof, but "the church," implying the *whole* church, just as when we speak of "a city," we mean the whole city—

agree with my view of the case, we have the fact that a body of those indwelt by the Holy Spirit, and so capable of having the mind of Christ, are of one judgment in the matter; and then if the offending brother will not hear and submit to the church, he must be treated as a Gentile and a publican, that is, he must be regarded, while contumacious, as not of the church fellowship. When the church thus *unanimously* deals with a case, the Lord assures us that we may be certain of doing the right thing, and that "what things soever ye shall bind on earth shall be bound in heaven," for the simple reason, that it is the will of our Lord in heaven that, through the Spirit, we have done on earth.

So, again, Paul having instructed the Corinthian church thus to deal with a wicked person (ch. 5, 1st ep.), upon learning that the disciples had produced in him the desired repentance, instructs them (ch. 2, 2nd ep.) now to forgive and to receive back the offender and to restore him to the joy of the fellowship of saints; and having invoked the name of the Lord Jesus for the former measure, he now claims the authority of the Lord for the latter course; and thus the one who had been "bound" over to Satan as an evil-doer for the destruction of the flesh, is now, upon repentance, "loosed" by the church from the sentence, that no advantage may be gained by Satan.

Thus, in this practical matter also the Lord indicates His willingness to recognize the decision of a church, if that decision be reached by spiritual men through spiritual means, that is, through patience, prayer, and attention to the Word, and be unanimous; nor is there one single precept or example in His Word to indicate or even appear to sanction the thought that He allows the authority of His name to be attached to the will of a section only of those of His people who have to decide a question. They may, and, it may be allowed, sometimes do, by that means decide according to His will; but they have no Scriptural right to claim His authority and profess to act in His name; such authority being given to the company of His people, and to them only, who act unanimously.

Against the application of Acts 15 to the matter in question it has been urged that the plan there shown is doubtless advisable and possible in matters of such great importance as the one then discussed, but that it is neither needful nor likely that unanimity should be reached in details say connected with the construction or fitting up of a hall or schoolroom, most of the church being unacquainted with such matters. But surely this is a very irrational objection, for if the Lord has undertaken to produce oneness of mind upon important and intricate questions, why should there be any difficulty in His doing so upon questions comparatively simple and unimportant? And as to the necessity of these latter things being brought within the rule, is it not often over absurdly trifling matters that personal differences most frequently arise? And ought not these things therefore to be dealt with in the way most likely to produce and preserve peace?

These numerous passages are written, and this clear example is given, for our guidance, and it is for us to conform our practice to the scriptural pattern, nor is there the least suggestion in the Word of God that any other than this procedure was followed, whatever the question to be decided by the church might be.

9. There are usually more women than men in a church, and very frequently their interest is keener and they attend meetings in larger numbers. Hence majority voting really puts the government of affairs into their hands, which is against the divine ordering that authority is vested in the man, not the woman (Gen. 3:16; 1 Cor. 11:3; 14:34; 1 Tim. 3:12).

10. It has, indeed, been suggested that *tōn pleionōn*, in 2 Cor. 2:6, "Sufficient to such a one is this punishment which was inflicted *by the many*"—(Gr., "the more"), means "the majority," and that the excommunication of the wicked brother was not unanimous. I am referred to Alford in support. But Alford's suggestion of there having been an anti-Pauline party in the Corinthian Church, not likely to bow to the Apostle's instructions to "put away" the brother, seems quite unsupported by the passages he cites, and is directly negatived by Paul's own statements (2 Cor. 7:13–16) that "the spirit of Titus hath been refreshed by you *all*" and "he remembereth the obedience of you *all*," expressions impossible if a distinct party had refused obedience. Nor, had there been such resistance, could the Apostle's joy have been so strong and unrestrained as he reveals it to have been.

Therefore "the many" (R.V.) of 2:6 will mean all the church contrasted with the one member put under discipline by them all, which is confirmed by the statement in ver. 5 preceding, that they "all" had been grieved by the sin of the *one*. Paul uses the expression thus in the first epistle (10:5) when he says, "with most of them (*en tois pleiosin autōn*) God was not well pleased," where "most of them" means *all* but *two* out of more than six hundred thousand adult men (Num. 2:32; 26:63–65).

Thus Bloomfield on ch. 2:6 takes it: "*hupo tōn pleionōn*, 'at the hands of the many,' the general body of the Church—the *plethos*, meaning all except the persons so punished. So 1 Cor. 5:4, *sunachthentōn humōn*;" in which last cited chapter, as in ch. 6 and all the epistle, the "you" and "ye" plainly are the whole community. And so Darby (*New Translation*, note) says, "the body at large," and Bengel comments "the church at large."

In Matt. 11:20, the terms mean, not majority, but that in one certain area the Lord did more mighty works than in any other one district: in 1 Cor. 9:19 and 2 Cor. 4:15, it signifies "as many as possible"; in 2 Cor. 9:2, it equals "very many"; in Acts 19:32, it has the force of "the vast majority," that is, practically all of the immense throng save the few who had engineered the tumult; and in only the two remaining places can it clearly mean a simple majority (1 Cor. 15:6; Phil. 1:14). That it may mean a majority is thus allowed, but of *what proportion of the whole* that majority consists must be separately ascertained.

That gifted teacher, C. F. Hogg, wrote to me as follows:

> The suggestion recently made that majority action is assembly action gives me much concern. It seems to reduce the Church of God to the level of a club, or other association controlled in a purely human way. Whereas I had thought of it as a superhuman institution, controlled by the Lord and guided by His Spirit. I had thought of the discipline in patience while brethren waited for unity of judgment as a prime means to holiness.
>
> But, of course, if Scripture teaching, whether by direct precept or by example, is that majorities rule, then all such false conceptions must be dismissed.

That *hoi pleiones* may mean a majority is clear; that it ever means a bare majority is not. The passage, 2 Cor. 7:16, points rather to an interpretation of the term in accord with 1 Cor. 10:5. As at present advised, I still understand that the errant brother is the minority in this case. The alternative seems to be to denude the Church of God of its supernatural character, to take away the justification of the epithet "of God," and to make this another *Ecclesia* after the pattern of Acts 19:39, where, presumably, matters would be so decided. Paul could assume that the Philippians would be united in soul and spirit (1:27), though he had to exhort them to unity of mind (2:2; 3:15). A church should forbear action until this fruit of the Spirit is manifested. Long-suffering is an acknowledgment of the presence and sufficiency of the Lord.[1]

11. It now only remains to offer some concluding and confirmatory remarks.

It may be asked—Is this plan really possible? In divine things the question is both irrelevant and irreverent. For the believer in *Almighty* God there is but one question—not, Is it possible? but, Is it Scriptural? not, Can it be done? but, Does God, in His holy Word, bid us do it? Is it Scriptural? Then it is also possible! It was impossible humanly for the man with the withered hand to stretch it forth. He would have done so long since had he been able. But when the Lord bade him do the impossible, it was at once done, for the question of power rested with Him who gave the command. Thus it is with this question, and all other His commandments.

The apostles uniformly insisted that they were men of like passions with others (Acts 10:26; 14:15). The believers, also, who gathered at that pattern church meeting had very deeply rooted prejudices, very stubborn human wills, yea, all those infirmities of mind and spirit which some fear must render this plan of church government inoperative in our days. But the thing was not impossible then, and, therefore, is not now on this account.

The affairs of Bethesda Church, Bristol, numbering many hundreds of members, from its founding on August 13th, 1832, by the late George Müller and Henry Craik, were constantly settled in this

---

1 On another occasion C. F. Hogg summed up the situation in his pithy way: "Majority rule is bad; minority rule is worse!"

way. In the year 1900 James Wright, Mr. Müller's son-in-law and successor, wrote as follows:

> ...reference has been made to a church in Bristol, the affairs of which have, since its founding in 1832, been conducted upon a Scriptural principle, namely, that of waiting, before deciding any matter, until unanimity of judgment has been arrived at.
>
> As one who has been connected with this church for the last sixty years, I very gladly testify that I firmly believe that simple obedience to the directions of the Word of God on this subject has been one of the chief causes of the remarkably uninterrupted peace and harmony which, through the goodness of God, have characterized this church all these years.
>
> The reason is not far to seek. The plan of waiting, before coming to a decision regarding any step, until the indwelling Holy Spirit has brought all minds into unity of purpose, yields to our Lord Jesus Christ His proper place as the One Lord and Master in His House, and keeps us His brethren in our proper place of humility, dependence, and subjection.

In the same year (1900) the Secretary of the China Inland Mission wrote to me that since the founding of the Mission in 1865 the affairs of its great work had been conducted on the plan proposed by Scripture.

Thus, dealing with these two cases only we have, in the aggregate, 103 years of modern and satisfactory experience of the method; simply proving, as might be safely expected, that in the "keeping of His commandments there is great reward" (Psa. 19:11).

What reward? it will perhaps be asked. Is there not great risk of matters needful to be decided promptly being delayed, to the injury of the work? Let the Secretary of the China Inland Mission answer. He was asked—Has any matter which it would have been for the good of the Lord's work to have had decided promptly been delayed to the prejudice of the work by the waiting for unanimity? He replied—No, decidedly not. Whenever there has been delay, it has always proved to have been a wise step, and the necessary guidance has come later on.

He was asked also—Has the experience of this plan shown any distinct advantages accruing therefrom? The reply was that after experience has proved that by this method mistakes have been avoided which might otherwise have been made, and that *no* inconveniences have been found to arise from the plan.

Is it not a great gain to avoid mistakes? Does not this method wholly cast us upon the Lord, and so, by our dependence, glorify Him? Do we not thus corporately "acknowledge Him in all our ways"? and should we not so secure the fulfilment of the accompanying promise "He shall direct thy paths"? (Prov. 3:5-6).

Unanimity is the divine plan of action in both the Godhead and the people of God, and it is attainable. Nor is it in church action only that this is the divine method. Any number of believers from two and upward (a husband and wife, two fellow workers in the gospel, e.g. who are jointly involved in any matter), should delay action until oneness of judgment is gained. R. C. Chapman wrote of his co-operation with William Hake:

> Our fellowship has been ever growing, and during its fifty-nine years' continuance never was strife or bitterness between us.... For guidance of our steps, the ordering our ways, the rule of our household, we always waited on God together for His mind. If on conferring together we found ourselves of one mind, we laid our unity before God for His perfecting—we remembered the fault of Nathan and David who, knowing in part the will of God as to the building Him a temple, failed to lay the matter before God for the perfect revelation of His will. If judgments did not agree, we waited on God to give us oneness of mind, and neither of us ever took a step against the judgment of the other—hence no strife, no bitterness! The obligation of John 17 to oneness between the children of God, like unto the oneness between the Father and the Son, will be fulfilled in a coming day—if not now fulfilled—the obligation is immutable, as is the Fountainhead, God the Father's love in His Son.
>
> We have endeavoured, in foreview of the judgment seat of Christ, to tread the path in which the whole Church of God should be found walking; the fruit of such obedience could not but be a keeping the unity of the Spirit in lowliness, meekness and love—schism and division far away. (*Seventy Years of Pilgrimage, A Memorial of William Hake*, pp. 6, 7.)

To many busy Christians in this age of deadly rush the foregoing may read as a description of the antique and curious ways of people of some distant country. Which is what it is, for these men belonged to the heavenly country. I have ample evidence from personal experience that their principles can be practised in church life also. It is indeed "the path in which the whole church of God should be found walking."

At my suggestion the large assembly in Unity Chapel, Bristol, adopted the following Resolution: "It is unanimously resolved that in future no proposal shall be deemed to be carried or be recorded as a resolution until the church unanimously consents to the same at a duly convened church meeting: it being understood that the absence of any objection to a proposed motion may be taken to signify its acceptance." It was the practice to give one month's notice of proposed changes.

In that assembly a large party were determined to introduce carnal methods. They pressed for these, raised storms in the business meetings for eighteen months, but *never brought forward a single resolution*, for under the above rule there never was any hope of one being carried. So determined were they, that under the other plan it would have been very possible for them to have packed a meeting and carried the day by a majority vote. The Scriptural method put the situation into the hands of the spiritual of the church. These had but quietly and persistently to refuse the proposed alterations, and to possess their souls in patience till the storm wore itself out. The carnally-minded, being irreconcilable, at length withdrew. On the other hand, the unspiritual are not able thus to obstruct the godly; for in believing, steadfast prayer the latter have a resource the former lack, by means of which a pressure can be exerted upon the situation which the unspiritual cannot escape. By conflict-prayer the efforts of wicked spirits can be frustrated, and by appeals to God His power can be brought to bear to secure, in His good time, the accomplishing of His will.

By attention to three things all difficulty in this matter may be removed, and unanimity be always attained when the Lord deems it desirable for His purposes.

1. The most diligent and careful inquiry in ascertaining that candidates for church fellowship are (*a*) scripturally converted to God through faith in our Lord Jesus Christ, and indwelt by the Holy Spirit, Whose working it is produces unanimity; and (*b*) that there is every reason to suppose from their past life and present conduct that they are really desirous of knowing and doing the will of God.

2. The sedulous cultivation of personal communion with God the Father, through our Lord Jesus Christ, in the power of the Holy Spirit; by regular meditation upon the Scriptures, so as to advance in the knowledge of His will; and by habitual prayer, wherein all doing and thinking passes beneath His inspection, and discrepancies and evils are revealed; and whereby grace is received to do those things which are pleasing to Him.

3. The due and loving exercise of discipline towards any on whose conduct the Word of God commands discipline.

So a church's corporate life would be lived beneath the eye and under the control of God; the Spirit of the Lord would obtain continually increasing power, working to will and to do of God's good pleasure; so would there be oneness in action in and through the Spirit, even as the Father and the Son are One in the communion of the Spirit, and thus would our Lord's desire and prayer be fulfilled more and more perfectly; so would the harmony and love of church life be secured and promoted; and so should our joint testimony before the world be unceasing and effective, to the honour and praise of Him to whom belongeth the glory for ever and ever.

Chapter 12

# The Public Ministry of Women

THIS much controverted topic is here touched by way of inquiry whether some points, important for ascertaining the meaning of the scriptures in question, have not been much overlooked, and whether the giving of due weight to these does not help to a harmonious exposition so much to be desired.

The first passage is 1 Cor. 11:4-5: "Every man praying or prophesying, having his head covered, dishonoureth his head. But every woman praying or prophesying with her head unveiled dishonoureth her head."

As the first clause certainly implies that men prayed and prophesied, so as certainly does the second imply that women also did so, which other scriptures also show to have been the fact. It were idle to direct how persons should be dressed when doing certain acts if in fact they were forbidden to do them at all. And as the men certainly prayed and prophesied in the public assemblies of the church, and as no limiting clause in this regard touching the women is introduced, the natural presumption is that they also prayed and prophesied in public. Ch. 14:4, 5, 22, 24, 29–33 make it unquestionable that prophesying is a gift for exercise in the public gatherings of the church.

That the apostle is speaking of matters that were the concern of the *churches*, and not family or private affairs, is clear from the way he finally settles the case: "we have no such custom, neither the *churches of God*" (ver. 16). That the whole of this paragraph is dealing with public matters is also clear from the next clause (ver. 17): "But in giving you this charge (that is, including the immediately preceding directions now in question), I praise you not, that YE COME TOGETHER not for the better, but for the worse," and there is no question that from this point forward to the end of ch. 14 his instructions, including those upon prophesying, concern the public assemblies of saints. And so Bengel rightly says on ch. 11:4: "*praying or prophesying* especially *in the church*, ver. 16, and *in the assembly* [*the coming together*], ver. 17." And so Alford takes it as "praying in public." Indeed, were this the only statement of Scripture upon this theme would any thought ever have entered any reasonable mind but that in the apostolic assemblies women prayed and prophesied as moved by the Holy Spirit?

The next scripture to be considered is 1 Cor. 14:34-35: "Let the women keep silence in the churches: for it is not permitted unto them to speak; but let them be in subjection, as also saith the law. And if they would learn anything, let them ask their own husbands at home: for it is shameful for a woman to speak in the church."

When seeking to form in the mind a picture of an early Christian "church" it is indispensable to dismiss completely every notion of a stately building, a pompous, carefully-ordered ritual, or even a decorous, routine service.

The first believers assembled in the open courts of the temple, where many were coming and going; in the homeliness of a house, where one perched himself on the window-ledge; amidst the informalities of a "school," or the gloom of an underground tomb (catacomb). Such varied and secular externals lent no adventitious sense of sacrosanctity to the gathering. Its profit and impressiveness must needs arise from other circumstances, the spiritual.

This is one feature not usually, or sufficiently, taken into account in judging of what was seemly or unseemly in the gatherings of believers. Conduct which would appear highly offensive in a stately ecclesiastical edifice might not seem so in the more genial atmosphere of a humble Christian home. It is most needful to consider that the New Testament is not a description of public worship according to the rites of the Church of England as prescribed by law, nor even of the Church of Scotland, and not even of the present-day meetings of the people called Brethren, though these last, in principles and in some features, certainly approximate to the apostolic type far more closely than such as the former. Yet even these, who do at least aim at conformity to the New Testament, may reflect that perchance they have something still to learn. To groups of churches, as to individuals, the saying may be addressed: Remember, brethren, that none of you is infallible, not even the youngest of you.

Moreover, the persons who mostly formed the first churches (as that at Corinth, which is particularly here in question), were not educated, disciplined Westerners, to whom routine and decorum (not to say deadness), especially in public worship, have become second nature and seem wholly proper. On the contrary, they were Orientals, Greeks, Latins; nervous, restless, emotional people, even as today; impulsive, vivacious, talkative; to whom routine was irksome and dullness intolerable. Then, also, the more part of them were poor, such as artisans, labourers and slaves, illiterate, uncultured, undisciplined. To such Easterners (as we have seen with our eyes) much in public meetings passes as natural which to the average English Christian would seem distracting.

Nor had those first believers been trained to a deadly propriety in public services. Their heathen temples had seen large concourses, with little semblance of order or sense of stillness, seething masses of humanity, swaying hither and thither; and those occasions were too often disgraced by uproarious and scandalous revelry. Hence the unholy gluttony and drunkenness at Corinth which the Apostle so sternly rebukes as making it impossible for them to eat the holy Supper of their Lord.

Neither was even the synagogue, in which believing Jews had been reared, marked by the degree of propriety and orderliness to which we in the west are today accustomed in the churches of God. It was indeed much more orderly than heathen worship, but at certain points of the proceedings extemporary prayers were permitted,[1] also a person desiring to read could rise in his place and the ruler of the synagogue cause a roll to be handed to him, and after having read he might address the congregation (Luke 4:16-17); or the rulers, seeing strangers, might invite them to address the people (Acts 13:15). Often many of the people would stand throughout the service or sit on the ground, both of which positions induce a good deal of movement in the crowd. Doubtless then, as now, there was much

---

1  Edersheim, *Sketches of Jewish Social Life*, ch. XVIII. *Life and Times*, etc., book III, vol. 1, 438.

freedom as to entering and leaving during the service; and in the summer the heat would cause restlessness, fanning, some leaving for the outer air and returning. But in addition to these natural causes of disturbance the Scriptures reveal other features. The emotional temperament excited by prejudice threw a whole congregation into a sudden tumult, with the alarming accompaniment of the attempted assassination of the offending teacher (Luke 4:28-29). We know (Edersheim, *Sketches*, 276) that if anyone expressed, even in prayer, what were regarded as false notions he was immediately stopped, while Acts 13:45 shows the leaders violently and offensively interrupting Paul while discoursing, calling forth from him a solemn rejoinder (46-47), which last utterance caused an outbreak of approbation from a section of the audience; an intense scene, repeated later (18:6). This same Oriental excitability caused the uproar in Ephesus among heathen (ch. 19), and the murderous riot in even the sacred temple at Jerusalem (ch. 21). But earlier than this we mark the indecorous interruptions to which Christ was subjected when teaching in synagogue or temple (John 7:30; 8:3, 59; 10:31, 39), treatment afterwards meted out to the apostles (Acts 4:1–3; 6:12; 7:51, 58; 17:32).

The narratives of John show also that instruction very often took the form of *dialogue* (chs. 6, 7, 8, etc.), a feature clearly seen in the Acts also, for the word translated "reasoned" (Acts 17:1, 17; 18:4, 19; 19:8-9) is "dialogued." The same word is rendered "disputing" in Acts 24:12, and again "reasoned" in ver. 25. In ver. 26 it is followed by "communed" as showing the nature of the intercourse usual between the two men in question. It is rendered "discoursed" at ch. 20:9, of Paul addressing a *Christian* assembly, being followed there (ver. 11) by "talked" as indicating the style of "discourse" on that occasion. Now the words "communed" and "talked" are the word "homilized," meaning to converse familiarly, and we know that this was a usual form of instruction in the early synagogue and then in the early Christian assemblies, and that it continued to later times. Thus the discourse or dialogue or homily contained the essential idea of interchange of thought and the notion of *disputing* was often prominent (Mark 9:34; Jude 9).

All these features reveal that assemblies at that time were marked by a familiarity, freedom, vivacity not common today among Teutonic peoples; but even now when one visits Latin, Slav, Oriental and notably Jewish circles exactly these features are in evidence.

It is necessary to appreciate this tone or temper of those early Christian gatherings, and to allow for this sense of the (to us) somewhat indecorous and commonly disturbed proceedings, otherwise it will be difficult to feel, as the apostle and the Corinthians felt it, the force of his remark that "it is *shameful* for a woman to speak in assembly." It is a very strong expression. The word is from a root which pictures conduct that is base, disgraceful.[1] Why should it be *disgraceful* for a woman to speak in such an assembly as we have described? A company of Christians, humble folk, are met in friendly fashion in the lowly home of one of them. There, after a social meal (the *agape*), they continue in praise to God, in supplication, exhorting one another to love and good works; or they break the bread and drink of one cup in grateful remembrance of that Death which is their way to life. The proceedings are spontaneous, with no externals that awe; there is a family atmosphere as of brothers and sisters communing at the table of their father: *why* should it be *shameful* that the daughters of the house should express themselves, as well as the sons? Why were it nothing less than *disgraceful* that one of them should speak to her Father (prayer), or repeat to the rest of the circle something He has just said to her (prophecy)?

It will be said that Christian assemblies were not *simply* family gatherings: the unconverted might be present. It is true: yet this was usually somewhat rare. Public dislike or open hostility, or the fact that private houses were so frequently the place of meeting, probably made it only occasional that non-Christians were present. Hence in our chapter we read at ver. 23: "*If* there come in (= suppose there should come in) one unlearned or unbelieving." And hence also the wild calumnies that wicked deeds were done as part of the worship of the Christians, slanders that were impossible if the world freely

---

1 As, e.g. for a woman's head to be shorn (ch. 11: 6), where the same word is used. In Eph. 5: 4, a derivative is rendered "filthiness." See also Col. 3: 8, where the meaning is obscene language.

and usually attended. Therefore the family sense remained strong in the gatherings of those days, and any who urge that because an occasional outsider was present *therefore* women must be silent are under obligation to justify that opinion.

But was not GOD present? Was not worship directed to the High and Holy One? It was so. It was the true glory of the gathering. But He was there as, and was worshipped as, *Father*: "We cry, Abba, Father.... Blessed be the God and *Father* of our Lord Jesus Christ." *This* knowledge of God was indeed the chief differentiating feature of *Christian* worship, distinguishing it from heathen and even Jewish worship. The question is not answered: Why, in the presence of the Father, must His daughters be silent?

But was not the Lord Jesus Christ present, and was not the worship offered in His holy name? It is true; He was there, according to His great promise (Matt. 18:20), a promise given in connexion with *prayer*, and by no means to be limited to, or even *specially* connected with, a gathering for breaking bread. Therefore the Lord was present with those gathered in His name in the upper room during the days directly after His ascension, and we are distinctly told that the women equally with the men continued steadfastly in prayer, and one woman is mentioned by name as so doing (Acts 1:14). As regards anything that is said, it is as possible to say that the men did not pray audibly as that the women did not.

But was not the Holy Spirit present, and were not all under His direct control? Most certainly; which mighty fact determined the form of the proceedings, and secured that all was spontaneous, solemn, animated, not formal or routine. But why must women *therefore* be silent? It was in direct connexion with the promised coming of the Spirit that God had said that the "daughters" and "handmaids" should prophesy; which prediction the Spirit Himself moved Peter to include when explaining the partial fulfilment of that prophecy at Pentecost (Joel 2:28-29; Acts 2:17-18).

Moreover, at the time the Spirit fell women as well as men were present, for the "all" of ch. 2:1: "they were all together in one place," must include at least all the persons mentioned in ch. 1:14-15. And it is distinctly said that the tongues as of fire "sat upon *each* one of them. And they were *all* filled with the Holy Spirit, and began to speak with other tongues, as the Spirit gave them utterance" (Acts 2:1–4). But since on that occasion it was an immediate consequence of the Holy Spirit's presence that women spake with tongues in the general assembly of believers, why should they be forbidden to do so in His presence in Corinth?

But were not MEN present, and is it not the divinely appointed status of the woman to be in subjection to the man? It is so: indeed it is a truth much to be stressed in our times, when in this, as in other particulars, forces are working for a thorough inversion of the divine orderings. And this is to be emphasized as much in the true interests of womankind as for other reasons. But men were present on the day of Pentecost, yea, the apostles of Christ themselves; and if at that time it was of the Spirit that women should speak with tongues in public why should the presence of men impose complete silence in later gatherings?

To these questions no straightforward answer seems to be forthcoming, or is, we think, possible. There seems nothing in the nature or conduct of Christian assemblies to demand that women *must* be silent. Her relation of subjection to the man demands that she wear the appointed sign thereof, a covering on the head, but it does not seem to demand that she must not *speak* in his presence, so long as her demeanour and the utterance itself be consistent with her subjection.

The case stands (1) that it was foretold that the Spirit should use women as well as men as His prophetic mouthpiece; (2) that this was cited as explanation of what took place at Pentecost, which citation on that occasion would have been unnecessary as regards women prophesying if they had not then and there been prophesying, for in the absence of the fact the explanation of it were inappropriate; (3) it is shown that they joined the men in public prayer and that they spake with tongues in assembly; (4) it is laid down later that when thus praying or prophesying they must be covered as to the head.

Now all this testimony of Scripture becomes confused and contradictory only when *absolute* silence is supposed to be the requirement of the words, "Let your women be silent in the assemblies, for it is not permitted unto them to speak" (1 Cor. 14:34). Ought not the necessary rule to apply that later statements must be construed in harmony with earlier, unless they avowedly repeal the earlier? In that case the position of the matter will be that praying and prophesying having been before sanctioned are excepted from the command of silence, which applies to different modes of speech.

Of these there were two. The one was joining in the "dialogues," those often animated discussions mentioned. Surely all will feel it inharmonious with the modesty and natural subjection becoming the woman that she should in this act as the men, springing to her feet, interjecting observations, opinions, questions, objections, thus interrupting the teacher speaking, as we have seen from Scripture was done, and also have ourselves watched in Jewish and Gentile meetings. *Such* behaviour *would* be generally felt "shameful" in a woman, something of which she *ought* to be ashamed, as indeed it easily becomes on the part of men, when they become excited.

That it had reached this stage at Corinth is to be inferred from the apostle's commands that only one person may address the assembly at one time; that they must show deference to one another by one speaking yielding place to another who is moved of the Spirit to communicate something; that each must control his own spirit, not lose that control himself, nor yield it to any other spirit; that order, not confusion, becomes assemblies where the God of order is worshipped. And as regards the women he prohibits them intervening in *such* manner of speaking.

That it is this element of the assembly proceedings he has in mind is suggested by the immediately following sentence. It would be replied: But the public teaching will raise problems in the minds of women as well as of men. Are these to be left unsolved? To which the apostle replied: "If they would learn anything, let them ask their own husbands[1] at home: for it is shameful for a woman to speak in

---

1 The suggestion that the injunction applies only to the married woman, and leaves the unmarried free, cannot be maintained. For (1) there are in the East practically no unmarried women. It is deemed a misfortune and disgrace. (2) The principles and arguments apply to the unmarried. (3) Paul appeals to the law in support of his statement of the divine will, and under the law the daughter was as fully subject to her father as the wife to her husband.

assembly," that is, by way of thrusting herself forward with her questions or remarks.

The other form of speaking that would be covered is best expressed by the word chattering. Because anything so unseemly is happily unknown in the West today let it not be imagined that it is unknown elsewhere. To be sure, the argument that *laleō*, the verb used here, properly means chattering, is inadmissible, because while it had that sense in classical Greek, it is the normal verb meaning "to speak" in biblical Greek. In the New Testament the kind of speaking envisaged must be determined from the context. What kind of speaking, then, is envisaged in 1 Cor. 14:34f.?

There is not the least question that among such excitable, undisciplined people as are in view the obnoxious, irreverent habit of chattering or gossiping was and is common. We ourselves have had to reprove it in Christian assemblies, and have heard other leaders do so, whilst in more than one land converted Jews have informed me that they have not infrequently known the rabbis in the synagogue obliged to exhort the women to cease chattering. It must be remembered that in almost all such lands it was, and is, customary for the women to sit together, often packed together, in a separate part of the room, which facilitated this annoying habit. This was so in the synagogues of New Testament times (Edersheim, *Life and Times*, I, 434, 436).

Is there not therefore sufficient ground for the required silence without throwing this passage into irreconcilable conflict with preceding scriptures by insisting that it demands entire silence?

But we further inquire whether in discussion on this topic proper force has been given to the clause "as also saith the law." The subjection enforced on the woman in the church is thus that subjection which was imposed under the law. But the law did not hinder women from praising and prophesying. Even before the giving of the Sinaitic law there was a woman prophetess, Miriam, one inspired by the Spirit, who led all the women in public praise. The natural relationship between man and woman was not created by the law, but preceded Sinai; if therefore that relationship were a ground for the absolute silence of women before men that outburst at the Red Sea had been improper. Yet stolid of soul must he be whose heart does not throb with the ecstasy of that hour of Jehovah's triumph and feel that those dancing feet and clanging timbrels and ringing voices were a fitting accompaniment to that thrilling moment.

Compare with that scene this in a Christian assembly, and say honestly if the latter is to be condemned as unseemly and unscriptural. In *How Christ Came to Church* (ch. 7), Dr. A. J. Gordon contrasts the days of worldliness in his church, when the praise was led by hired professionals from the opera, with the spiritual worship after the temple had been cleansed, and says: "The Spirit has had liberty to break forth in song in unexpected ways now and then, as when a joyous young disciple going down to be baptized sang the strains of 'My Jesus, I love Thee, I know Thou art mine,' as her feet touched the water, all the congregation uniting with overpowering effect." Ought that dear girl to have stifled the joyous outburst because men were present? Was the impulse thus to pour out her love to her Lord of His Spirit or of her carnal nature?

Neither did Eli, the high priest and chief administrator of the divine law, interrupt or reprove Hannah's inspired prayer and worship, though it was poured forth in his presence and in the temple of God (1 Sam. 2:1–10). The law did not hinder Anna, the prophetess, from worshipping, supplicating, giving thanks and testifying in public, for she passed her whole time in the temple, and at the very hour of the Lord being presented to God there she "spake of Him to *all* them that were looking for the redemption of Jerusalem" (Luke 2:36–38). Nor did it hinder Huldah from being a prophetess to whom public men went openly, at the bidding of the king himself, to learn the mind of God. Josiah had just before heard the book of the law read. Evidently that book contained nothing to forbid a woman prophesying before men. The law did not prevent Deborah, a woman, from prophesying, nor Barak, a man, from joining her in a public song of praise.

Praise, prayer, and prophesying in public, as moved by the Spirit, being, therefore, not inconsistent with the subjection of woman according to the law, how can they be prohibited by a passage which expressly says that its requirement corresponds to that of the law?

Does not this consideration further support the suggestion that the silence imposed does not apply to these exercises?[1]

If it be asked how this view can be harmonized with Paul's unequivocal words: "I permit not a woman to teach" (1 Tim. 2:12), the simple answer is, By taking him to mean just what he says, and nothing more. He does not say "praise" or "pray" or "preach" or "evangelize" or "prophesy," but "teach," which term has its own proper sense, especially in contrast with the term "prophesy." As far as I recollect, this distinction has been too much omitted from the discussions upon our subject. Much confusion has resulted. Paul has been made to contradict himself, and exegetes have been driven to various devices to explain away one or other of his statements.

That prophets and teachers were separate gifts is clear from Acts 13:1; 1 Cor. 11:29; Eph. 4:11; and they were still distinguished in times later than the apostles, as may be seen in the *Didache*, ch. 15, which, agreeably to these scriptures, speaks of "the ministry of the prophets and teachers."

The difference between prophesying and teaching is simple and uniform. The prophet spoke by immediate impulse of the Spirit, without premeditation or preparation for that particular occasion,[2] whereas the teacher pondered the divine oracles, the Word of God, and delivered to the people the fruit of his meditations thereon.

In Israel the priests were the official teachers of the people. On the day of the consecration of Aaron and his sons, they were forbidden to touch intoxicants while about the Sanctuary. Was not this that their mind might be wholly clear for this task, with the subtle distinctions required between things clean and unclean (Lev. 10:8–11; *cf.* Hag. 2:10–13)? Thus the people were to "ask the priests concerning the law," "for the priest's lips should keep knowledge, and they

---

1  Since writing as above, I have found in Tertullian (c. A.D. 200) the following remark: "In precisely the same manner, when enjoining on women silence in the church, that they speak not for the mere sake of learning (although that even they have the right of prophesying, he [Paul] has already shown when he covers the woman that prophesies with a veil), he goes to the law for his sanction that woman should be under obedience" (*Against Marcion*, 411. Ed., Clark).

2  See Note at end of this chapter (pp. 162 ff.).

should seek the law at his mouth: for he is the messenger of Jehovah of hosts" (Mal. 2:6-7). Specially difficult matters of judgment were to be referred to them, and their sentence was so authoritative that presumptuous rejection thereof was made a capital offence (Deut. 17:8–13; Num. 5). They were to be perpetually prepared for this duty of teaching by continual occupation with the law. Similarly, Paul enjoined upon Timothy: "give heed to reading, to exhortation, to teaching.... Be diligent in these things.... Continue in these things" (1 Tim. 4:13-16).

But the prophets were not of this type. They were persons selected by the Spirit from various walks in life (Amos 1:1; Jer. 1:1, etc.), and of both sexes. To them the message they were to deliver came as a sudden vision (Num. 24:3, 4, 15, 16), or a vision communicated to the inner sight, not by meditation upon the Book (1 Kings 22:17–23). It was commonly given at the time for utterance (Ex. 4:11–12; 2 Chron. 20:14; 24:20, etc.) and if restrained became as a fierce fire in the heart burning its way out in impassioned speech (Jer. 20:9). The teachers read in the law consecutively, and explained its sense systematically (Neh. 8:1–8); the prophets rather enforced than explained its requirement, charged upon the conscience of men its infringement and denounced the divine wrath against obduracy, or promised the divine blessing to the obedient. Thus the work of the teacher was regular and permanent, that of the prophet supplementary and occasional, though continuing throughout such periods as it was needed. The teacher explained divine oracles already given, the prophet was often the agent to add fresh revelations, though this last feature was not of the essence of prophesying, nor indispensable thereto.

Of course, the same person might be used by the Spirit in both offices—Jeremiah as a priest might teach the law and also be an inspired prophet; so also the apostles: but the functions were distinct; a priest *as a priest* was a teacher, though God might also employ him as a prophet.

We have noted above that the priest, as the appointed teacher of the will of God, was invested with *authority*; the hearer was laid under definite obligation to obey. This is inherent in the very idea of a teacher; hence, in all lands and times, some authority to discipline the scholar is conceded to the secular school teacher. Hence also Christ said: "The scribes and the Pharisees sit on Moses' seat: all things, therefore, whatsoever they bid you, these do and observe: but do not ye after their works; for they say and do not" (Matt. 23:2-3). For the office carries authority even though the holder of it does not practise his own precepts. We read of our Lord: "He *taught* them as having *authority*" (Matt. 7:29). So Paul to Timothy: "These things *command* and *teach*. Let no man despise thy youth" (1 Tim. 4:11-12); and to Titus concerning his teaching: "These things speak and exhort and reprove with all *commandment*. Let no man despise thee" (ch. 2:1, 7, 15). But the prophet had no formal authority, but only the moral influence accompanying the truth he declared and the character and life he displayed. Whereas the qualified teacher in the Christian church has received from the Head of the church authority to discipline: the elder was to be a teacher and a *ruler* (1 Tim. 3:2–5; 5:17).

Now it is obvious that there *can* be no authority but of God, for it is in His right and power to delegate and to withdraw authority: "He removeth kings and setteth up kings," a philosophy of history completely ignored by most historians (Dan. 2:21). Under the law Aaron had no formal authority till God conferred it, but then it was real. So with the elders of a church. The Lord has graciously given to the church not only "helps," but "*governments*" (1 Cor. 12:28), directors who, when they act according to His word and Spirit, have as full authority and power as a steersman has to direct the ship, for such is the word here used.[1] Solemn for the present age of self-will in both the world and the church is the word: "the powers that be are ordained of God. Therefore he that resisteth the power withstandeth the ordinance of God: and they that withstand shall receive to themselves judgment" (Rom. 13:1-2).

But as between the man and the woman, God has delegated authority to the man, as is the uniform declaration of Scripture, beginning from the words of God to Eve in Eden: "he (Adam) shall

---

[1] Compare its allied noun in Acts 27:11; Rev. 18:17. These are all the places where the two words are found in N.T.

rule over thee" (Gen. 3:16). This was heavily emphasized under the law (see e.g. Num. 30), and confirmed in the church, as by the passages now before us (1 Cor. 11:2–16; 14:34; 1 Tim. 2:8–15). The notion that these last injunctions are mere prejudices of Paul and his age is refuted by the whole of Scripture, and, indeed, of human experience and history. Now, because authority is thus vested by God in the man, therefore the woman is prohibited from that public function in the church which presupposes authority: "I permit not a woman to teach"; to which the appropriate context is: "Let her learn in quietness with all subjection," and let her not attempt to exercise "dominion over man." But as neither praying nor prophesying involves authority, these exercises do not fall within this prohibition.

Such as accept the foregoing exposition will feel that it allows each of Paul's statements to be taken in its simple surface sense, so that they require no reconciling, and are harmonious with all the other testimony of Scripture, older and later.

The headship of the man the Scripture founds on definite facts. Now facts are facts, nor can wisdom be learned save by accepting them heartily and in practice. (1) It is a fact that God is the head of Christ; Christ of man; man of woman (1 Cor. 11:3). Christ is not humiliated by acknowledging the headship of God the Father, neither is the man by owning that of Christ, nor the woman by submitting to that of the man. On the contrary, it is the unique glory of Christ that He, in the ordering of the whole universe, stands, as the Son, nearest of all to God; it is the special honour of man that (through the Son of God becoming incarnate as man) he of all created intelligences stands most nearly connected to Christ; it is the corresponding dignity of woman that she is the closest connexion of the one who stands next in dignity under the Son. (2) The second fact is that man by creation is peculiarly "the image and glory of God" (1 Cor. 11:7). He, in the universal Kingdom of God, exhibits the likeness of the all-glorious Creator. Equally so does the woman, being taken out of the man, correspond to him who is the image of God. So high honour woman could not have had, unless indeed by having been created in the image of God independently of the man, *which she was not.* (3) This involves the third fact—that "Adam was first formed, then Eve" (1 Tim. 2:13). Priority in creation demonstrates priority of position according to the purpose of the Creator. She who refuses to accept this fact thereby rejects the mind and will of God upon this matter. (4) Lastly, by contrast, the woman was the first to be entangled in transgression (1 Tim. 2:14). "Adam was not deceived (*apataō*) but the woman being beguiled (thoroughly deceived, hoodwinked, *exapataō*[1]), hath fallen into transgression." The completeness of Eve's deception is emphasized in 2 Cor. 11:3 by the word being joined to two others which mean that the serpent thoroughly blinded (*exapataō*) and corrupted (*phtheirō*) the mind of Eve by his craftiness (*panourgia*), which last has the force of the English idiomatic expressions that one stoops to anything and sticks at nothing to gain his end. Now this greater susceptibility to deception is revealed as a fact, and a fact inherent in the original constitution of woman as compared with man. Probably it was through discerning this that Satan resolved to attack Eve first, and while she was apart from Adam. It is, therefore, no fault or discredit to woman, and it is compensated by a wealth of emotion above that of the man, fitting her admirably to be the help answering to, that is, complementing him; but *it remains a fact*, and a feature accentuated by that derangement of all the human nature produced by the loss through the fall of the divine grace.

This fact remains in startling evidence today, in that women have been leaders in so many of the mighty spiritual deceptions ensnaring myriads. Madame Blavatsky and Mrs. Besant in Theosophy, Mrs. Baker Eddy in Christian Science, Mrs. White in Seventh Day Adventism are prominent instances, and the frequency with which women are séance mediums is well known, even as in heathenism they were, and are, the common prophetesses declaring the oracles of the gods (see Acts 16:16, e.g.).

The foregoing consideration leads to a pertinent reflection. It will be seen that I would allow more liberty to women to serve publicly than many would do, but in view of the persistent and universal

---

1 Compare all its other occurrences, Rom. 7:11; 16:18; 1 Cor. 3:18; 2 Cor. 11:3; 2 Thess. 2:3.

attempt of wicked spirits in the present day to force forward the woman into public life, to the degradation of her womanliness, to the neglect of her normal private duties, and to the general corruption of society, it becomes Christian women to be very careful in the use of their freedom, and especially that their style and tone in its exercise be wholly becoming. Otherwise such exercise may easily afford opportunity to Satan to infect the Christian circle wherein they move with the baneful spirit that is fast ripening for destruction his own sphere, the world. This is, indeed, not necessary, but it is possible.

Moreover, when any assembly or its elders conscientiously object to sisters speaking in public, it affords opportunity to the sisters who see otherwise to display grace by yielding their rights, according to the law of love, as applied to other matters in Rom. 14, 15. Edification of the church is necessary to justify *any* public ministry (note the sevenfold emphasis on edification in the chief passage on Christian gatherings, 1 Cor. 14), and this cannot be gained by forcing oneself upon hearts that feel outraged by the attempt. To divide a church in the asserting of such a right would be wholly indefensible, and, on the other hand, to *leave* the fellowship of the house of God because one cannot get all the liberty one feels is one's right would argue a very low state of soul, a feeble sense of the dignity of the fellowship of saints, and would be quite unjustifiable from Scripture, which grants no wider grounds for alienation from fellow Christians than a denial by them of Christ, or flagrant wickedness. Other evils or errors in saints must be tolerated patiently and with prayer for their enlightenment. I preach only what I practise. As a matter of right I claim the same liberty to teach what I deem the true meaning of prophetic scriptures that other brethren exercise, but I have never felt it proper to exercise that right by introducing my views where they would be resented.

It is to be further observed that the injunctions against women teaching or ruling over men condemn emphatically their being elders, pastors, ministers, moderators, presidents, chairmen. Their election of late to such posts is a serious proof of that thorough rejection of the Word of God as authoritative which marks much Western

Nonconformity. I speak of the *election* of women to ruling place. The Head of the church is above His rules by which He binds His people. *He*, on occasion, may employ a Deborah to be *judge* of His people (Jud. 4:4) and to summon and to direct the soldier who shall lead the fighting. But *His people* have no leave from Him themselves *to appoint* a woman to such a post. Those who study history in the light of the Old Testament will have no difficulty in seeing the hand of God in putting the great Victoria upon the throne of the greatest of modern empires, and in keeping her there so long. I myself knew an elderly sister in Christ, one of God's princesses, who actually, though not nominally or obtrusively, was "bishop" over two or three country assemblies, guiding them with a heavenly wisdom that no brother then in that district possessed. And I have seen the same thing in foreign lands. But in none of these cases did the sister seek such influence, nor was she chosen by the people, or appointed by men, nor did she exercise the power in any unseemly or domineering manner. Where there is no man that the Lord can use, it is better far that He raise up a woman to judge than that Israel be left a prey to enemies and to chaos. But this must be *the Lord's* doing, and it is exceptional. There was only one Deborah in Israel's history.

What, then, is the real, harmonious teaching of the Word? I understand the Scripture to deal specifically with praying, prophesying and teaching, sanctioning the two former and forbidding the last. But these passages regard only the gatherings of saints, and therefore do not pronounce upon the matter of women evangelizing, that is, preaching the good news in spheres outside the assembly of believers. This service, therefore, is not restricted by these scriptures, or by any others, as far as I see. Gospel preaching is an individual service, carried on, according to the New Testament point of view, in the world, not in the gatherings of saints. And the spreading of the good news, and the saving of souls from perdition, is so urgent a matter that all disciples may well devote themselves thereto, as the Lord may be pleased to lead. I feel quite unable to require, in effect, that men must perish eternally rather than that a woman should tell them the good tidings. Let any good brother who feels strongly in the other direction consider whether, if *he* were unconverted, he would prefer to go to hell rather than be saved through a woman preaching!

For myself, having been called by God to see with my own eyes and feel with my own soul the unutterable need of the millions of mankind yet in Satanic darkness I can but thank God from the depths of my heart for everyone, man or woman, that takes to them the Word of life. I appreciate keenly the incident recorded by Dr. A. J. Gordon: "We vividly remember, in the early days of women's work in the foreign field, how that brilliant missionary to China, Miss Adele Fielde, was recalled by her Board because of the repeated complaints of the senior missionaries that in her work she was transcending her sphere as a woman. 'It is reported that you have taken upon you to preach,' was the charge read by the chairman: 'is it so?' She replied by describing the vastness and destitution of her field—village after village, hamlet after hamlet yet unreached by the gospel—and then how, with a native woman, she had gone into the surrounding country, gathered groups of men, women and children—whoever would come—and told out the story of the cross to them. 'If this is preaching, I plead guilty to the charge,' she said. 'And have you ever been ordained to preach?' asked her examiner. 'No,' she replied, with great dignity and emphasis—'*no, but I believe I have been foreordained.*'"[1]

To my still objecting brother I present the case this way—a case of daily occurrence in other lands: Suppose you were to find a stranger woman from a foreign land—say a French Roman Catholic nun—talking with your wife and daughters and those of some near neighbours. Suppose, upon inquiry, you learned that she was instructing your womenfolk in a new religion. Would you not feel it only right that you should be permitted to join the group and consider the nature and probable issues of this instruction? And if your neighbours were at hand might not they also deem it their right to hear? And if the stranger excused herself on the ground that her religion did not allow a woman to speak before men, might not a distrust of her arise in your heart and a suspicion of the motives that prompted her to wish to indoctrinate your family privately? In any case, would you, in the face of such refusal to enlighten you, readily believe her

---

1   *The Ministry of Women*, 20, 21.

assertion that your eternal welfare hung absolutely upon your believing the doctrines she refused to impart to you? This situation our sisters preaching Christ in heathen and Moslem lands constantly meet.

Thus much as regards preaching the gospel. But now as touching the practical aspects of women praying in public. For many years I attended a prayer meeting where it was permitted. There came regularly a brother, rough, unlettered, whose prayers for some time were a sore trial. Elder brethren at length proposed to ask him to desist. But one pleaded for longer forbearance, in the hope that the Spirit might yet teach him to pray more as he ought. And He did. In due time he became a real asset to our waiting upon God.

There attended also an elderly widow. Her prayers likewise were almost unbearable. Brethren desired that she, too, be restrained. In her case also patience was urged, and presently she also developed a marked gift of helpful intercession. In sixty years I do not remember any other person, woman or man, who could helpfully and reverently employ in addressing God such a wealth of appropriate Old Testament scriptures. But if it was not the same divine Spirit who helped this sister's infirmity in prayer, who was it? Why give Him praise in the case of the man and not of the woman? Why in her case give His glory unto another? But if the Holy Spirit must be acknowledged as helping a woman to pray in public, how can He be supposed to have positively forbidden the act? Must we not re-examine our exegesis?

In another land I visited a church distracted by fierce strife. The discussions were long and painful, for hearts were hard. Brethren flung at each other the bitterest accusations and reproaches. Remonstrance, and even application of the solemn warnings of the Word, seemed to make no impression. But one evening, during a heart-breaking altercation between two brethren, an elderly sister, the mother of one of them, rose and poured out her heart in prayer. She stirred up herself to take hold on God; she prevailed; her supplication proved the crisis in that diseased community, the fever abated, softening of heart set in. She had carried all into the presence of the Holy One. It is difficult to believe that the Holy Spirit thus mightily helped and used her in flagrant breach of peremptory regulations of His own to the contrary.

I have heard women pray not to edification. I have heard men do the same, and more often. The argument is worthless. Are there no assemblies, who now prohibit women from praying, bold enough to remove the embargo and discover whether the participation of the sisters might not enable the spirit of prayer to requicken many a moribund prayer meeting?

But it ought also to be mentioned, as another point almost entirely forgotten but most important, that the New Testament knows nothing of one gathering of saints being of a different order or rank to another. The "breaking of bread" has its own peculiar and choice blessedness, but it is not more *sacred* than a gathering for prayer or ministry. It is the altar that sanctifies the gift, the temple the gold, and the Indweller the temple (Matt. 23:16–22). Who does not see that it is the Presence of God, not the bread and the cup on the table, that makes the assembly sacred? Therefore conduct permissible in that Presence in one meeting of saints is permissible in any other meeting.

Indeed, the apostolic believers do not appear to have met at this hour for breaking bread alone, at that for preaching the gospel, at another on Monday for prayer, and on yet another day for Bible teaching. *Whenever* they met in general assembly it was to wait in the promised presence of the Lord, subject *always* to the direction of His Spirit as to what should occupy the time on each occasion. And so on the occasion at Troas (Acts 20:7–12), while it says that the disciples had "met to break bread," it records that Paul "discoursed until midnight," then, after the exciting interruption of the fall, death and resuscitation of Eutychus, the bread was broken, and then this was followed by further prolonged instruction by the Apostle. The actual breaking of the bread, precious as it was, was only a brief incident in the long assembly. It was thus when our Lord instituted the ordinance. It was dovetailed into the fraternal intercourse of the Passover solemnities and followed by the much instruction by Christ preserved in John 13–17. A close study of 1 Cor. 11 and 14 reveals the same feature, for the gathering of believers is shown to have been the occasion of a social meal (the *agape*), of the Lord's Supper, of prophesying, speaking in tongues, interpretation thereof, teaching, revelation, praying, psalms (presumably singing thereof, Col. 3:16; Eph. 5:19).

The fact that psalms are included in the Corinthian passage, which deals with the assembly proceedings, forbids the confining of the Colossian and Ephesian passages to private occasions. Now "speaking to one another," "teaching and admonishing one another," is not performed by *congregational* singing. There can be no doubt that the Spirit prompted believers to sing individually, and the word "hymn" included praise to God either in songs already known or inspired at the moment.[1]

Hence the notion that at *any* meeting only this or that exercise is permissible—only the breaking of bread now, only prayer at another time, and so on—is not Scriptural, and really involves a dictating to the Lord the Spirit Himself as to what He shall or shall not incite on each occasion.

I speak of the general gatherings of believers. To meet the emergency of Peter's impending murder the Spirit drew together many specially for prayer (Acts 12). To encourage the saints to glorify God, Paul and Barnabas gathered the church at Antioch to hear an account of what God had wrought through them during their journey. A sufficient precedent for "missionary" meetings (Acts 14:27). To settle once for all a question fundamental to the very gospel of our salvation special meetings of the church in Jerusalem were held (Acts 15). But even at these exceptional gatherings, as in all others, the lordship of the Spirit was acknowledged, as is seen in the last case by the discussion being open to all to express what the

---

1   See Alford, Meyer, Ellicott, Lightfoot. But the attempted distinction between "divine service" and other gatherings of Christians is not in the New Testament, but made in the interests of human ecclesiasticism.
    We know this was so 150 years later. Tertullian (*Apol.* c. 39), rebutting the charge that the *agape* was a revel, says: "After the washing of the hands and the bringing in of the lights, each is asked to stand forth and sing, as he can, a hymn to God, either one from the Holy Scripture, or one of his own composing—a test of the measure of our drinking."

Spirit gave. Is it conceivable that a chairman decided whether Paul or Barnabas should give the first account of their tour and how long each should speak? We may surely be sure that if, during that night of prayer, the Spirit gave to anyone instruction or encouragement to strengthen faith, no one would have said, "We are met for prayer and do not wish to hear ministry."

This means that those who allow to women liberty to pray or to prophesy must get rid of the sacerdotal notion that they ought not to do so before elder or ministering brethren (which is close to priestcraft), and get rid of the sacramentarian idea that they ought not to take part if the bread and cup are on the table, giving a *false* sanctity to the symbols, as if they were more sacred than the presence of Him they represent.

In a Continental capital I found a small gathering of humble Christians whose meetings were nearer than anything else I ever knew to what I conceive the apostolic worship to have been. I had known those gatherings when dull and inanimate, but in 1926 I found all was changed, vivified. Fasting and prayer had prepared the way for the Lord to come to His temple. Also the following change had been momentous. Following the usual practice in the liturgical services out of which they had escaped at conversion they had continued all to kneel together for prayer. It resulted that the spirit of worship was interrupted by some unconverted person, or someone not able physically to kneel for long, fidgeting or rising, whereupon all rose. I had often pointed out that thus the real control of the proceedings was taken from the Holy Spirit and given to the feeble or the least spiritual or even to the unregenerate. But now they had adopted the plan of the individual leading the exercises alone standing or kneeling, and at once the gracious Spirit asserted His power. These fifteen or so believers I found continuing in worship, praise, ministry, breaking of the bread, for two and a half hours without effort, without haste, without wearisomeness; just a fervent, joyous, solemn overflow of full hearts glorying in God through our Lord Jesus Christ.

So remarkable, so edifying was it that unbelievers were finding their way to that humble room on a third storey, and were sitting quietly throughout the long meeting, marvelling at the contrast with the formal worship of Roman or Lutheran services or of the synagogue. And most notable of all, so powerful was the work of the Spirit, that some Romanists and Jews had been converted to Christ in those meetings, though there was no direct preaching to them. One morning I saw a woman at the other end of the room rise, commence to pray, break down in sobs, fall upon her knees, struggle for self-control, and then further pour out her heart to God. A solemn hush was upon all present. She was a Roman Catholic making her first confession of faith in Christ. Such scenes were a manifest fulfilment of the Scripture: "If there come in one unbelieving, or unlearned, he is convicted by all, he is judged by all; the secrets of his heart are made manifest; and so he will fall down upon his face, and worship God, declaring that God is among you indeed" (1 Cor. 14:24, 25).

And yet in all those gatherings sisters took part as freely as brethren, and, I may add, as decorously and as profitably. Apparently the Spirit of God did not regard this as the outrage, the lawlessness, that I have known it proclaimed. Surely we must re-examine our interpretation of His words, and consider whether it really is justifiable to base this policy of repression of spiritual gifts in women virtually upon a rigid unconditional sense of one single word, *sigato*, "keep silence," for this, it seems to me, is the position to which the supporters of that view are finally reduced.

For that some women are actually *gifted* in prayer and some in power of exhortation cannot be denied by such as know. But the conferring of a gift proves the intention of the Giver that it should be used: "To each one is given the manifestation of the (otherwise unseen) Spirit to profit (the rest) withal" (1 Cor. 12:7). And it is clear that the repression, the quenching, of the Spirit, the despising of prophesyings, on the ground that they come through a woman, must be a hindrance to His working and a corresponding loss to the church, if it be that it is His desire to use women in such service.

In this discussion it is a basic presupposition that a sister shall pray or prophesy only when the Holy Spirit impels. There is no liberty for any and every woman to express herself. But these principles are as necessary and as applicable to men. Would that the latter always observed them!

And if it be said that prophesying, in the New Testament sense, was a gift not intended to be permanent in the church and is not now known, we simply refuse both propositions; for of the former the Word of God offers no proof, but rather the contrary; and, as to the latter, what we understand by prophesying, namely, the delivering of a message given by the Spirit at the time, fitting the exact need of the moment, and charged with holy unction to the hearer, this many must have often experienced.[1] Such ministry is probably the most clamant need in the church of God today, as in all former times.

Our inquiry, therefore, is whether the first scripture considered (1 Cor. 11) does not obviously imply the public praying and prophesying of women; whether the second passage (1 Cor. 14) is not harmonized therewith and fully explained by the circumstances of the apostolic meetings as described; and whether the last scripture (1 Tim. 2) is not kept in perfect accord with the testimony of the whole Word of God by the distinction shown between "prophesying" and "teaching."

And finally, it may be noted, as an incidental but not unimportant consequence of this last distinction, that it puts to rest the long dispute as to whether premeditated ministry in certain meetings of saints is of the Spirit. As He gave to the church prophets *and* teachers both these forms of ministry are needed and proper, and as only *one* type of meeting is known to the New Testament room for both should be given therein. In any church where the Lord truly rules both will be known. A chief trouble in the western world is that believers can (or will) give so *little time* to the supremely momentous

---

[1] It is, we trust, fairly generally understood that the predicting of future events is not a necessary element in "prophesying." The revealing of new truth is not a necessity for prophetic speech, nor is now possible, for John 16:13 has been fulfilled; "all the truth" has been revealed that God purposes to give to men, and the Word (message) of God has been completed by the revelation of "the things that are to come" and of the Mystery (Col. 1:25-26; 2:2-3; reading "mystery in which are all the treasures of wisdom and knowledge hidden." See Alford, and Darby, *New Translation*).

privilege of waiting together before God. In consequence, the Spirit can work and bless but little. Short meetings mean restricted ministry and diminished unction. The older and eastern habit is better, of persons who *cannot* remain quietly departing, the rest remaining till the Spirit ceases to move their hearts and to hold them together.

In all these questions concerning Christian assemblies the supreme principle is that the Lord the Spirit should actually control, neither restrained by human preferences, forms, rules or self-assertion, nor grieved by any disregard of His written Word or violation of the law of love which seeks only the edification of others. And the spirit of love is patient and forbearing with those who differ from it and grieve it; and it is humble, and readily concedes that another may have light upon the mind and Word of God which itself has not yet perceived.

## Note—Extracts Concerning Prophesying

ALFORD on 1 Cor. 12:10. *Prophēteia*, SPEAKING IN THE SPIRIT. Meyer gives an excellent definition of it: "discourse flowing from the revelation and impulse of the Holy Spirit, which, not being attached to any particular office in the church, but improvised—disclosed the depths of the human heart and of the divine counsel, and thus was exceedingly effectual for the enlightening, exhortation and consolation of believers, and the winning of unbelievers. The *prophet* differs from the *speaker with tongues*. . . in that he speaks *with the understanding*, not ecstatically, from the *didaskalos* (*teacher*) thus: *Ho men prophēteuōn panta apo tau pneumatos phengetai, bo de didaskōn estin hopou kai ex oikeias dialegetai*. [*He who is prophesying utters everything from the spirit, but he who is teaching there are places where* (*he*) *argues* (*or converses*) *out of his own inner consciousness as well*], as Chrysostom on ver. 28."

ELLICOTT. 2 Cor. 11:5. *Propheteuōn*; "speaking under the more immediate influence of the Holy Spirit." Cremer, *Lexicon*, 600–602. The fact moreover that the earlier name for prophet was seer, 1 Sam. 9:9, shows that what really constitutes the prophet is *immediate intercourse with God*, a divine communication of what the prophet has to declare. . . . That the special element of prophesying was not prediction but a *showing forth of God's will*, especially of His saving purpose, is confirmed by 1 Cor. 14:3: "he that prophesieth speaketh unto men to edification and comfort and consolation." Cf. Jer. 1; Isa. 1; Ezek. 2, and other passages. Two things therefore go to make the prophet, *an insight granted by God* into the divine secrets or mysteries, and a communication to others of these secrets. N.T. [prophets were] "messengers or media of communication between the upper and the lower world," as they have been aptly called.

OLSHAUSEN. 1 Cor. 12:7–11. In both [prophesying and speaking with tongues] the divine efficacy predominated over the human, but so that the prophet's consciousness of facts which might have reference to the circumstances and hearers, remained undisturbed, while on the contrary, in those speaking with tongues all worldly knowledge was subject to the consciousness of God, they held as it were converse with God. The *prophesying* is therefore the real gift of awakening the soul, the principal Charisma for the *arising* church, while the *teaching*, the gift of *knowledge*, appears to be the chief Charisma for the church firmly established, but ever *increasing in itself*.

HATCH, Hibbert Lectures, 105–115. I will ask you, in the first instance, to note the broad distinction which exists between what in the primitive churches was known as "prophesying," and that which in subsequent times came to be known as "preaching." I lay the more stress upon the distinction for the accidental reason that, in the first reaction against the idea that "prophecy" necessarily meant "prediction," it was maintained—and with a certain reservation the contention was true—that a "prophet" meant a "preacher." The reservation is, that the prophet was not merely a preacher but a spontaneous preacher. He preached because he could not help it, because there was a divine breath breathing within him which must needs find an utterance. It is in this sense that the prophets of the early church were preachers. They were not church officers appointed to discharge certain functions. They were the possessors of a *charisma*, a divine gift which was not official but personal. "No prophecy ever came by the will of man; but men spake from God, being moved by the Holy Ghost." They did not practise beforehand how or what they should say; for "the Holy Ghost taught them in that very hour what they should say."

In the course of the second century this original spontaneity of utterance died almost entirely away. It may almost be said to have died a violent death. The dominant parties in the church set their faces against it. The survivals of it in Asia Minor were formally condemned. The Montanists, as they were called, who tried to fan the lingering sparks of it into a flame, are ranked among heretics. And Tertullian is not even now admitted into the calendar of the saints, because he believed the Montanists to be in the right.

It was inevitable that it should be so. The growth of a confederation of Christian communities necessitated the definition of a basis of confederation. Such a definition, and the further necessity of guarding it, were inconsistent with that free utterance of the Spirit which had existed before the confederation began. Prophesying died when the Catholic Church was formed.

In place of prophesying came preaching. And preaching is the result of the gradual combination of various elements. In the formation of a great institution it is inevitable that, as the time goes on, different elements should tend to unite. To the original functions of a bishop,[1] for example, were added by degrees the functions—which had originally been separate—of teacher. In a similar way were fused together, on the one hand, teaching—that is, the tradition and exposition of the sacred books and the received doctrine, and, on the other hand, exhortation—that is, the endeavour to raise men to a higher level of moral and spiritual life. Each of these was a function which, assuming a certain natural aptitude, could be learned by practice. Each of these was consequently a function which might be discharged by the permanent officers of the community, and discharged habitually at regular intervals without waiting for the fitful flashes of prophetic fire. We consequently find that with the growth of organization there grew up also, not only a fusion of teaching and exhortation, but also the gradual restriction of the liberty of addressing the community to the official class....

Such are some of the indications of the influence of Greek Rhetoric upon the early churches. It created the Christian sermon. It added to the functions of church officers a function which is neither that of the exercise of discipline, nor of administration of the funds, nor of taking the lead in public worship, nor of the simple tradition of received truths, but that of either such an exegesis of the sacred books as the Sophists gave of Homer, or such elaborated discourses as they also gave upon the speculative or ethical aspects of religion. The result was more far-reaching than the creation of either an institution or a function. If you look more closely into history, you will find that Rhetoric killed Philosophy. Philosophy died, because

---

1 That is, of a post-apostolic bishop. In the New Testament the "bishop" and "elder" are one, and he was to be "apt to teach" (1 Tim. 3:2).

for all but a small minority it ceased to be real. It passed from the sphere of thought and conduct to that of exposition and literature. Its preachers preached, not because they were bursting with truths which could not help finding expression, but because they were masters of fine phrases and lived in an age in which fine phrases had a value. It died, in short, because it had become sophistry. But sophistry is of no special age or country. It is indigenous to all soils upon which literature grows. No sooner is any special form of literature created by the genius of a great writer than there arises a class of men who cultivate the style for the style's sake. No sooner is any new impulse given either to philosophy or religion than there arises a class of men who copy the form without the substance, and try to make the echo of the past sound like the voice of the present. So it has been with Christianity. It came into the educated world with the simple dress of a Prophet of Righteousness. It won that world by the stern reality of its life, by the subtle bonds of its brotherhood, by its divine message of consolation and hope. Around it thronged the race of eloquent talkers who persuaded it to change its dress and to assimilate its language to their own. It seemed thereby to win a speedier and completer victory. But it purchased conquest at the price of reality. With that its progress stopped. There has been an element of sophistry in it ever since; and so far as in any age that element has been dominant, so far has the progress of Christianity been arrested. Its progress is arrested now, because many of its preachers live in an unreal world. The truths they set forth are truths of utterance rather than truths of their lives. But if Christianity is to be again the power that it was in its earliest ages, it must renounce its costly purchase. A class of rhetorical chemists would be thought of only to be ridiculed; a class of rhetorical religionists is only less anomalous because we are accustomed to it. The hope of Christianity is, that the class which was artificially created may ultimately disappear; and that the sophistical element in Christian preaching will melt, as a transient mist, before the preaching of the prophets of the ages to come, who, like the prophets of the ages that are long gone by, will speak only "as the Spirit gives them utterance."

G. H. Pember, *The Church, the Churches, and the Mysteries*, ch. 35.—
The second order, that of prophets, consists of men who are caused to speak under the immediate inspiration of the Holy Spirit; so that, when the power is upon them, they do not necessarily know what they may be guided to say.

The gift of prophecy has not, however, been confined to the present dispensation; from the earliest times there were men through whom God chose to communicate His wishes and purposes to their fellows. Such were Enoch and Noah, among the antediluvians, and Joseph and Moses in a subsequent period.

But when the Israelitish polity was established, the spiritual instruction of the people was committed to the priests; for they were to "teach the children of Israel all the statutes which the Lord had spoken to them by the hand of Moses" (Lev. 10:11). This they did for a while; but during the times of the Judges they became debased and lost their spiritual power, so that they performed the ritual of the Sanctuary mechanically, and no longer instructed the people as to its real meaning. Hence the Lord began to transfer His work to prophets, whom from the time of Samuel He used, more systematically than before, as His mouthpieces to Israel. For the regularly appointed priests and Levites continued to fail in their duty until they had made the oblations vain, the incense an abomination, the new moons and Sabbaths, and the calling of assemblies, things that He could not away with. He would, therefore, choose men after His own heart, and, filling them with His Holy Spirit, send them forth, without any human ordination or permission, to preach His Word, to be instant, in season and out of season, to reprove, rebuke, and exhort, with all long-suffering and teaching (2 Tim. 4:2)....

Prophets, however, as Paul declares, are an order that belongs to the present dispensation, as well as to that which has passed by; and they are men who receive communications directly from God, just as apostles do. But they are not, like the latter, endowed with all the gifts of the Spirit, and their inspired utterances are usually intended only for the benefit of the churches, and are rarely addressed to those who are without. "Prophesying," says Paul, "is for a sign, not to the unbelieving, but to them that believe" (1 Cor. 14:22).

And so the apostle regarded it as a power that should be commonly found in the churches, and ought to be earnestly desired and prayed for, both of which points are pressed in his epistle to the Corinthians.

For, first, he speaks of prophecy as a divine institution in the church; that is, in the whole body, as its members succeed each other upon the earth during the times of the church-period or present dispensation. For he says: "God set some in the church, first apostles, secondly prophets, thirdly teachers, then miracles, then gifts of healing, helps, governments; divers kinds of tongues" (1 Cor. 12:28). . . . The need of such rules as these (Rom. 12:6; cf. 1 Cor. 12:10; 1 Cor. 14:29-33) testifies to the frequency of the prophetic gift. And we may find examples of it in the prophets who came from Jerusalem (Acts 11:27), in those that were afterwards found in the church at Antioch (Acts 13:1), and in the four prophesying daughters of Philip at Cæsarea (Acts 21:9).[1]

Indeed, it would seem that a church assembly could scarcely be complete unless one prophet, at least, were present. For prophecy was the means of communication by which the Spirit signified the will and purpose of God, and conveyed the necessary instruction, exhortation, or reproof to His people.

Hence we find Agabus predicting the famine that was to come in the days of Claudius Cesar (Acts 11:27-28), and the bonds that awaited Paul at Rome (Acts 21:10-11).

So, too, at Antioch, the Spirit said, doubtless through one of the prophets: "Separate Me Barnabas and Saul for the work whereunto I have called them" (Acts 13:21). Again, to Timothy, Paul says: "Neglect not the gift that is in thee, which was given thee by prophecy, with the laying on of the hands of the presbytery" (1 Tim. 4:14). From which it appears that the Holy Spirit signified, through a prophet, the call of Timothy to the ministry and that when, in obedience to this intimation, the hands of the presbytery—among whom Paul included himself (2 Tim. 1:6)—had been laid upon him, he received the necessary gift. In reference to the same event, Paul also says: "This charge I commit unto thee, my child Timothy, according to

---

[1] Compare ver. 1, which mentions the presence of prophets in the assembly.

the antecedent prophecies concerning thee, that, in conformity with them, thou mayest war the good warfare" (1 Tim. 1:18).

A consideration of these three cases of Paul, Barnabas and Timothy certainly suggests the thought that there can be no real ordination or, at least, no certainty of a real ordination, to an office requiring spiritual gifts, unless the Holy Spirit has previously intimated His choice. If so, we can well understand why the vast majority of recognized ministers exhibit no spiritual power, either in promoting the sanctification of the saved or in effecting the conversion of the unsaved.

In early times, before the canon of Scripture had been completed, prophets were used to convey to believers those things which afterwards appeared in the written Word. So Paul explains to the Ephesians: "Ye can perceive my understanding in the mystery of Christ, which in other generations was not made known unto the sons of men, as it hath now been revealed unto His holy apostles and prophets in spirit" (Eph. 3:4-5).

By "in spirit " he, of course, means in the spiritual sphere in which apostles and prophets, being what Paul calls *pneumatikoi*, or "spiritual" (1 Cor. 3:1; 12:1; 14:37), could be made conscious. And the fact that the mysteries of God were thus revealed to, and declared by, apostles and prophets explains the meaning of those other words of Paul in which he affirms that believers are "built upon the foundation of the apostles and prophets" (Eph. 2:20); that is, upon the foundation which they laid, or in plain terms, upon the revelations and doctrines which they taught.

Lastly, a true prophet, as one having access to the spiritual sphere, ought to have discernment in spiritual things; and, on this ground, Paul puts forth the challenge: "If anyone thinketh himself to be a prophet or spiritual, let him recognize the things which I write unto you as being commandments of the Lord" (1 Cor. 14:37).

The passage in the fourth chapter of Ephesians tells us that the prophetic gift, like the others there mentioned, was intended to remain in the churches until the end of their period.[1] And hence it is

---

1 Presumably the writer had in mind the statement in ver. 13, that the gifts were given "unto the building up of the body of Christ; till we all attain unto the

that Paul urges the Corinthians to "desire earnestly the greater gifts" (1 Cor. 12:31). He does, indeed, add that he will point out a way still more excellent, and that love is to be desired even more earnestly than gifts. Nevertheless, his argument on that point is concluded with the words: "Follow after love, yet desire earnestly spiritual gifts, but rather that ye may prophesy" (1 Cor. 14:1). For, as he explains, the prophet has a greater power of edifying the churches than all other spiritually-gifted persons. And so he sums up the whole subject with the commands: "Wherefore, my brethren, desire earnestly to prophesy, and forbid not to speak with tongues. But let all things be done decently and in order" (1 Cor. 14:39-40).

Yet inestimably valuable as the prophetic gift is, it was not long before it passed out of recognition, and was supplanted by orders of human appointment. We do, however, find it mentioned in the *Didache*,[1] where, as in Scripture, the prophet stands next in dignity to the apostle; but unlike the latter, is acknowledged also as a local minister who might attach himself to a single church, and for whose maintenance provision must be made. . . .

If a church has no prophet it is directed to give its first fruits to the poor. From this we may infer that there were at the time some congregations which had no prophet. Already the prophetic gift was failing, and the guidance of the churches was being transferred from those who had special gifts of the Spirit and were called of God only, to the presbyters and deacons whom men had elected for themselves.

Descending now to the times of Justin Martyr,[2] we find in the *Dialogue with Trypho* (lxxxii) a statement that the prophetic gift was still lingering in the churches; and Justin thinks that such a fact ought to convince the Jews of the transference of the grace of God from themselves to Christian believers. Yet in his account of Baptism, the Lord's Supper, and the Christian mode of keeping the first day of the week, there is no mention of either apostles or prophets, but only of a president and deacons (*First Apology*, c. lxi, lxvi, lxvii).

---

unity of the faith, and of the knowledge of the Son of God, unto a fullgrown man, into the measure of the stature of the fulness of Christ."—G. H. L.

1   One of the earliest known Christian writings after the apostles.
2   Middle of second century A.D.

What the compiler of the *Apostolical Constitutions* (century five) has to say on this subject does not give us a very exalted idea of the prophets of his period, if, indeed, there were any true prophets at all. His chief anxiety, in the two chapters (viii. 1, 2) which treat of spiritual gifts, seems to be to teach those who possess them not to think more highly of themselves than they ought to think. Evidently the gifts had been perverted and were dying out, at least in their purer and more powerful development. And, while they were failing, the unauthorized bishop had become the centre of power.

For our present purpose, it will not be necessary to trace the history of prophecy, real or false, through the centuries. We are only concerned to show what the Lord originally gave, and the fact that His gift gradually disappeared, or, at least, ceased to be recognized and seemed to disappear, for it is possible, that, of the fervent and effective preachers, whose tongues of fire have from time to time awakened the slumbering churches, not a few may be found on the Great Day, standing in the goodly fellowship of the prophets. There are certainly not many among us in these times who receive, and act upon, the command to covet earnestly the best gifts, and especially the spirit of prophecy; but there may be some who have done so, and have obtained the reward of their obedience. The chief characteristic of such men would, of course, be the power of speaking weighty but yet altogether unpremeditated words, in which the closest scrutiny would fail to detect any divergence from the revealed Scripture of Truth. And if a prophet be moved to foretell things to come, he has given his prediction as a credential, and upon its precise and clear fulfilment his reputation must depend. Should it fail, he has been convicted as a false prophet, inspired, not by the Spirit of the Living God, but by the spirit that now worketh in the children of disobedience.[1]

Concerning *false* prophesyings in modern times, both of the great Tongues movements of the last and this century have produced

---

[1] On prophets in the Early Church see also F. F. Bruce, *The Spreading Flame*, pp. 92, 214 ff.

abundance.[1] Prophets, under the power of another spirit, confirmed as being of God Edward Irving's fatally false teaching concerning our Lord as having a sinful nature, doctrine more than once set forth in the present-day Tongues circles. And of false predictions of coming events we may mention that a leading woman in the Tongues movement in India predicted on September 23, 1907, that Colombo would be destroyed by an earthquake, and Ceylon be sunk in the sea within ten months. This was at once widely published in their magazine in India. About the same time the then most prominent leader in England announced, under power, the recovery to health of the son of a neighbour, and sent her brother to inform the father of this. But upon reaching the house the child was found to have already died.

As regards true predictions of future events, there can be no doubt that God has so used godly men in modern times.

In the *Autobiography* of C. H. Spurgeon, chapter 5, the great preacher says: "The story of Mr. Knill's prophesying that I should preach the gospel in Rowland Hill's Chapel, and to the largest congregations in the world, has been regarded by many as a legend, but it was strictly true. Mr. Knill took the county of Essex in 1844, and... spent a little time at Stambourne Parsonage... all the family were gathered to morning prayer. Then, in the presence of them all, Mr. Knill took me on his knee, and said, 'This child will one day preach the gospel, and he will preach it to great multitudes. I am persuaded that he will preach in the chapel of Rowland Hill, where (I think he said) I am now minister.' He spoke very solemnly, and called upon all present to witness what he said. Then he gave me sixpence as a reward if I would learn the hymn,

> God moves in a mysterious way
> His wonders to perform.

I was made to promise that, when I preached in Rowland Hill's Chapel, that hymn should be sung.... After I had begun for some little time to preach in London, Dr. Alexander Fletcher was engaged

---

1 See my *The Early Years of the Modern Tongues Movement* (London, 1958).

to deliver the annual sermon to children in Surrey Chapel[1] but as he was taken ill, I was asked in a hurry to preach to the children in his stead.... Still, I fancy that Surrey was not the chapel which Mr. Knill intended. How was I to go to the country chapel? All unsought by me, the minister at Wotton-under-edge, which was Mr. Hill's summer residence, invited me to preach there."

The history of John Welch, son-in-law of John Knox, given in *The Scots Worthies*, narrates several fulfilled predictions of the great Covenanter and saint, for example: that a fop of the town of Kirkcudbright should succeed him as minister there: that a profligate man near Ayr should lose his estate for refusing Welch's written protests against his open profanation of the Sabbath; that two packmen who sought entrance to the town for business had the plague in their packs and should be refused admittance, which being done, and they going to a neighbouring town, the plague at once spread there in the houses where their goods were received; that a certain nobleman should lose his estates and honours, because he had failed to keep his word and afterward had lied in saying that he had done as he had promised.

In his *Autobiography*, chapter 10, C. G. Finney, the mighty revivalist of the last century, says:

"As soon as the revival broke out [at Gouverneur]... a set of young men joined hand in hand to strengthen each other in opposition.... Brother Nash addressed them very earnestly, and pointed out the guilt and danger of the course they were taking. Towards the close of his address he waxed exceedingly warm, and said, 'Now, mark me, young men! God will break your ranks in less than a week, either by converting some of you, or by sending some of you to hell. He will do this as certainly as the Lord is my God.'.... The house was still as death.... For myself, I regretted that Brother Nash had gone so far. He had committed himself, that God would either take the life of some of them, and send them to hell, or convert some of them, within a week... before the week was out nearly all if not all of that class of young men were hoping in Christ."

---

[1] Which was Rowland Hill's London chapel.

Chapter 13

# Some Aspects of Gospel Service

WE have learned (chapter 3) that the mighty revolution which destroyed the primitive independence of the apostolic churches and created a vast tyranny, commenced by the holding of conferences, convened by some prominent and influential person, to consider matters of common interest. These were "more or less informal," claimed no power of jurisdiction, nor were their recommendations binding upon any; yet from this innocent beginning "a confederation was thereby established which placed dissentients at a great disadvantage" (pp. 23, ff.).

I. Resident or Itinerant Missionaries?—In apostolic days those separated unto the gospel were almost invariably nonresident, but moved from place to place as guided by the Spirit (Acts 16:6–10), or driven by circumstances (Acts 13, 14, 16, etc.). Today perhaps a majority of workers are resident. Here is not so much departure from as reversal of the apostolic practice. Into the numerous causes and effects of this change I cannot now enter. Two principal effects are that evangelization advances slowly, and the churches formed rarely become self-maintaining and self-propagating. Hatch has shown that the restricting of itinerant ministry was an early act of the confederated Church! (p. 23).

From various causes the primitive churches were often quite early bereft of their founders. How did these little groups of newly converted Jews or pagans, or both, manage to thrive? Acts 13 and 14 narrates a lengthy missionary tour in Asia Minor, covering some three hundreds of miles in each direction, occupying only some months, issuing in the gathering of several churches. At none of these did the evangelists stay any length of time. The converts, so recently emerged from Judaism or heathenism, were just *left to them-*

*selves*; yet observe this material fact—that on their return journey after so short an interval, Paul and Barnabas found in *every church* men who had already developed the high qualifications demanded for eldership (14:23)! Nor was it a case of a cultured, trained, naturally competent race among whom leaders might easily arise. The Lycaonians are described by Dr. Howson as being "illiterate idolaters," a "rude and unsophisticated people," bound by "mythology and superstition," marked by the "wild fanaticism of a rustic credulity," "proverbially fickle and faithless."[1] My brethren in many regions will apply this description locally, and will inquire why those converts grew thus, whereas those around themselves commonly do not.

The answer may be given in the striking words of another: "The apostles did not trust their converts, but *they trusted the Holy Spirit in their converts.*" I humbly invite my fellow-labourers unto the kingdom to do two things. First, to cease assuring converts that they did, by and because of regeneration, necessarily receive, not only eternal life as a gift by the Spirit of God, but also the *indwelling* of the Spirit *as a person*, and instead to instruct them to receive the Spirit of God by faith, as the divine Indweller, as definitely as they received the Son of God by faith as Redeemer. The two matters are strictly parallel. The Son of God was promised beforehand, duly came, and accomplished that portion of the divine counsels (principally redemption) which was allotted to Him at that time. The message of the gospel informs the hearer concerning Him, and the hearer receives Him by an act of faith in that message. So also the Spirit of God was promised beforehand, duly came, and remains on earth to carry on that further portion of the divine counsels (the perfecting of the saints) allotted to Him at this time. Of Him also the gospel informs the hearer, and the hearer is to receive Him also by an equally definite act of faith in that message (Gal. 3:14).

When the apostles found that this had not taken place at conversion they took steps to see that it did take place (Acts 8:14–17; 19:1–7). They did *not* assure these believers that they had received what, in fact, they had *not* received. Saul of Tarsus also was not filled with the Spirit till some days after his conversion (Acts 9:17).

---

1 Conybeare and Howson, *St. Paul*, c. vi.

Repentance, regeneration, eternal life are truly gifts from the Spirit, but they do not require His personal, indwelling presence.[1] According to John 3:36, the apostles and all believers in the Son of God had these gracious gifts before Pentecost, but not till then did the Spirit enter into them as a *person*. In this distinction is an open secret why many Christians today resemble the disciples in the days of the Gospels, and not in the days of the Acts and the Epistles. Such *cannot* prosper alone, even as the apostles could not stand without the presence of the Lord Jesus.

That the Spirit *may* take up His abode in a believer at conversion is seen in Acts 10:44; and doubtless this is the ideal, and no doubt it often so takes place; but there is nowhere such a general participial assertion concerning the indwelling of the Spirit as John 3:36 makes concerning the present possession of eternal life ; it is nowhere said, "The one believing upon the Son is indwelt by the Holy Spirit." When Paul reached Ephesus he found certain "disciples" (Acts 19:1). He did not know they had been only imperfectly instructed: it was his later questioning which elicited that. He faced them simply as baptized believers, as disciples of Christ; and he asked: "Did ye receive the Holy Spirit when ye believed?" If Paul had held that every believer, without any possible exception, does necessarily receive the Spirit when he believes, he never could have asked that question. No one who so teaches would think of asking it, for it challenges the teaching.

A bishop was making his annual visitation to a church. He learned that it was full at all services; that the communicants were so many as not to be counted; that all was instinct with life. He inquired how the vicar kept the people together; had he clubs, benefit societies, socials, or how was it done? The churchwarden answered: "It's like

---

1 Rom. 8: 9 is used to the contrary, but by inference only. I take it the passage should read: "But ye are not in flesh [the old unregenerate nature], but in spirit [the new regenerate nature]. If at least spirit of God [no articles] dwells in you. But if anyone has not spirit of Christ [no article] this one is not of Him."

It appears that the Holy Spirit as a person does not come distinctly into view in this chapter until ver. 16: "The Spirit himself witnesses together with our spirit" [the new nature], conferring a God-consciousness that we are children of God.

this, my lord: our vicar first gets the people properly converted; then he gets them filled with the Holy Spirit; and then the Holy Spirit keeps them together!"

The second recommendation is that the believers being really, as a fact, not merely as a doctrine, indwelt by God the Spirit, the evangelist should be ready, at any time, at the call of God, to leave them. In a great emporium like Ephesus, the capital of a populous province, Paul stayed three years (Acts 20:31), not only, it would seem, for the sake of the local church, but that all the dwellers in the whole province should hear the word of the Lord (Acts 19:10). Similarly at Corinth, another strategic centre, he stayed eighteen months. *These are the longest visits recorded* while his movements were free.

Here is a cheering testimony of the year 1925 from a brother in China, who had been long absent in this country: "You will be glad to know that the work has gone on well during our absence. Thirty have been baptized during the past year, and the church has made distinct progress along the lines of independence and self-support." Let us trust the Holy Spirit in our converts; *but He must first be in them.*

It arises from the itinerant character of ministry that unmarried women, and married persons with binding local ties, can be regarded only as an exceptional type of worker, not the normal. Their services are feasible in an altogether exceptional period of general public peace, such as the nineteenth century, but involve serious problems in the more usual public conditions. That young single women should be engaged in spreading the gospel away from their own sphere or land scarcely seems contemplated in the New Testament. We may give hearty thanks for all such have been able to accomplish, and yet recognize that only under certain favourable conditions of country and social conditions is their going forth desirable. And the married brother should be ready to be often from home (as Peter and other apostles, and Philip the evangelist, clearly must have been), both for reaching the unevangelized and in order that the local church may not feel him to be indispensable, for they who always have a crutch will always halt.

Quite to the purpose is this paragraph, which I have much pleasure in quoting, from *Echoes of Service* ("Remarks With Annual Account," April, 1925, 76, 77):

> More and more we are persuaded that in the little time that is left to us, those who labour in the gospel are called upon to guard against the tendency of settling down as pastors in so-called "stations," and to seize every opportunity of pressing on from place to place, remaining only as long as the Lord indicates is needful for the establishment of churches, and looking to Him to raise up in the midst the necessary pastoral gifts. The methods of missionary work as exhibited in the New Testament are our permanent and reliable guide. They were Divinely appointed and directed. They can never, therefore, be out of date. Wheresoever there has been a tendency to depart therefrom, there is need for a return to the Apostolic pattern, if we are to obey the command of the Lord, and districts yet lying without are to be reached. A missionary is first and foremost an evangelist.

The normal missionary of the cross is the younger, unmarried brother who can itinerate, or the married man who may rightly be much from home. But how shall it be known which of such are *called of the Lord* to this whole-time service?

The New Testament contains no suggestion of one informing the church that he feels called to devote his life to the work of the gospel, and inviting their commendation. Those whose spirit was pressed to public ministry went about that work in the power of that inward compulsion (Acts 9:20; 18:25-26), saying, "*Necessity* is laid upon me, for woe is unto me if I preach not," and the Lord's endorsement of their testimony became their sufficient commendation. I remember a youth who thus, on his own account, in sheer faith in God, commenced village work, though the elder brethren of the meetings in his district had discountenanced it. I was only a visitor, but I felt bound to encourage him privately, my spirit feeling clear and constrained to do so. He soon became one of the most God-used evangelists in that area. Thus it was that Apollos gained the approval of the brethren, and then they commended him to saints in another country. But he had given himself boldly to the work without waiting for human commendation (Acts 18:26). So it was with Paul also. He emphasizes that as to his ministry he did "not confer with flesh and blood," or seek approval even from the apostles (Gal. 1:16-17): Such men could have said:

> Christ, *the Son of God*, hath sent me
> Through the midnight lands,
> Mine the mighty ordination
> Of the pierced Hands—

and with or without human encouragement this type of man *will go forward*. If only such, and no others, had gone forth it would have been well indeed.

It is also shown that older ministers of the word took the initiative in inviting another to join them. Thus Barnabas took a journey to find Saul (Acts 11:25-26); thus Saul chose Silas as a companion (Acts 15:40); and, later, Timothy (Acts 16:1–3). It is especially to be noted that nothing is said of the local brethren "commending" Timothy *for the work*. It is simply mentioned that they spoke well of him personally. His giving himself to the work was his matter, and Paul's. Commendation was to the Lord for the work, not to the work itself (Acts 14:26; 15:40).

A third method was that the Lord Himself directly and distinctly informed other leaders that certain brethren were to be sent forth for specific service: "Separate Me Barnabas and Saul for the work whereunto I have called them" (Acts 13:2). This is preceded by the significant information that it was "as they [the prophets and teachers] ministered to the Lord, and *fasted*, the Holy Spirit said, Separate, etc." Today the going out of a missionary is usually celebrated by a *feast*; but" then, when they had *fasted*, and prayed and laid their hands on them, they sent them away." This was no "ordination," for these were already accredited ministers of the word of God; nor was it a "commendation" of them as deemed fit to be "foreign missionaries," for this misleading term had not been invented, the false distinction between "home" and "foreign" work being unknown. It holds large, if latent, place today, and some will help earnestly "foreign" work who will scarce bestir themselves for souls near at hand, so that, e.g.

workers in spiritually needy English villages are overlooked by many who would give liberally to workers in African or Indian villages.

The Lord is still well able thus to make clear His mind concerning one or more of His servants. It is to be noted that in the case cited He made it clear to the two who were called as well as to their fellow-labourers, for *all* are just before named and are included in the "as *they* ministered. . . the Spirit said." I am tempted to give modern illustrations known to me of this order of divine call, only space forbids; but it takes place as clearly today as of old.

But the New Testament does not warrant the notion that a formal responsibility to reject or commend a candidate devolves upon the assembly or its elders. He who is sure of the will of God *must* get on with the work, he cannot help himself; in due time *the Lord* will lead from place to place, in this or that land, and the Lord will secure to that servant the approval of the godly.

The true way in this or any land to avoid the evil (as far as it may be avoidable) of uncalled persons getting into the ministry is to leave matters *completely* in the hands of God by following *exactly* His methods as indicated in the New Testament. Here is a striking contrast between the occasion when the Lord Himself calls and the occasion when one *offered himself* publicly to join those separated unto the ministry: "He *calleth* unto him whom *He himself would*: and *they went* unto Him" (Mark 3:13): "*There came* a scribe, and said unto Him, Teacher, I will follow Thee whithersoever Thou goest. And Jesus saith unto him, "The foxes have holes, and the birds of the heaven have nests; but the Son of Man *hath not where to lay His head*" (Matt. 8:19–20).

II. RELATIONS WITH THE STATE.—The confederating of the primitive churches was accelerated and consolidated by pressure from the State. This is intelligible from the State point of view. Officials necessarily have much greater labour in investigating, supervising and controlling many independent individuals than in dealing with a few senior representatives of an association to which all belong. By this arrangement the State can much more easily control, and *crush*, any individual, *and*, when it wishes, the *association*!

Consider, moreover, the autocratic power thus concentrated in the senior representatives of the association. The State officials intimate to these their wishes; if a hapless individual or a local church refuses submission, he or it must oppose not only the association, but finally the State! (pp. 25, 26). Thus personal liberty is filched from the individual and the local assembly.

But presently the confederated Church grew so powerful that it dominated the State, and the Popes reigned in temporal glory and with unapostolic pride. Thus first spiritual liberty was forfeited and then the power of world tyranny was gained. But what a woeful loss was that gain. The gentleness, purity, humility, which are of Christ, and which can take the *subject* place, were supplanted by the fierceness, foulness, pride of the Devil.

In 1922, the workers from several large spheres in one country met in annual conference, and it was urged by some that they, as a body, should seek Government "recognition." The subject was deferred to the next year, and to one in that land I wrote as follows:

> I am glad that the workers' conference deferred the question of Government recognition. It will be well if they defer it till the Lord shall come. Scripture knows not of anything corporate to be recognized except the local assembly. Governmental *toleration* of the individual Christian, and of such meeting together as a local church, is the most we should desire from the authorities: *recognition* by them of *groups* of churches or workers involves the essence of sectarianism, by the formation of a defined circle larger than the local assembly yet smaller than the whole church of God, and it brings ultimately, either favours which are ruinous to our real separateness from the world, or oppression, which is more effective by being on a body corporate instead of having to be applied to each individual.
>
> It is deeply sorrowful that, with the lessons of church history so clear and solemn and uniform, any who profess separation from the world system should entertain any notion of applying for or even of accepting formal sanction from its Governments. We already hold commission and command from the King of Kings, and are bound to go on with His business on His lines, whether rulers like it or oppose it.
>
> State "recognition" is the first step towards State control, and the first thing for which the State asks is something like itself, corporate, organized, visible, that it can recognize. Such a visible body the Head of

the church did not institute and nowhere in Scripture sanctions; so that any group of His people or servants that form themselves into somewhat that can have formal corporate relations with Governments or other bodies corporate are a somewhat that Christ does not recognize, though the State may; and thus they enter a path in which they cannot find guidance in His Word, nor can count upon the aid of His Spirit, nor the protection of His hand. This assures decay and disaster.

This snare of visible corporate unity is Satan's chief present method of unifying his control over all human institutions, religious and secular, in preparation for Antichrist and the war with the Lamb. It is only to be expected that he should strenuously attempt to enmesh all free assemblies, as all other circles of Christians, and only to be expected that he should, with his usual prudence and subtlety, commence the attack by suggesting no more apparently dangerous plans than combined property trusts for districts, conferences for given areas, delegates from various regions to central committees for such useful purposes as the issue of literature, and the like worthy ends, and then proposals for accepting or securing Government recognition for our work viewed as philanthropic and utilitarian. The end will be certain, even deterioration by adopting the inevitable "suggestions" of officialdom, or repression for refusing to conform to their wishes.

There is only one course that will certainly command the endorsement of our Lord, namely, to go on with our testimony to Him as individuals and as local churches. Anything beyond this originates from the fertile mind of our Enemy and plays into his hands.

I had not thought to write so much on this point, but the matter is of prime and urgent importance, and you may make known my considered views to any who may be interested and helped. May the Lord keep the feet of His saints.

The following year one wrote to me regarding the proposal that, "It was not even discussed. . . . But that it should ever have been proposed, and last year hotly championed, is sad."

It was a matter of thanksgiving that this untimely proposal came to a timely end. But the incident indicates the need for watchfulness, for warning, for education.

My letter quoted refers to a "literature committee," which was formed by representatives from several districts, speaking several languages. It was hoped to co-ordinate thus the output of Scriptural literature, to increase its volume, to widen its circulation; and efforts were made to secure for the committee its own printing establishment. A sensible, business-like proposal, with, it would seem, everything to commend it *except* its ultimate spiritual effects. One of the most probable of these would be that in due time only the literature approved by that small committee would be accepted in those areas; or, in the alternative, should some individuals secure and circulate other literature in preference, there would be the great likelihood of heart-burnings, heart-separations and strife, of complaints that the efforts of the committee were not appreciated, of disloyalty to "our" organization, and so on.

In any case, the power of the committee would become great, the possession of the printing plant would enable them to issue more economically than a private person could do through the usual trade channels, and the individual would assuredly find himself at a "great disadvantage." Now, it is a changeless economic law that anything that discourages individual enterprise, *anything* that decreases individual responsibility and incentive, finally depreciates the quality and diminishes the quantity of output.

The following further facts will show what deadly dangers may be involved in accepting binding relations with Governments.

One of the great missionary pioneers and explorers opened up to the gospel, to the knowledge of Europe, to trade, a vast, untrodden tract of Africa. His sufferings and labours resulted, under God, and through the service of others who followed, in thousands being delivered from the degradations of the devilish paganisms of the forests. A European Power duly seized the territory, and has exploited it for its own aggrandisement. In 1922 it demanded of the whole missionary force (who are mostly English) that this Declaration be signed in the presence of the consul of the country of the signatory:

> I, ……………………(age, civil rank, profession, nationality, and residence), declare by this document that I disclaim (or relinquish) all the rights which by my nationality I may have, in everything that has reference to concessions of land in this Province, and that in virtue of my relinquishing entirely my national privilege, *I subject myself to all the*

*decisions of the* (name of country) *authorities and courts* in the terms of the diploma of concessions and other provisions of the present, and *also future* (name of country) *legislation.*

*I bind myself* also, by this, to maintain and support the constituted authority, *always,* when my help may be officially required.

The covering letter from the Vice-Governor forwarded lengthy "*instructions,*" which covered all manner of matters, such as the forbidding of the teaching or use of the native language, save only as a help to teaching the language of the governing power; an *obligation* to give *industrial* instruction; *regulations* for minute annual reports by the missionary to the Government; power to the Governor to suppress missions; and so forth. The letter stated that these "instructions" were "for the carrying on of foreign religious missions in this Province," and would "*serve as a regulation for the work of the same missions*"; that they "must be *considered to be in force,* for which reason you must *completely and exactly fulfil them, in whatever* may be applicable to you." (The italics are mine.)

Thus it was proposed that missionary work should be wholly under Government control, and that the missionary should bind himself to support officials *always,* no matter what their proceedings. Thus would the Lord's servants have been stamped before the exploited natives with the hall-mark of their oppressors. An English medical missionary, with twenty-five years' experience of a similar district under British control, said to me that he would not give such an undertaking to *British* officials, let alone to those of the country in question.

Officialdom blandly explained that this proposal applied only in connexion with concessions of land; but inasmuch as resident missionary effort cannot be carried on without the worker dwelling on land somewhere, and seeing that the foreign Government had deprived native chiefs of the power to cede land, it meant in effect that the settled missionary must always seek a concession of land from Government, and so come under the bondage prescribed.

I understand that the foreign workers did not yield to these demands, and that they have not been pressed, but the proposals show the impossibility of conducting the work of God along His lines if State patronage and consequent control be accepted.

The Christian acknowledges that rulers have real authority from God in the civil sphere, and therefore he obeys "every ordinance of man for the Lord's sake," Who gave rulers power to rule (Rom. 13:1–7; 1 Pet. 2:13–17), however irksome be the ordinance, but always supposing that their ordinances do not require acts that God has universally prohibited (Ex. 20:1–17, e.g.), or that Christ has forbidden to His personal followers (Matt. 5, e.g.). But God has given the government of His "house," the church, not to States or princes, but to *His Son*, the Lord Jesus Christ (Heb. 3:6; Col. 1:18), and what authority the Son has delegated He has placed in the elders of each local assembly, and in *no other persons*; therefore, on the same ground that we resist bishops and synods of every sort, we refuse to princes and senates any right of dictation as to the ordering of the house of God and its various services.

It is for the Christian respectfully, but firmly, to instruct rulers upon this matter; not to succumb to their blandishments or their threats. If they insist on having their way by force the Christian must resist to the last, but passively, never actively. If he take the latter course he forfeits any guarantee of divine protection: "All they that take the sword shall perish with the sword" (Matt. 26:52); if he endure unto the end he will certainly please his Lord by following in His steps, and nearly always he, or his successors, will carry the point at last. Noble and significant were the words addressed to Charles IX, in 1562, by Theodore Beza, as he protested against the persecution of the Huguenots: "Sire, it belongs in truth to the Church of God, in whose name I speak, to endure blows and not to inflict them. But it will also please your Majesty to remember that *she is an anvil that has worn out many hammers.*"

In a certain European country God has worked with power and has gathered many churches in widely separated areas. Urged probably by the bloodthirsty, persecuting Orthodox Church, and partly from a suspiciousness and sensitiveness arising from perilous political conditions, begotten through Bolshevik influences, the State, in 1923, took cognizance of these scattered, energetic, evangelizing communities. The Minister of Religion sent for a beloved, zealous, impulsive brother, a leader, and informed him that there must be lodged a full, binding declaration of beliefs and practices, or the meetings would be stopped by force, and personal penalties might follow. Also, that he (the Minister) was not prepared to deal with many local companies, but required that a corporate body be formed, with President, Secretary, and Treasurer, whom he might hold responsible for the doings of all represented.

The good brother, being comparatively lately converted, and an evangelist by spirit and gift, and insufficiently instructed in Scripture or history upon such a situation, agreed, drew up a lengthy memorial, unwisely discussed and settled this with the Minister before going over it fully with his brethren, and then, having thus committed himself, urged upon the other leaders their joining him in adopting the scheme.

By one of those divine orderings which they can receive who walk with God by daily guidance, I and a brother in that country arrived at the place where the conference was to be held on the day it was to be held. Being invited to give my thoughts upon the circumstances, I pointed out:

(*a*) That the State was pressing them to become a mere sectarian organization, which would entirely destroy their testimony to the oneness of the Body of Christ as composed of all believers.

(*b*) That the New Testament sanctions in the church no other organization than the local assembly, and no other rulers than its local elders.

(*c*) That vast controlling power would be vested in the few officials to be created, greatly increasing the power of the State to oppress, and duly leading to strife amongst the churches by dissatisfaction, arising with the actings of those few officials.

(*d*) That the declaring of dogmas would create a creed which would shut out believers who might not agree with any item thereof, and the fellowship of the Spirit in the bond of peace would be impossible. For example, such brethren as objected to military service (a serious question in that country) would be driven out, or kept out, if the memorial declared in favour thereof, whilst those who allowed believers to bear arms would be shut out by a declaration against such service.

(*e*) That it would be very difficult ever after to go to the Minister and say: "Please, sir, we have changed our views, or altered our practices"; and so further knowledge of, or obedience to, the mind of God revealed in His Word would be blocked; which attitude would be disloyalty to Christ and crippling to spiritual growth.

(*f*) That Government had a right to know what its subjects believed, taught, did, but that the New Testament sufficed to show our beliefs and practices, and that our meetings were public, and could be visited by officials.

(*g*) That any memorial presented to the Minister, even if always in the same form, should be presented from each local church separately, and on no account by groups of churches; and it should be pressed upon the authorities that the separateness of the assemblies, the absence of inter-church organization, coupled with the uniform publicity of their gatherings, was the very safeguard required by Government that sinister political ends were not in view, but religious and moral ends only.

It is to be noted that these instances have occurred within this present century. They come from three continents, Asia, Africa, Europe, and affect eight or nine large missionary spheres, and indicate therefore a present and general element which must be carefully and resolutely faced by the Lord's servants. Therefore do I enlarge upon it.

Nor is the tendency to be seen only in foreign lands. If I go back a few years and look out over the world, I see some hundreds of earnest persons carrying the gospel to many countries on no apparent *plan* of campaign. If I inquire under whose auspices they work, they will all return the one answer, that they labour in direct dependence upon the Lord alone for guidance and support. If they are asked by what name their society is known, they will reply that there is no society, and that they own only the name Christian.

But should I today ask the same questions of many that have followed or joined these, they will still give the same answers if replying with formal care, but some of them, if expressing their heart's natural sentiments, will be likely to acknowledge some other corporate title.

Surely here is another sign of that influence of the State which we have considered in ancient and modern workings, operating this time in England, as elsewhere. For I can suppose no other ends to be sought by the coining of such a corporate title, save securing reductions on travel charges, facilitating dealings with passport officers, customs officials, and their superiors, and other such purposes. But for these purposes of travel and of service to the Lord God the Almighty, schemes not devised by Him are neither necessary, nor reverent, nor of faith; and I ask again, in all love, if it be not an unconfessed want of faith in Him as an actual controlling Leader, that begets in our hearts these devices for dealing with difficulties? It will not do to plead that the late wars have left a public international condition of such complexity as our predecessors had not to meet. This is only very partially true. Who today meets severer difficulties than Groves overcame in the Baghdad venture, 1829–1833, or F. S. Arnot faced in faith and conquered by prayer and patience?

But when He laid His plans, settled His methods, wrote His Word, the Lord foresaw beyond today, even to the End-days. During and since the 1914–1918 war, I travelled and stayed in some thirty foreign countries (half of them in Europe), several of these being what were war areas, where the acutest of the difficulties exist. I have crossed frontiers perhaps seventy times, with passport inspection, customs examination, and endless police registrations, all this in addition to obtaining the many necessary visas and permits from British and foreign officials. And by the help of God, in answer to the prayer of faith, the unavoidable emergencies and perplexities have been solved, even on those occasions when no one was at hand who understood my speech. Our Master has no favourites: He who has done so much for one so unworthy will do as much, and more, for others, and I venture to think He will do better for those who trust Him fully than for those who turn aside to plans not authorized by Himself.

I affectionately beg my fellow-workers unto the kingdom to consider whether a dread of trouble, reproach, delay, and seeming failure be not a deep, unacknowledged motive in the resort to corporate action. When that Minister of Religion was pressing his proposal, the leader he had skilfully selected pressed, in his turn, upon his brethren that, should they not submit to the Minister, persecution and the breaking up of the work would follow. To which one of the others answered with the searching question, "But what has become of the *cross*?" All these heavy risks the first Christians accepted as a true portion of their fellowship with the Son of God, the *Lamb*, who suffered that He might reign. For His follower to avoid the suffering is to imperil his prospect of reigning.

III. THE TRIAL OF FAITH.—Moreover, it is by the *impossible* conditions which He allows or arranges for His people that the Lord shows them what He is and can do, thus strengthening faith and perfecting character. Red Seas, barren deserts, Jericho's walls, deaths oft, are the grandest of places and conditions for learning to know God and to trust Him.

> In the *desert* God will teach thee
> What the God that thou hast found;
> Patient, gracious, powerful, holy—
> *All* his grace shall *there* abound. (Darby.)

But a large part of the anxious thought of Christians seems to be directed to discovering some other route to Canaan than the desert, some other means of inheriting than fighting. It is a futile endeavour, and such as attempt it lose heart-fellowship with our divine Leader, Who is Moses, Aaron and Joshua in one.

At Dohnavur, S. India, I revelled in the profuse table decorations with that most fascinating and brilliant tropical flower, the *Glorioso Superba*. Miss Carmichael has told us that if it be planted in a well-prepared rich bed it languishes, but left to a desperate fight amongst the soil-exhausting giant aloes and prickly pears it flourishes, and flowers worthily of its grand name. The natural *habitat* of the Christian life, in our case as in His, when in this world, is trial; it cannot flourish without it: "In the world ye have tribulation: but be of good cheer; I have overcome the world" (John 16:33).

It is fire that purifies gold. Nothing but the fire of world opposition keeps churches pure. The place outside the camp where Jesus is found is designedly a place of reproach that only the sincere may seek it. The necessary condition of gospel work, in order that only those sent by the Lord may engage in it, is severe trial. It is the privilege of the church to support those "separated unto the gospel of God"; it is disastrous if that loving support be rendered by such methods as make acute trial unlikely or faith less imperative, or such as take the *actual, constant* control of the *detail* of matters out *of the Lord's* hand.

I write from conviction burned into my soul by nearly sixty years' experience of being in the hollow of that Hand. It is a safe, a blessed place. Times without number have I gone about my Master's business penniless, sometimes for days together, and in many places, from the streets of London to those of Cairo and Rangoon. Now journeying through many lands according to His will; now detained a day, a month, three months in His place for me by financial inability to leave: often ministering temporally to others, sometimes hungry oneself—it is a fascinating life, deeply instructive as to the ways of the Lord, highly beneficial if faith humbly accepts its lessons, a manner of life not to be exchanged for the safest scheme man can devise.

But it must be remembered that only the man of faith can walk this road, and he only when called thereto by his Lord. A well known Presbyterian minister of the last century, seeing the mind of God, surrendered his stipend to depend upon freewill offerings. Being asked by fellow-ministers if he would have them all to do as he had done, he is said to have given the witty but searching reply: "Which the Egyptians assaying to do were drowned" (Heb. 11:29). On the other hand, a young brother and his wife, who had been most distinctly led by the Lord alone into this path, wrote to me thus (April, 1925): "Many thanks for sending on the gift. Your prophecy came true—that after a time we should have some severer tests of our faith. When we received this gift we were just without a penny and had had no bread for over a week, and it would have been awkward for us had not a sister been moved to give us some potatoes. *But we would not be without these tests, for they draw us nearer the Lord.*

*Who knows how we might wander from Him if He did not seem to hide His face sometimes?"*

The highest posts in the ancient "mysteries"—the secret religious orders that largely dominated the pagan world—were reached only by a lengthy process of initiation, under the supervision of the high priest of the order, the tests in which were stringent and severe. It is to this Paul refers when he speaks of the training the Lord had put him through by temporal trials. His words in Phil. 4:11–13 may be thus expanded: I speak not of my privations; for as regards myself I have learned in whatever circumstances I happen to be placed to be satisfied in myself, independently of my condition (cf. John 4:13, 14). I know both how to be abased and I know how to abound. In everything and in all things I am initiated both to be full and to be hungry, both to abound and to suffer privation. I have strength for all things in Him that gives me power.—Happy apostle, to be prepared unto *every* good work by being equal to *every* condition of trial: thine shall be the highest service in the most impossible spheres, such as Nero's palace and supreme court of the Empire, and thine shall be the highest honours in the kingdom of thy Lord!

Now no one but our High Priest has wisdom enough to control this initiation, or can impart to the one being initiated strength enough to endure the long and severe tests.

And if at times, or frequently, He permits His servants to share His own poverty, known when He was here, this but enriches the heart with experimental fellowship with Himself in His sufferings. Frederick Stanley Arnot, the great African missionary pioneer, speaking in Bristol early in this century, remarked that life in England was far more difficult than in Central Africa. Here, he said, rent day comes round with such terrible regularity, and all the necessities of life are dear; yet it would be dishonouring to our Master to live in a disreputable condition; "but," he added, "in Africa you can starve—I mean, you can live on a sack of potatoes till something more comes along!"

It is not pleasant to be "abased," that is, to be known as in poverty, but it may be a prime advantage in gaining our end of helping those whose good we seek for Christ's sake. A Bedouin youth, converted in Egypt in 1914, and instantly reduced from affluence to beggary, casually, in conversation one evening, said to me, "I have had only bread and bananas to eat today." I replied, "Abd el-Messiah, and I have had only bread and dates today." From the moment the lad thus knew that I, the English hawaga (gentleman), as he regarded me, was really, for his sake, down on his level of need, his heart was mine; the truculent Arab spirit no more resented my counsel, his growth in grace was marked, and from him, to whom before his conversion the very notion of purity was utterly foreign, the last remark I heard when leaving the country was: "One thing I ask of my Heavenly Father, that He will *keep me holy*."

Chapter 14

# Conclusion and Appeal

THE Christian needs fellowship. In these days of alarming declension it is for many an urgent question where fellowship on the lines here set forth as Scriptural can be found.

I trust the true principles of church life and service have been made clear and attractive, so that others may adopt them, and that any departures therefrom may give place to conformity thereto. But this is by no means to suggest that anyone should "join the Brethren," or any other comparable body. That supposes that there is something general and corporate that can be joined, which is exactly what I have written to repudiate as unscriptural. Nor is it even Scriptural to speak of "joining" a local assembly. He who has been so joined to the Lord as to be one spirit with Him (1 Cor. 6:17), and who has been publicly added to the church of God (Acts 2:41), does thereby belong to any local company of saints where he may at any time be. It is simply for the individual to acknowledge this by associating with that company while in that place, and for that local assembly to acknowledge it by receiving him to their love and fellowship, being satisfied, through intercourse with him, or personal recommendation, or by a letter of commendation, that he is a child of God, or at the first on his own testimony. Any *formality* of reception into a local assembly of an already baptized person is unscriptural, as also the deeming of such a person as not a member of "an assembly," unless his name has been inserted in "our list of members." Such requirements are nothing less than a challenging of the believer's actually existing status in the church of God acquired by his regeneration, baptism, and the indwelling of the Spirit.

I further make clear—what will be evident to the instructed reader—that I have not attempted to argue fully any of the topics touched, except, perhaps, the first, the independence of the local assembly. The treatment is intentionally suggestive, not exhaustive, for one must warn and exhort, but may not seem to legislate. Direct dependence upon the Head of the church, by both the assembly and the individual, is a postulate fundamental to my position. Hence I have no manner of right to dictate to anyone but myself what is the will of the Lord; neither has anyone a right to prescribe to me my individual service or conduct. Each church must decide its own duty to the Lord and its own members; each Christian must walk by what light he receives; while for both the Word of God is the sole and sufficient standard.

1. THE HOLY SCRIPTURES THE SOLE STANDARD.—Consequently my first appeal to all my beloved brethren in Christ is for a real reinstatement of the written Word of God, the Holy Scriptures, as the *sole* criterion for all conduct and action, united or personal.

We who assert the divine inspiration of the very words of Scripture accept, above all others, the obligation to conform to the *least hint* therein given of the mind of God. We deny to ourselves the slightest right to neglect a jot or a tittle of His Word, or to sanction the least thing not sanctioned thereby. It is our duty and wisdom and privilege to act in all things upon the holy resolution of the Psalmist: (1) "I thought on my ways, (2) and turned my feet unto Thy testimonies [that is, to guide every step thereby]. (3) I made haste, and delayed not, *to observe* Thy commandments" (Psa. 119:59-60). Therefore "let us *search and try* our ways, and turn again to Jehovah" in any points in which we have turned from His ways (Lam. 3:40).

Here is a primary secret of George Müller's mighty life from its first years. Speaking of how, in the year 1830, he came to see the truth concerning the immersion of believers, and to escape from the error of infant baptism, he says: "It had pleased God, in his abundant mercy, to bring my mind into such a state, that I was willing to carry out into my life whatever I should find in the Scriptures" (*Narrative*, Part I, 65).

Where this frame of mind obtains, changes of practice are made without sorrow or friction. The Ukrainians are a musical people. Their native music is akin to the Welsh—wild and minor. I have heard a group of peasants sing "Diadem" as I have heard it nowhere out of Wales. Thus singing held a large place in their meetings, and a choir was a regular feature in their congregations. At a question meeting in a Ukrainian assembly in the then Eastern Poland, it was asked in writing whether it was right that the conductor should beat time in public worship. Experience and observation of choirmasters makes me think of the saying that the deacon is worse than the devil, for if you resist the devil he will fly *from* you, but if you resist the deacon he will fly *at* you. On this occasion the conductor sat before me on the front seat. I replied by reminding the church that they had lately suffered not a little by separating from former associates in order to maintain the fundamental principle that in the house of God the Word of God was the only authority. If, therefore, they found in that Word the idea of a certain number of the saints sitting together to lead the rest in song, or to sing to them, well and good, but if not they would know what to do. Thus, for their own education and development, I left the responsibility upon themselves. After the meeting I learned, with interest, that it was the choirmaster who had put in the question, and on a later visit it was gratifying to find that the choir was no more. The spirit of humble obedience to the Word, applied to the *ceasing* to do what was *not* found in the Word, had solved without any trouble what has divided and wrecked many a church elsewhere.

I make this appeal the more confidently since the theory is widely accepted: but let us apply the theory, rigidly and minutely, to our practice. I address myself in particular to those believers who are feeling compelled to abandon some former, perhaps lifelong, religious system so as to be faithful to the Son of God and His Word. With such I sympathize from personal experience. The strain is great, the uprooting painful; but be of good comfort; the One who is the holy and the true sets high value upon our keeping His Word and not denying His Name, and gives magnificent promises to such as overcome in these severer tests (Rev. 3:7–13). But when at last the dreaded break has been made, do not look around for another church system as near as possible to the one left, only as yet not so unfaithful to Christ. Or if it be that several have left together, do not form a new church with the former familiar and cherished features preserved for the sake of "auld lang syne."

No; since the old must be abandoned, though the cost be great, seize so favourable an opportunity to make a thoroughly new start on the only right principle of seeking in every detail to conform to the New Testament pattern. Look most carefully into the Word of God to discover exactly His mind concerning His church and work. Since you must move to a new spiritual dwelling, or must build one, do examine minutely the plan and specification of the divine Architect, and look around for the house where the present builders or inhabiters seek honestly to follow the pattern set; or if none such are near, and yourselves must build, do follow the divine mind and not any human style of building.

With an honest mind inquire (1) whether the New Testament sanctions a federation of churches, or only many local separate churches; (2) whether it sanctions one minister to conduct public worship, or the actual immediate leadership of the Holy Spirit; (3) whether unregenerate persons, sprinkled or even baptized, ought to be of the church; (4) whether baptism was of infants or only after personal faith in Christ, and was by sprinkling or immersion.

As these and similar questions arise let them be settled honestly by the Word only, *and the light thus gained be obeyed*, and most blessed progress of soul will follow, with richer fellowship with the Lord and knowledge of His mind. This will lead to increased fitness for service and usefulness therein, with corresponding glory to His name and blessing to men.

So fundamental is this matter that I propose to show how it lay at the root of that most fruitful of all lives of the whole wonderful nineteenth century, the life of George Müller, of Bristol. In his *Narrative of some of the Lord's Dealings* (part I), Mr. Müller speaks of his experiences when he came first to England, in 1829, for the purpose of being trained as a worker with the London Society for Promoting Christianity amongst the Jews. This was not long after his conversion. He had been educated in Germany, his native land, to be a pastor in the Lutheran State church in that country. He says:

I will mention some points which God then began to show me. 1. That the Word of God alone is our standard of judgment in spiritual things; that it can be explained only by the Holy Spirit; and that in our day, as well as in former times, He is the teacher of His people. The office of the Holy Spirit I had not experimentally understood before that time. Indeed, of the office of each of the Blessed Persons, in what is commonly called the Trinity, I had no experimental apprehension. I had not before seen from the Scriptures that the Father chose us before the foundation of the world; that in Him that wonderful plan of our redemption originated, and that He also appointed all the means by which it was to be brought about. Further, that the Son, to save us, had fulfilled the law, to satisfy its demands, and with it also the holiness of God; that He had borne the punishment due to our sins, and had thus satisfied the justice of God. And further, that the Holy Spirit alone can teach us about our state by nature, show us the need of a Saviour, enable us to believe in Christ, explain to us the Scriptures, help us in preaching, etc. It was my beginning to understand this latter point, in particular, which had a wonderful effect on me; for the Lord enabled me to put it to the test of experience, by laying aside commentaries, and almost every other book, and simply reading the Word of God and studying it. The result of this was that the first evening that I shut myself into my room to give myself to prayer and meditation over the Scriptures I learned more in a few hours than I had done during a period of several months previously. *But the particular difference was that I received real strength for my soul in doing so.* I now began to try by the test of the Scripture the things which I had learned and seen, and found that only those principles which stood the test were really of value... (p. 48). 3. Another truth into which in a measure I was led during my stay in Devonshire respected the Lord's coming. My views concerning this point up to that time had been completely vague and unscriptural. I had believed what others told me without trying it by the Word. I thought that things were getting better and better, and that soon the whole world would be converted. But now I found in the Word that we have not the least scriptural warrant to look for the conversion of the world before the return of our Lord. I found in the Scriptures that that which will usher in the glory of the church and uninterrupted joy to the saints is the return of the Lord Jesus, and that till then things will be more or less in confusion. I found in the Word that the return of Jesus, and not death, was the hope of the apostolic Christians; and that it became me, therefore, to look for His appearing. And this truth so entered into my heart that though I went into Devonshire exceedingly weak, scarcely expecting that I should return again to London, yet I was immediately on seeing this truth, brought off from looking for death, and was made to look for the return of the Lord. . . 4. In addition to these truths, it pleased the Lord to lead me to see a higher standard of devotedness than I had seen before. He led me in a measure to see what is my true glory in this world, even to be despised, and to be poor and mean with Christ. I saw then in a measure, though I have seen it more fully since, that it ill becomes the servant to seek to be rich and great and honoured in that world where his Lord was poor and mean and despised.

I do not mean to say that all that which I believe at present concerning these truths, and those which, in connexion with them, the Lord has shown me since August, 1829, were apprehended all at once; much less did I see them all at once with the same clearness as, by the grace of God, I do now (1837). . . . My light increased more and more during the months of September, October, and November. At the end of November it became a point of solemn consideration with me whether I could remain connected with the society in the usual way. My chief objections were these: (1) If I were sent out by the society it was more than probable, yea, almost needful, if I were to leave England, that I should labour on the Continent, as I was unfit to be sent to Eastern countries, on account of my health, which would probably have suffered, both on account of the climate and of my having to learn another language. Now, if I did go to the Continent it was evident that without ordination I could not have any extensive field of usefulness, as unordained ministers are generally prevented from labouring freely on the Continent; but I could not conscientiously submit to be ordained by unconverted men, professing to have power to set me apart for the ministry, or professing to communicate something to me for this work which they have not even themselves. Besides this, I had other objections to being connected with any State church or national religious establishment, which had arisen from the increased light which I had obtained; all of which were brought to me through the reception of this truth, that the Word of God is our only standard, and the holy Spirit our only teacher. For as I now began to compare what I knew of the establishment in England and those on the Continent with this only true standard, the Word of God, I found that all establishments, even because they are establishments, i.e, the world and the church mixed up together, not only contain in

## Conclusion and Appeal 199

them the principles which necessarily must lead to departure from the Word of God; but also, as long as they remain establishments, entirely preclude the acting throughout according to the Holy Scriptures. Then again, if I were allowed to stay in England the Society would not allow me to preach in any place indiscriminately where the Lord might open a door for me; and to the ordination of English bishops I had still greater objections than to the ordination of the Prussian Consistory. (2) I further had a conscientious objection against being led and directed by *men* in my missionary labours. As a servant of Christ it appeared to me I ought to be guided by the Spirit, and not by men, as to time and place; and this I would say with all deference to others who may be much more taught and much more spiritually minded than myself. A servant of Christ has but one master. (3) I had love for the Jews, and I had been enabled to give proofs of it; yet I could not conscientiously say, as the committee would expect from me, that I would spend the greater part of my time among only them. For the scriptural plan seemed to me that in coming to a place I should seek out the Jews and commence my labour particularly among them; but that if they rejected the gospel I should go to the nominal Christians. The more I weighed these points the more it appeared to me that I should be acting hypocritically were I to suffer them to remain in my mind without making them known to the committee.

The question that next occurred to me was how I ought to act if not sent out by the Society. With my views I could not remain in Prussia; for I must either refrain from preaching, or imprisonment would be the result. The only plan that showed itself to me was that I should go from place to place throughout England, as the Lord might direct me and give me opportunity, preaching wherever I came, both among the Jews and nominal Christians. . . . At the same time, it appeared to me well that I should do this in connexion with the Society for Promoting Christianity among the Jews, serving them without any salary, provided they would accept me under these conditions. . . there remained now only one point more to be settled; how I should do for the future as it regarded the supply of my temporal wants, which naturally would have been a great obstacle, especially as I was not merely a foreigner, but spoke so little English that whilst I was greatly assisted in expounding the Scriptures, I could only with difficulty speak about common things. About this point, however, I had no anxiety; for I considered that as long as I really sought to serve the Lord, that is, as long as I sought the kingdom of God and His righteousness, these my temporal supplies would be added unto me. The Lord most mercifully enabled me to take the promises of His Word and rest upon them, and such as Matthew 7:7-8; John 14:13-14; Matthew 6:25–34, were the stay of my soul concerning this point. In addition to this, the example of brother Groves, the dentist before alluded to, who gave up his profession and went out as a missionary, was a great encouragement to me. For the news which by this time had arrived of how the Lord had aided him on his journey to Petersburg, and at Petersburg, strengthened my faith.

At last, on December 12, 1829, I came to the conclusion to dissolve my connexion with the Society, if they would not accept my services under the above conditions, and to go throughout the country preaching (being particularly constrained to do so from a desire to serve the Lord as much as in me lay BEFORE HIS RETURN), and to trust in Him for the supply of my temporal wants. Yet at the same time it appeared well to me to wait one whole month longer, and to consider the matter still further before I wrote to the committee, that I might be sure I had weighed it fully... (p. 55). During the first days of January, 1830, whilst still at Exmouth, it became more and more clear to me that I could not be connected with the Society under the usual conditions; and as I had an abundance of work where I was, and little money to spend in travelling (for all I possessed was about five pounds), it appeared best to me to write at once to the committee that whilst they were coming to a decision respecting me I might continue to preach. I therefore wrote to them, stating what had been my views before I became acquainted with them, and what they were now. I also stated my difficulty in remaining connected with them on the usual terms, as stated in substance above; and then concluded, that as, however, I owed them much as having been instrumental in bringing me to England, where the Lord had blessed me abundantly; and as I would also like to obtain from them the Hebrew Scriptures and tracts for the Jews; I would gladly serve them without any salary, if they would allow me to labour in regard to time and place as the Lord might direct me. Some time after I received a very kind private letter from one of the secretaries, who had always been very kind to me, together with the following official communication from the committee:

"London Society for Promoting Christianity amongst the Jews.

"At a meeting of the Missionary Sub-Committee, held January 27, 1830, Society House, 10, Wardrobe Place, Doctors' Commons, a letter was read from Mr. G. F. Müller.

## Conclusion and Appeal

"Resolved, that Mr. Müller be informed that while the committee cordially rejoice in any real progress in knowledge and grace that he may have made under the teaching of the Holy Spirit, they nevertheless consider it inexpedient for any society to employ those who are unwilling to submit themselves to their guidance with respect to missionary operations; and that while, therefore, Mr. Müller holds his present opinions on that point the committee cannot consider him as a missionary student: but should more mature reflection cause him to alter that opinion, they will readily enter into further communication with him."

Thus my connexion with the society was entirely dissolved. Twenty years have passed away since, and I never have even for one single moment regretted the step I took, but have to be sorry that I have been so little grateful for the Lord's goodness to me in that matter. The following part of the Narrative also will prove to the enlightened reader how God blessed my acting out the light He had been pleased to give me... (p. 64). About the beginning of April (1830) I went to preach at Sidmouth. While I was staying there three sisters in the Lord had in my presence a conversation about baptism, one of whom had been baptized after she had believed. When they had conversed a little on the subject I was asked to give my opinion concerning it. My reply was: "I do not think that I need to be baptized again." I was then asked by the sister who had been baptized, "But have you been baptized?" I answered, "Yes, when I was a child." She then replied, "Have you ever read the Scriptures and prayed with reference to this subject?" I answered, "No." "Then," she said, "I entreat you never to speak any more about it till you have done so." It pleased the Lord to show me the importance of this remark; for whilst at that very time I was exhorting everybody to receive nothing which could not be proved by the Word of God, I had repeatedly spoken against believers baptism without ever having earnestly examined the Scriptures or prayed concerning it; and now I determined, if God would help me, to examine that subject also, and if infant baptism were found to be scriptural I would earnestly defend it, and if believers baptism were right I would as strenuously defend that, and be baptized.

As soon as I had time I set about examining the subject. The mode I adopted was as follows: I asked God repeatedly to teach me concerning it, and read the New Testament from the beginning, with a particular reference to this point. But now, when I earnestly set about the matter, a number of objections presented themselves to my mind.

1. Since many holy and enlightened men have been divided in opinion concerning this point, does this not prove that it is not to be expected that we should be able to come to satisfactory conclusion about this question in the present imperfect state of the church? This objection was thus removed: If this ordinance is revealed in the Bible, why may I not know it, as the Holy Spirit is the teacher in the church of Christ now as well as formerly? 2. There have been but few of my friends baptized, and the greater part of them are opposed to believers baptism, and they will turn their backs on me. Answer: Though all men should forsake me, if but the Lord takes me up I shall be happy. 3. You will be sure to lose one half of your income for such and such reasons if you were to be baptized. Answer: As long as I desire to be faithful to the Lord He will not suffer me to want. 4. People will call you a baptist, and you will be reckoned among that body, and you cannot approve of all that is going on among them. Answer: It does not follow that I must go along on all points with all those who hold believers baptism, although I should be baptized. 5. You have been preaching for some years, and you will have thus publicly to confess that you have been in an error should you be led to see that believers baptism is right. Answer: It is much better to confess that I have been in error concerning that point than to continue in it. 6. Even if believers baptism should be right, yet it is now too late to attend to it, as you ought to have been baptized immediately on believing, Answer: It is better to fulfil a commandment of the Lord Jesus ever so late than to continue living in neglect of it.

It had pleased God in his abundant mercy to bring my mind into such a state that I was willing to carry out into my life whatever I should find in the Scriptures concerning the ordinance, either the one way or the other. I could say, "I will do His will," and it was on that account I believe that I soon saw which *doctrine is of God*, whether infant baptism or believers baptism. And I would observe here, by the way, that the passage to which I have just now alluded, John 7:17, has been a most remarkable comment to me on many doctrines and precepts of our most holy faith. For instance: "Resist not evil, but whosoever shall smite thee on thy right cheek, turn to him the other also. And if any man will sue thee at the law, and take away thy coat, let him have thy cloak also. And whomsoever shall compel thee to go a mile, go with him twain. Give to him that asketh thee, and from him that would borrow of thee turn not thou away. Love your enemies, bless them that curse you, do good to them that hate you, and pray for them which despitefully use you, and persecute you." Matthew 5:39–44. "Sell that ye have and give alms." Luke 12:33. "Owe no man anything, but to love one another." Romans 13:8. It may be said, surely these passages cannot be taken literally, for how then should the people of God be able to pass through the world. The state of mind enjoined in John 7:17 will cause such objections to vanish. WHOSOEVER IS WILLING TO ACT OUT these commandments of the Lord LITERALLY will, I believe, be led with me to see that to take them LITERALLY is the will of God. Those who do *so* take them will doubtless often be brought into difficulties hard to the flesh to bear, but these will have a tendency to make them constantly feel that they are strangers and pilgrims here, that this world is not their home, and thus to throw them more upon God, who will assuredly help us through any difficulty into which we may be brought by seeking to act in obedience to His Word.

As soon as I was brought into this state of heart I saw from the Scriptures that believers ONLY are the proper subjects for baptism and that immersion is the only true Scripture mode in which it ought to be attended to. The passage which particularly convinced me of the former is Acts 8:36–38, and of the latter, Rom. 6:3–5. Some time after I was baptized. I had much peace in doing so, and never have I for one single moment regretted it. Before I leave this point I would just say a few words concerning the result of this matter so far as it regards some of the objections which occurred to my mind when I was about to examine the Scriptures concerning baptism. 1. Concerning the first objection, my conviction now is this, that of all revealed truths not one is more clearly revealed in the Scriptures, not even the doctrine of justification by faith, and that the subject has only become obscured by men not having been willing to take the *Scriptures alone* to decide the point. 2. Not one of my true friends in the Lord has turned his back on me as I supposed, and almost all of them have been themselves baptized since. 3. Though in one way I lost money in consequence of being baptized, yet the Lord did not suffer me to be really a loser, even as it regards temporal things; for what I lost in one way He more than made up to me in another. In conclusion, my example has been the means of leading many to examine the question of baptism and to submit from conviction to this ordinance, and my seeing this truth has led me to speak on this as well as on other truths, and only since I have been in Bristol, now more than seventeen years, nearly nine hundred have been baptized among us... (p. 67). In this summer also it appeared to me scriptural, according to the *example* of the Apostles, Acts 20:7, to break bread every Lord's day, though there is no *commandment* given to do so, either by the Lord, or by the Holy Ghost through the apostles. And at the same time it appeared to me scriptural, according to Eph. 4, Rom.12, etc., that there should be given room for the Holy Ghost to work through any of the brethren whom he pleases to use; that thus one member might benefit the other with the gift which the Lord has bestowed upon him. Accordingly at certain meetings any of the brethren had an opportunity to exhort or teach the rest if they considered that they had anything to say which might be beneficial to the hearers. I observe here that as the Lord gave me grace to endeavour to carry out at once the light which he had been pleased to give me on this point, and as the truth was but in part apprehended, there was much infirmity mixed with the manner of carrying it out. Nor was it until several years after that the Lord was pleased to teach me about this point more perfectly. That the disciples of Jesus should meet together on the first day of the week for the breaking of bread, and that that should be their principal meeting, and that those, whether one or several, who are truly gifted by the Holy Spirit for service, be it for exhortation or teaching or rule, are responsible to the Lord for the exercise of their gifts: these are to me no matters of uncertainty but points on which my soul, by grace, is established through the revealed will of God.

On October 7, 1830, I was united by marriage to Miss Mary Groves, sister of the brother whose name has aleady been mentioned.... About this time I began to have conscientious objections against any longer receiving a stated salary. My reasons against it were these:

1. The salary was made up by pew-rents; but pew-rents are, according to James 2:1-6, against the mind of the Lord, as in general the poor brother cannot have so good a seat as the rich. (All pew rents were therefore given up, and all the seats made free, which was stated at the entrance of the meeting-house.) 2. A brother may gladly do something towards my support if left to his own time; but when the quarter is up he has perhaps other expenses and I do not know whether he pays his money grudgingly and of necessity or cheerfully; but God loveth a cheerful giver. Nay, *I know it to be a fact*, that sometimes it had not been convenient to the brethren to pay the money when it had been asked for by the brethren who collected it. 3. Though the Lord had been

pleased to give me grace to be faithful so that I had been enabled not to keep back the truth when he has shown it to me; still I felt that the pew-rents were a snare to the servant of Christ. I was tempted, at least for a few minutes, at the time when the Lord had stirred me up to pray and search the Word respecting the ordinance of baptism, because £30 of my salary was at stake if I should be baptized.

For these reasons, I stated to the brethren at the end of October, 1830, that I should for the future give up having any regular salary. After I had given to the brethren my reasons for doing so, I read to them Philippians 4, and told them that if they still had a desire to do something for my support by voluntary gifts I had no objection to receive them, though ever so small, either in money or provisions. A few days after it appeared to me that there was a better way still; for if I received personally every single gift offered in money, both my own time and that of the donors would be much taken up; and in this way also the poor might through temptation be kept from offering their pence, a privilege of which they ought not to be deprived; and some also might in this way give more than if it were not known who was the giver; so that it would still be doubtful whether the gift were given grudgingly or cheerfully. For these reasons especially there was a box put up in the meeting-house over which was written that whosoever had a desire to do something towards my support might put his offering in the box.[1]

At the same time it appeared right to me that henceforth I should ask no man, not even my beloved brethren and sisters to help me, as I had done a few times according to their own request, as my expenses on account of travelling much in the Lord's service were too great to be met by my usual income. For unconsciously, I had thus again been led in some measure to trust in an arm of flesh, going to man instead of going to the Lord at once. *To come to this conclusion before God required more grace than to give up my salary.*

About the same time also my wife and I had grace given to us to take the Lord's commandment, "Sell that ye have and give alms," Luke 12:33, literally, and to carry it out. Our staff and support in this matter were Matthew 6:19–34; John 14:13-14. We leaned on the arm of the

---

1   In 1841 George Müller and his co-worker, Henry Craik, ceased to have their names put on boxes for offerings, so as to avoid any sense of themselves being officially superior to other ministering brethren in the church. The full reasons are spiritually instructive. See *Narrative*, Part III, vol. I, 411–415.

Lord Jesus. It is now nineteen years since we set out in this way and *we do not in the least regret the step we then took*. Our God also has in his tender mercy given us grace to abide in the same mind concerning the above points, both as it regards principles and practice; and this has been the means of letting us see the tender love and care of our God over His children, even in the most minute things, in a way which we never experimentally knew them before; and it has in particular made the Lord known to us more fully than we knew him before *as a prayer hearing God*.

I lay these weighty personal utterances before my readers, being well assured that such as read them with a heart truly set upon pleasing God will be as richly profited thereby as I myself was in my early manhood. There is grace available to strengthen each of us to follow George Müller as he followed Christ. We are not all called of God to found an orphanage, as he did, but we are called to imitate his faith. And the evidence of faith is obedience.

II. INDEPENDENCE OF THE LOCAL CHURCH.—I appeal next for clear recognition and most careful maintenance of the administrative independence of each local church. The following excellent letter was addressed by E. H. Broadbent, in June, 1923, to an important conference of the Ukrainian believers before-mentioned. It had a most helpful influence, and was translated into Russian, Polish, and German. I have inserted the Scripture references.

DIRECT DEALINGS WITH GOD BY THE INDIVIDUAL AND BY THE CHURCH

Each individual soul has the right of direct communication with the Lord. He says, "Come unto Me" (Matt. 11:28). Great efforts have been made to prevent this, and to bring a priest or saint or other intermediary between the soul and God. We have learned to break through these hindrances and to have direct communion with the Lord (2 Cor. 12:8-9; 1 John 5:14-15). We believe in *Him* to our salvation (Acts 16:31); we walk in fellowship with *Him* (1 Cor. 1:9; 1 John 1:3); we obey *His Word* (John 14:23-24); we depend on *Him* (Prov. 3:5-6; Jer. 17:7-8); and we are responsible to *Him* in all things (1 Cor. 4:1–4; 2 Tim. 2:15; 2 Cor. 5:9-10). We do not allow anyone to rob us of this invaluable right of direct, personal relation to God.

It is the same with a church or assembly of believers. Each such company has the right of direct dependence on the Lord (Acts 4:23–31; 14:23; 20:32), and of obeying His word (2 Thess. 2:15; 3:6; 1 Cor. 11:2), and of receiving the gifts of the Holy Spirit (1 Cor. 1:4–7), and the supply of all its needs of every kind (Phil. 4:19; 2 Cor. 9:8). This is clear throughout the New Testament. The Lord says, "On this rock will I build *My* church" (Matt. 16:18). In the Acts we find no federation of churches, but each church independent. Fellowship was maintained, not by rules aiming at bringing about uniformity, but by frequent visiting and personal intercourse. In the Epistles each church is considered as directly responsible to the Lord (Eph. 5:24; Col. 1:9-10), as also in the Revelation (Rev. 1, 2, 3). Paul writes: "*The called of Jesus Christ*, to all that are in Rome, beloved of God, called to be saints" (Rom. 1:7), and "to the church of the Thessalonians in *God the Father and the Lord Jesus Christ*" (1 Thess. 1:1), and so on. The direct relation to the Lord of each congregation is made clear.

Great efforts have been made, and are still made, to come between the Lord and His churches. A great variety of religious organizations endeavour to control the churches; to decide what they shall believe and practise; to undertake the guidance and to supply the needs of those who minister the Word; and in every way to prevent churches from depending on the Lord and make them dependent on men. To enforce this the strongest measures are used, of persecution, or exclusion, cutting off supplies, etc.

We have to maintain the right of each assembly to direct dependence on the Lord. Otherwise believers cannot make progress in faith and knowledge and obedience, because when they reach a certain point the rules or traditions of the organization or system that controls them step in and forbid further progress, on the ground that it would be contrary to the rules of the organization. This is the chief cause of the lack of growth and development among the Lord's people.

Just as every soul is directly under God and no one may come between, so is each assembly of believers directly under the Lord, and subject to the leading of His Holy Spirit according to His Word, and no organization or federation of churches may intervene.

If this feature be fully observed no danger of general division can arise, for each separate assembly will deal only with matters and individuals as each of these becomes locally and directly its concern, and will neither impose its decisions upon, nor feel bound by the actions of, any other assembly.

III. REGARD THE LOCAL CHURCH AS THE ONLY BODY CORPORATE.—I appeal further, and most earnestly, for the full acknowledgment in practice that the local church is the only visible body corporate sanctioned by the Head of the church. Joint action by two or more assemblies, groupings of churches for any purpose whatever, associations of believers into "societies," "classes," "missions," public lists and funds, all trespass against this vital feature of the divine arrangements for the church. Readers will have discerned that almost all, if not all, the departures surveyed impinge upon this truth. Hence the due maintenance thereof constitutes a powerful safeguard against declension.

Probably a sense of this prompted a remark by the late William Dudgeon, shortly before his death. A younger worker asked him for such advice as his sixty years' experience as a servant of Christ might suggest as useful. He concentrated all into the single word: "Never start a mission!" and said nothing more. "No one *can serve two masters*," or objects. God calls us to found and to build up local churches; let us not create circles of our own devising, which can only absorb affection and divert energy, even though honestly *intended to help* the church.

IV. CHRISTIAN SERVICE IS INDIVIDUAL—This involves the further principle that gospel service and other good works are to be rendered by individuals as individual efforts. This does not mean that two or more persons may not co-operate when and as long as the Lord indicates. But that their work is to be deemed *their* work and responsibility, not that of a *body* of persons.

The commencement of the Scriptural Knowledge Institution will illustrate what is meant. In George Müller's *Narrative* (part I, 109), under date February 21, 1834, we find this statement (italics mine): "*I was led* this morning to form a plan for establishing, upon scriptural principles, an institution, etc." Notice, "I was led" to do a certain thing; it was an individual guided *to do something*, not to consult his brethren *whether* he should do this thing, and defer to their judgment and planning. Again (p. 112): "March 5th.—This evening, at a public meeting, Brother Craik and I stated the principles on which we *intend to carry on* the institution which *we* propose to establish." There was no submitting to the church the question of whether the thing was or was not to be done. They took their orders from their Lord and set to work, simply informing their friends of their purpose, because, of course, it could not but become known, and love so required.

Workers thus joining together should form no formal or binding partnership, but ever be ready to dissociate, even at short notice, should the Lord so indicate. Thus nothing corporate will be formed, but all individuals will look directly to the Lord with personal faith for control, direction, support.

V. Love.—I next appeal most earnestly to myself and to all saints that we open wide our hearts for a *rich inflow of the love of God*. These pages have been written with the desire to inform the understanding as to the mind of God, so as to form a right judgment as to the ways of God; but a yet deeper necessity is that the spirit be suffused with the love of God. The purest love may take a wrong course if the judgment be unenlightened as to what is right; but the most instructed mind may yet do the right thing in such wise that the effect be hurtful, from the unloving spirit in which action is taken.

God is a Person, and His love is towards persons: "The Father loveth the *Son*"; "God so loved the *world*"; "The Father Himself loveth *you.*" The heart filled with His love loves the *brotherhood*. It is fatally easy to love a denomination, a creed, doctrines, my own views of truth (especially dispensational and prophetic truth) more than I love my *brother*.

Love studies how many it can embrace: it is extremely reluctant to exclude and will do so only under utterly unavoidable duty. Hence it will welcome to communion on the smallest valid ground, making its tests of fellowship as few and light as possible. It has a greater dread of shutting out one that ought to be received than of receiving one who ought to be shut out. Love counts the latter risk the lighter.

It welcomes eagerly the injunction, "receive ye one another, even as Christ also received you, to the glory of God" (Rom. 15:7). Christ, in His divine love, received each upon the least signs of true repentance and the most meagre measure of genuine faith, in spite of colossal ignorance, a thousand defects of character, and obvious, persistent blemishes of conduct. Love, His love, in His people constrains them thus to act.

Almost the earliest known post-apostolic writing, the *Didache*, shows that the primitive Christians so acted in the generation immediately following the apostles. It says: "And whosoever cometh in the name of the Lord, let him be received; and then when ye have proved him ye shall know him" (ch. 12). First receive, then test: honour the Name in which he comes, then prove him whether he bear it worthily.[1]

The practice of the early Brethren was stated at the time (1836) by one of the first and greatest, Anthony Norris Groves, as follows:

> Was not the principle we laid down as to separation from all existing bodies at the outset, this: That we felt ourselves bound to separate from all individuals and systems, *so far* as they required us to do what our consciences would not allow, or restrained us from doing what our consciences required, and no further? and were we not as free to join and act with any individual, or body of individuals, as they were free *not* to require us to do what our consciences did not allow, or prevent our doing what they did? And in this freedom did we not feel brethren should *not* force liberty on those who were bound, nor withhold freedom from those who were free? ... As any system is in its provisions narrower or wider than the truth, I either stop short, or go beyond its provisions, but I would INFINITELY RATHER BEAR *with all their evils*, than SEPARATE from THEIR GOOD. These were the *then* principles of our separation and intercommunion.

And, again:

> ... when weak you can be liberal and large, but when holpen with a little strength, the *true* spirit of sectarianism begins to bud; that being "*one of us*" has become a stronger bond than oneness of the power of the life of God in the soul.

---
1 Always, of course, supposing one does not already know of the individual what would bring him under 2 John 10.

And, again:

> Some will not have me hold communion with the Scotts, because their views are not satisfactory about the Lord's Supper; others with you, because of your views about baptism; others with the Church of England, because of her thought about ministry. On my principles, I receive them all; but on the principle of witnessing against evil, I should reject them all. . . . I make use of my fellowship in the Spirit, to enjoy the common life together. . . .

When Groves thus wrote, Modernism and Romanism were scarcely known in the Protestant denominations. *Such* evils he would not have tolerated, nor may we. But as regards the matters he had in mind, if love shall *reign* again in our hearts we shall thus act, and once more the Lord will cause His assemblies to be attractive havens of refuge, homes of rest, schools of knowledge, spheres of service, for the at present starved and forlorn of His people. As He has received them, let us do so, and it shall be to the glory of God. But as we reject humanly-drawn creeds as tests of Christian fellowship, so also other believers will not come to us if they are first to be put through the items of an *unwritten* creed, which may be just as extensive, rigid, and oppressive as any other. Let us once and for all put far from us the spirit that will slaughter our very brothers who cannot pronounce aright our Shibboleth. Shall we not nail this evil heart to the bitter cross, and bury it in the grave of Him who died to atone for its guilt?

William Collingwood united with the Brethren before the first division. He confirmed Groves' statements as to those first days by writing, in 1899, as follows (*The Brethren*, 9, 11):

> The chief aim was to exhibit, in a Scriptural way, *the common brotherhood of all believers*. They recognized no special membership. That they belonged to Christ was the only term of communion; that they loved one another was the power of their fellowship. In principle, it embraced all whose faith and walk showed that they had spiritual life; in practice, all such of these as would avail themselves of it. . . . Their attitude toward other Christians was shown, for example, at Hereford, when Mr. Venn, the godly Rector, was holding a public discussion with a Unitarian, and they sent him word that they would spend the time in prayer for him.

It was, moreover, quite a common thing to see the clerical dress at their largest meeting in London.

The principles thus briefly stated were in full force when in 1844 the writer sought a place with them at the Lord's table. He plainly expressed his intention, at the time, of continuing to attend the ministry of the clergyman through whom he had received much spiritual blessing. The answer was that this would be no bar to their full and hearty fellowship; that so far as they were concerned though it was not likely to be profitable to himself—he was free to go to as many of the evangelical communities as he thought fit; but being recognized as a child of God, there would always be a place for him at the Lord's table whenever he would come. And this was not an exceptional case; it was the rule in those early days.

Love is tolerant; it forbears to the utmost limit of righteousness; and even when compelled to exert discipline, it does it sorrowfully, gently, with tears, seeking still only the good of the the offender. The *enemies* of the cross of Christ it *must* oppose, yet it *weeps* as it speaks of them (Phil. 3:18), even as He wept over murderous Jerusalem. Him whose practical life is a disgrace to the Holy Name it must and will put away; but as it issues this command it feels "much affliction and anguish of heart" and writes "with many tears" (1 Cor. 5:13; 2 Cor. 2:4).

Love is tolerant; it beareth all things; it can listen long and patiently to opinions from which it differs. What millenniums the God of Love has listened quietly to the hard things that ungodly men speak against Him! Yet are there children of His to whom a prophetic opinion contrary to their own is as a red rag to a bull; they can hardly keep their seats or hold their tongues. One solemnly urged his readers to leave the meeting in a body if the Revised Version should be read by a speaker! So little does he value order or fellowship in the House of God. But love is strong enough to be patient. It is not so conceited as to dream that it alone has wisdom; it is too humble to deem itself perfect in knowledge. Wesley said of certain he met that they had sundry excellent qualities, but unfortunately they knew everything and therefore they learned nothing. Let us be warned. This spirit is not of love.

## Conclusion and Appeal

Far nobler was the spirit of John Robinson's farewell address to the Pilgrim Fathers at Delft Haven, Holland, on September 5, 1620. As he bade good-bye to those who were suffering and venturing so much to gain for themselves liberty of religious opinion, he said:

> I am verily persuaded the Lord has more truth yet to break forth out of His Holy Word. For my part, I cannot sufficiently bewail the condition of the Reformed Churches, who are come to a period in religion, and will go at present no further than the instruments of their reformation. The Lutherans cannot be drawn to go beyond what Luther saw; whatever part of His will our good God has revealed to Calvin, they will rather die than embrace it. And the Calvinists, you see, stick fast where they were left by that great man of God, who yet saw not all things.
>
> This is a misery much to be lamented, for though they were burning and shining lights in their times, yet they penetrated not into the whole counsel of God; but were they now living, would be as willing to embrace further light as that which they first received, for it is not possible the Christian world should come so lately out of such thick anti-Christian darkness, and that perfection of knowledge should break forth at once.[1]

There is an unloving, intolerant spirit abroad which will not allow divergence of opinion from itself, and which will take the severest measures against offenders, all, of course, in the name of zeal for the truth and for Christ. We ought indeed to be deeply thankful to God for every resolute endeavour to prevent Modernism (misnamed) from entering the assemblies, but there is evident danger of zeal, if untempered by knowledge, mistaking for the fundamental, which must not on any account be surrendered, various matters of opinion upon which divergence may safely be tolerated. For example, the fact of Christ's eternal unchangeable Deity and true humanity may not be compromised in the smallest degree, but such a subordinate topic as the mode of the interactings of the three Persons in the Godhead is not in the same category. Neither are dispensational views, nor prophetic schemes, nor details concerning the Tribulation or the Rapture. Important they are; matters for deep, earnest investigation;

---

1 That is, a full stop.

but not just causes for controversy, bitterness, alienation of heart, division.

Another has well said:

> In the class of persons which has been mentioned, the spiritual life mingles more or less, and perhaps in nearly equal proportions, with the tendencies and activities of nature. The fire which blazes up from their hearts, and which often casts a broad light upon a surrounding multitude (they often have great gifts; they labour for God; they attract attention) is a mixed fire, partly from heaven and partly from earth. The natural unholy principles are not extinct, but can only be said to be partly purified, and to be turned into a new channel. Hence they will often-times fight for God with the same zeal, and almost in the same manner, that worldly men fight for their temporal and worldly objects; with great earnestness, with an unquiet and turbulent indignation, and sometimes with a cruelty of attack which vents itself in misrepresentations, and which persecutes even to prison and to death (T. C. Upham, D.D., *The Interior or Hidden Life*, 414-416).

From all these, and a thousand other evils, the warm glow of the love of God can preserve us. And it is written that "he that loveth not his brother whom he hath seen, *cannot* love God whom he hath not seen. And this *commandment* have we from Him, that he who loveth God love his brother also," and, "let us not love in word, neither with the tongue; but in deed and truth"; yea, "let *all* that ye do be done in *love*" (1 John 4:20-21; 3:18; 1 Cor. 16:14).

VI. PERSONAL HOLINESS—Finally, I appeal, most lovingly but solemnly, for a great increase of diligence in *the cultivation of personal holiness* in character and practice. This is the call of the Father: "Ye shall be holy, for I am holy" (Lev. 11:44-45; 19:2; 1 Pet. 1:15). It is the object of redemption: "Who gave Himself for us, that He might redeem us from *all* iniquity, and *purify* unto Himself a people for His own possession, zealous of good works" (Tit. 2:14). It is the work of the Holy Spirit: "but ye washed yourselves, but ye were sanctified, but ye were justified in the name of the Lord Jesus Christ, and in the Spirit of our God" (1 Cor. 6:11). It is the effect of the Word of God: Ye have *purified* your *souls* in your obedience to the truth unto unfeigned love of the brethren" (1 Pet. 1:22). This last passage shows that holiness and love are inseparable. A purified soul is one freed from every feeling towards another but love. I beg the controversialist to demand of his heart whether he can meet with unfeigned affection and ease the brother with whom he has contended. I beg one who feels himself wronged to test his heart in the same way. If the honest answer be in the negative love has been quenched and holiness sullied.

It is a most serious deficiency in theology if but a small place be given to the doctrine of sanctification. Far too much Eph. 5:25–27 has been treated as if it read that Christ loved the church (the foundation of all her blessings), and gave Himself up for her (redemption at the Cross, the ground of all blessing), that He might present the church to Himself (the bridal glory). But what the Scripture says is that Christ loved her and redeemed her *in order that* He might *sanctify her*, having cleansed her by the laver (composed of) water (the energy of the Holy Spirit) in the Word, *in order* that He might present the church to Himself, not having spot or wrinkle, or any such thing, but that she should be holy and without blemish. This last term is principally sacrificial and priestly, and always refers to *external* appearance (see Deut. 15:21; Lev. 21:16–24; 23:17–25; 24:19-20, etc.). The repeated *hina* (in order that), shows that redemption is with the view to sanctification, and sanctification with the view to glorification. The direct connecting of justification with glorification, by omitting the connecting link of sanctification, is contrary to the passage and injurious to piety. The truth connected with the altar and the holy place has been well taught, but we have too largely passed by the laver, with its ceaselessly repeated washing of the hands and feet. But to have walked from the altar to the holy place without each time washing at the laver rendered the priest liable to the penalty of death (Ex. 30:20-21; and cf. Acts 5:1–11 ; 1 Cor. 5:3–5; 11:30; Rom. 8:12-13; etc.).

We need to face the full and precise force of such a searching word as, "Pursue *peace* with all men, and the *sanctification* without which no one shall see the Lord" (Heb. 12:14). In this sentence the sanctification is not judicial, the imputed righteousness which justifies eternally, but that practical holiness caused by being set free from slavery to sin and becoming instead obedient slaves to do the will of God, which produces "fruit unto sanctification" (Rom. 6:22). *This* sanctification is practical; it means sexual purity, as opposed to fleshly uncleanness (1 Thess. 4:3–7); and it is this sanctification unto which God chose and called us "in sanctification of spirit and belief of the truth unto (*eis*, with a view to) the obtaining of the glory of our Lord Jesus Christ" (2 Thess. 2:13-14). In each of these passages the word is the same, and points surely to that holiness which has as its spring the purity of heart which will secure the blessedness of seeing God (Matt. 5:8). For "the Lord" in the above passage is God the Father, since everyone, including the wicked, must at some time see Christ (Matt. 26:64; Rev. 1:7; 20:12; Phil. 2:10-11), and so for this no sanctity whatever is required.

These things being so, it is high time to awake out of sleep, and to address ourselves with the utmost zeal to the task of becoming holy as God is holy; and he who is thus engrossed will cease from criticizing harshly, from making strife, from "weights" as well as sins, from all that hinders heart purity.

No doubt, where there has been cleaving to the Word of God it has maintained a general level of morality which is cause for thanksgiving, and has preserved from much gross worldliness elsewhere seen. But it is unwise for Christians to be measuring themselves by one another (2 Cor. 10:12). God is the true standard of holiness, Christ Jesus the perfect example, the Word the only rule. Tested thus, we may well be humbled.

He who would preserve himself pure must be diligent to "*cleanse* HIMSELF from all defilement of flesh [outward life] and spirit [the inward life], *perfecting* holiness [by a zeal that shall end only with life] in the fear of God" (2 Cor. 7:1). When the Oriental walks to a feast, and must needs pass through dark and muddy places, he gathers up his flowing robes into his girdle, and so, picking his way, arrives "unspotted" and with undefiled garments. Wherefore "gird up the loins of your mind," says Peter—gather up your thoughts and desires, let them not trail in the mire of worldly pleasures; that is, "bring every thought into captivity to the obedience of Christ," and then "set your hope perfectly" on His return, and the marriage feast to which you hasten. (1 Pet. 1:13; 2 Cor. 10:5). Oh for a resolute cultivation of that habit of mind described by old writers as a being "recollected in God"; the thoughts harnessed, gathered together again (re-collected) after necessary attention to right matters, so as to be occupied inwardly with God. Thus would the mind be preserved from aimless wandering, from flitting hither and thither, sipping from the world's bright but poisonous flowers.

Shall we not all heed our blessed Lord's solemn words: "I counsel thee to *buy* of me... *white garments* that thou mayest *clothe thyself*, and that the shame of thy nakedness be not made manifest?" (Rev. 3:18). For it is only they who, in this day of evil, overcome the world, so not defiling their garments (their outer life with which they array themselves in daily doings), who shall in His day be counted worthy to walk about with Him in white, as His chosen companions (Rev. 3:4-5). For the fine linen, bright and pure, in which the bride of the Lamb shall be permitted to array herself for the marriage, is the "righteous acts of the saints" themselves, wrought out by the grace of the Holy Spirit through detailed acts of obedience to the commands of her Lord (Rev. 19: 8).[1] The heavenly Bridegroom *freely* provides *all* the rich materials, but it is for the Bride to *make up* the trousseau, and only what she has made will be ready to be worn at the wedding. And the trifling price at which she must "buy" the costly white linen which He gives is this: "Be not fashioned according to this age, but be ye transfigured by the renewing of your mind" (Rom. 12:2). Be content, O heavenly pilgrim, to be despised in Vanity Fair for your heavenly costume and manners.

> O happy band of pilgrims,
> Look upward to the skies,
> Where such a light affliction
> Shall win so great a prize.

---

1 That the R.V. "righteous acts" is the correct rendering may be seen from ch, 15: 4, where the same word is rendered "judgments" (A.V.), "righteous judgments" (Newberry), "righteous acts" (R. V.).

"*dikaiōmata*. Its strict meaning is a *thing righteously done*. Its usual meaning is *an ordinance of justice*. But in one New Testament passage at least (Rev. 19: 8) it appears to mean a righteous act or course of acts" (Moule, *Cambridge Bible*, on Rom. 5: 18). The word is plural. In any case, it is here not the righteousness of God, but of the *saints*, and cannot mean imputed righteousness.

Here I conclude. In these pages I have concentrated the meditation, observation, and reading of perhaps sixty years. They have been written with travail of soul and prolonged prayer. I have pondered these words of Paul: "I am jealous over you with a godly jealousy: for I espoused you to one husband, that I might present you as a pure virgin to Christ. But I FEAR, lest by any means, as the serpent beguiled Eve in his craftiness, your thoughts should be corrupted from the simplicity and the purity that is toward Christ" (2 Cor. 11:2-3). I have weighed also this very early Christian exhortation, which is a striking application of this and similar scriptures:

> The Clementines put these words into the mouth of St. Peter: "Do ye as elders of the Church adorn with discipline the bride of Christ—and by the bride of Christ I mean the whole assembly of the Church—in moral purity: for if she be found pure by the bridegroom King, she herself will attain the height of honour, and ye, as guests at the wedding feast, will gain great delights: but if she be found to have sinned, she herself will be cast out, and ye will suffer punishment because, it may be, the sin has happened through your neglect." *Ep. Clem. ad Jacob*, c. 7. (Hatch, *Organisation*, 71-72).

If what has been here written is found in that day to have helped any disciples, still more any churches, to walk and to build more "according to the pattern," then they will be edified, Christ will be glorified, and I shall be satisfied.

To the reader who has persevered to the end of these pages I bid a loving farewell. See to it, my brother, that you meet your Lord with joy. Tolerate nothing, however slight, that may cause you to be "ashamed from Him at His presence" (1 John 2:28; Luke 19:20–26). Remember that if you consent to *die with Him* you shall also *live* with Him; if you endure what is involved in such dying, you shall also *reign* with Him (2 Tim. 2:11–13). Sell not your rights of the first born for any mess of pottage, any earthly, carnal, temporary gratification (Heb. 12:14–17). The prize of your calling is noble; the day of reward hastens: "Wherefore, beloved, seeing that ye look for these things, GIVE DILIGENCE that ye may be found in peace, without spot and blameless in His sight" (2 Pet. 3:14).

# Index

## A

Abraham, 57
Agabus, 167
*Against Marcion,* 147
Alford, Dean, 80, 129, 138, 157, 160, 162
Ananias, 61
Anderson, Sir Robert, 15
Anna, 146
Antioch, church, 125, 157, 167
Antioch, council of, 26
Apollos, 177
*Apologia* (Newman), 20
*Apology* (Tertullian), 91, 157
*Apostolical Constitutions/Apostolic Canons,* 26, 170
Apostolic succession, 17
Arles, Council of, 24
Arnot, F. S., 187, 190
Asa, King, 123
Augustine, 32
Aurelian, Emperor, 27
*Autobiography* (C. G. Finney), 172
*Autobiography* (C. H. Spurgeon), 171
Ayr, 172

## B

Baal, 122
Balaamites, 108
Baptismal regeneration, 56
Barak, 146
Begbie's *Life of William Booth,* 51
Bengel, 130, 138
Bennet, W. H., 102
Besant, Mrs. Annie, 151
Bethesda Church, Bristol, 105, 131
Beza, Theodore, 184
*Bible and Modern Criticism* (Anderson), 15

Bishops. *See* Elders
Blackie's Popular Encyclopaedia, 97
Blavatsky, Madame Helena, 151
Bloomfield, 130
Booth, William, 51, 60
Bowden, E. S., 99
Bowen, George, 95
Bread, unleavened, 72
*Brethren, The* (W. Collingwood), 211
Broadbent, E. H., 206
Bruce, F. F., 32, 170

## C

Cæcilian, 24
Caleb, 122
*Cambridge Bible* (Moule), 217
Carmichael, Miss Amy, 188
Ceylon, destruction foretold, 171
Chapman, R. C., 133
Charles IX, 184
Charles IX, Emperor, 184
China Inland Mission, 132
*Christian Ecclesia* (Hort), 16
Christian Institutions (Stanley), 56
Chrysostom, 162
Church of England, 15, 20, 21, 56, 98, 138, 211
Church of Scotland, 138
*Church, The, the Churches, and the Mysteries* (Pember), 166
Clementines, 218
Collingwood, William, 211
Colombo, destruction foretold, 171
Constantine, Emperor, 24, 27
Consubstantiation, 71, 77
Conybeare and Howson, 174
Cornelius, Bishop of Rome, 31
Cornelius (Caesarea), 60, 64

219

Craik, H., 105, 131, 205, 209
Cremer, 162
Cyprian, Bishop, 16, 24, 30, 31
Cyril of Alexandria, 46

## D

Darby, J. N., 51, 80, 98, 102–106, 130, 160, 188, 225
David, King, 28, 122
Deacons, 11, 14, 27, 38, 106, 169
Deborah, 146, 153
Delft, 213
Development, doctrine of, 10, 21
*Dialogue with Trypho*, 169
*Didache*, 57, 147, 169, 210
Diotrephes, 44
Dohnavur, 188
Donatists, 32
Dudgeon, William, 208

## E

*Early Years of the Modern Tongues Movement* (Lang), 171
Easter, observance, 23
*Echoes of Service*, 177
Eddy, Mrs. Mary Baker, 151
Edersheim, Dr. A., 139, 145
Elders (bishops), duties and status, 11, 14, 16, 17, 35, 38, 103, 105, 106, 109, 112, 126, 127, 149, 152, 179, 184, 185, 218
Elihu, 41
Ellicott, Bishop, 157, 162
Eutychus, 69, 87, 156
Exclusive Brethren, 48
Excommunication, 26, 27, 48, 103, 107, 110, 111, 112, 129

## F

Fasting, 70, 158
Fielde, Miss Adele, 154
Finney, C. G., 172

*Firstfruits and Harvest* (Lang), 58
Fletcher, Dr. Alexander, 171
Fox, George, 60
Free Church Council, 46

## G

Gifts, spiritual, 11, 97, 159, 168–170
Gordon, Dr. A. J., 105, 146, 154
Gouverneur, 172
Govett, Robert, 97
Gratian, Emperor, 28
*Greek-English Dictionary* (Kykkotis), 55
Grimm, 103
Groves, Anthony Norris, 104, 105, 187, 200, 210, 211
Groves, Miss Mary, 204

## H

Hake, William, 133
Hannah, 146
Hatch, Dr. Edwin, 15, 23, 43, 52, 108, 110, 113, 163, 173, 218
*Hibbert Lectures* (Hatch), 113, 163
Hill, Rowland, 171, 172
*History of My Religious Opinions* (Newman), 20
*History of the Plymouth Brethren* (Neatby), 103
Hogg, C. F., 130
Homer, 164
Hort, Dr. F. J. A., 16, 18
*How Christ came to Church* (Gordon), 146
Howson, Dr. J. S., 174
Huguenots, 184
Huldah, 146
*Hypatia* (Kingsley), 46

## I

Ignatius, 20
Individual communion cups, 74

# Index

Infant baptism, 56, 59, 60, 63, 65, 194, 196, 201, 202
*Influence of Greek Ideas and Usages upon the Christian Church, The* (Hatch), 113
*Interior or Hidden Life, The* (Upham), 214
Irving, Edward, 171

## J

Jezebel, 108
Joshua, 122, 188
Justin Martyr, 169

## K

Kelly, William, 111
Kingsley, C., 46
Kirkcudbright, 172
Knill, 171
Knox, John, 172
Kykkotis, I., 55

## L

Lang, G. T., 52
*Lectures on Philippians* (Kelly), 111
*Life and Times of Jesus the Messiah* (Edersheim), 139, 145
*Life of William Booth* (Begbie), 51
Lightfoot, 157
London Society for Promoting Christianity amongst the Jews, 196
Lutheran, 71, 159, 196
Luther, Martin, 59
Lydia, 64

## M

Majority Decisions, 115
Meyer, 157, 162
Miller, Andrew, 51
*Ministry of Women, The*, 154
Miriam, 145

Missions, 11, 12, 13, 36, 43, 50, 86, 99, 154, 157, 173, 177, 178, 182, 183, 186, 190, 199, 200, 201
Modernism, 211, 213
Montanists, 163
Morrish, Dr., 52
Moule, Bishop Handley C. G., 56, 57, 217
Müller, George, 102, 105, 131, 194, 196, 200, 205, 206, 208
Mysteries, heathen, 61, 78, 190

## N

*Narrative of Some of the Lord's Dealings* (Müller), 194, 196, 201, 205, 208
Nash, 172
Neatby, W. B., 103
Nestlé Greek, 37
Newberry, 217
Newman, 20–22
*New Testament Critically Emphasized* (Rotherham), 61
Newton, B. W., 102, 104
*New Translation* (Darby), 130, 160
Nicæa, Council of, 26
Nicolaitans, 108
Noah, 166
Nonconformists, 46, 83, 91, 153
Novatian, 31

## O

Old Catholic Congress, Berne, 19
Olshausen, 162
Omri, King, 122
Open Brethren, 86
*Organisation of the Early Christian Churches, The* (Hatch), 15, 44, 218
Organization, human, 16, 28, 35, 113, 164, 182, 185, 207
Origen, 31
Ozanne, Rev. J. A. F., 19

## P

Paget, Miss, 81
Paul, Apostle, 18, 33, 38, 40, 42, 45, 64, 67, 78, 87, 109, 126, 140, 156, 166, 207, 218
Paul of Samosata, Bishop, 27
Pember, G. H., 166
Peter, Apostle, 60, 64, 87, 127, 176, 216
Philip, evangelist, 56, 167
Pierson, Dr. A. T., 105
Pilgrim Fathers, 213
Plymouth, assembly, 97
Plymouth Brethren, 85, 97
Pope, 18, 47, 52, 180
*Popular Encyclopaedia* (Blackie), 97
Prophets, prophecy, 35, 95, 100, 141, 147, 160, 189

## R

Reservation (sacrament), 87
Rhetoric, Greek, 164
Robinson, John, 213
Roman Catholic Church, 29, 31, 32, 55, 108, 164
Rotherham, J. B., 61

## S

Sacraments, 32, 55, 63, 65, 71, 83, 87, 158
Salaries of Christian workers, 199, 204
Salem Chapel, Bristol, 102
Saul, King, 122
*Scots Worthies*, 172
Scriptural Knowledge Institution, 208
*Seventy Years of Pilgrimage, A Memorial of William Hake*, 133
Short, Dr. Rendle A., 101
Singing, 38, 61, 91, 157, 195
*Sketches of Jewish Social Life* (Edersheim), 139, 140
Solomon, King, 28

Sophists, 164
*Spreading Flame, The* (Bruce), 32, 170
Spurgeon, C. H., 69, 98, 171
Stanley, Dean, 56
State
  Christians and, 179
  Churches, 10, 24, 27, 36, 46, 83, 184, 196
Stephanas, 106
St. Paul (Conybeare and Howson), 174

## T

Taylor, J. Hudson, 45
Tertullian, 32, 91, 147, 157, 163
*Three Letters* (Tregelles), 97, 98, 102, 103
Tibni, 122
Tongues, 143, 157
Transubstantiation, 45, 70, 71, 77
Tregelles, Dr S. P., 97, 101, 103
Troas, 68, 69, 77, 84, 87, 91, 92, 156

## U

Ukrainians, 194
Unity Chapel, Bristol, 134
Upham, Dr. T. C., 214
Uzziah, 45

## V

Valentinian, Emperor, 28
Venn, 211
Victoria, Queen, 153

## W

Welch. John, 172
Wesleyan Methodism, 50
Wesley, John, 212
White, Mrs. Ellen G., 151
Wigram, George V., 51, 98, 102, 103
Wine, unfermented, 72
Wright, James, 132

*Also from Kingsley Press:*

# AN ORDERED LIFE
## AN AUTOBIOGRAPHY BY G. H. LANG

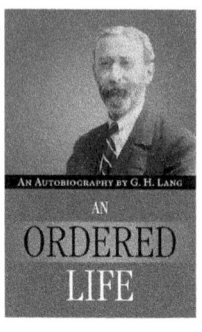

G. H. Lang was a remarkable Bible teacher, preacher and writer of a past generation who should not be forgotten by today's Christians. He inherited the spiritual "mantle" of such giants in the faith as George Müller, Anthony Norris Groves and other notable saints among the early Brethren movement. He traveled all over the world with no fixed means of support other than prayer and faith and no church or other organization to depend on. Like Mr. Müller before him, he told his needs to no one but God. Many times his faith was tried to the limit, as funds for the next part of his journey arrived only at the last minute and from unexpected sources.

This autobiography traces in precise detail the dealings of God with his soul, from the day of his conversion at the tender age of seven, through the twilight years when bodily infirmity restricted most of his former activities. You will be amazed, as you read these pages, to see how quickly and continually a soul can grow in grace and in the knowledge of spiritual things if they will wholly follow the Lord.

Horace Bushnell once wrote that every man's life is a plan of God, and that it's our duty as human beings to find and follow that plan. As Mr. Lang looks back over his long and varied life in the pages of this book, he frequently points out the many times God prepared him in the present for some future work or role. Spiritual life applications abound throughout the book, making it not just a life story but a spiritual training manual of sorts. Preachers will find sermon starters and illustrations in every chapter. Readers of all kinds will benefit from this close-up view of the dealings of God with the soul of one who made it his life's business to follow the Lamb wherever He should lead.

Buy online at our website: **www.KingsleyPress.com**
Also available as an eBook for Kindle, Nook and iBooks.

# FIRSTFRUITS AND HARVEST
## By G. H. Lang

Few writers have approached the subject of Biblical prophecy with more diligence and precise thinking than G. H. Lang. His purpose in studying and writing on the end-times and related themes was not to be controversial or sensational, but rather to encourage watchfulness and readiness. The serious reader will find much to challenge both mind and heart in these pages as the writer uses the prophetic Scriptures to give a strong call to holy and careful living.

The secret of G. H. Lang's power and persuasiveness as a writer must surely be attributed to his lifelong dedication to searching the Scriptures, not for the sake of aquiring more knowledge, but in order that he might know God more intimately and follow Him more closely. His great passion was that God's children everywhere would press beyond the shallow and superficial and into a deep understanding of the ways and workings of God. In this respect he was the true successor to such spiritual giants as George Müller, Hudson Taylor, Robert Cleaver Chapman and Anthony Norris Groves.

One of Mr. Lang's contemporaries, Douglas W. Brealey, wrote of him: "I think I may truthfully say that he was the most apostolic man I have ever met; perhaps for that very reason he was a very controversial figure; a correspondent suggested to me that he was the most controversial figure in Brethren circles since J. N. Darby; yet it would be true to say that he himself was not a controversialist. A very close student of the Word, and an independent thinker, he was not prepared to take traditional interpretations unless he were personally convinced that they were right.... To be in his presence was to realize that one was in the presence of a true saint of God whose holy life gave weight and authority to all he taught."

Buy online at our website: **www.KingsleyPress.com**
Also available as an eBook for Kindle, Nook and iBooks.

# The Revival We Need
## by Oswald J. Smith

When Oswald J. Smith wrote this book almost a hundred years ago he felt the most pressing need of the worldwide church was true revival—the kind birthed in desperate prayer and accompanied by deep conviction for sin, godly sorrow, and deep repentance, resulting in a living, victorious faith. If he were alive today he would surely conclude that the need has only become more acute with the passing years.

The author relates how there came a time in his own ministry when he became painfully aware that his efforts were not producing spiritual results. His intense study of the New Testament and past revivals only deepened this conviction. The Word of God, which had proved to be a hammer, a fire and a sword in the hands of apostles and revivalists of bygone days, was powerless in his hands. But as he prayed and sought God in dead earnest for the outpouring of the Holy Spirit, things began to change. Souls came under conviction, repented of their sins, and were lastingly changed.

The earlier chapters of the book contain Smith's heart-stirring messages on the need for authentic revival: how to prepare the way for the Spirit's moving, the tell-tale signs that the work is genuine, and the obstacles that can block up the channels of blessing. These chapters are laced with powerful quotations from revivalists and soul-winners of former times, such as David Brainerd, William Bramwell, John Wesley, Charles Finney, Evan Roberts and many others. The latter chapters detail Smith's own quest for the enduement of power, his soul-travail, and the spiritual fruit that followed.

In his foreword to this book, Jonathan Goforth writes, "Mr. Smith's book, *The Revival We Need*, for its size is the most powerful plea for revival I have ever read. He has truly been led by the Spirit of God in preparing it. To his emphasis for the need of a Holy Spirit revival I can give the heartiest amen. What I saw of revival in Korea and in China is in fullest accord with the revival called for in this book."

Buy online at our website: **www.KingsleyPress.com**
Also available as an eBook for Kindle, Nook and iBooks.

# Lord, Teach Us to Pray
## By Alexander Whyte

Dr. Alexander Whyte (1836-1921) was widely acknowledged to be the greatest Scottish preacher of his day. He was a mighty pulpit orator who thundered against sin, awakening the consciences of his hearers, and then gently leading them to the Savior. He was also a great teacher, who would teach a class of around 500 young men after Sunday night service, instructing them in the way of the Lord more perfectly.

In the later part of Dr. Whyte's ministry, one of his pet topics was prayer. Luke 11:1 was a favorite text and was often used in conjunction with another text as the basis for his sermons on this subject. The sermons printed here represent only a few of the many delivered. But each one is deeply instructive, powerful and convicting.

Nobody else could have preached these sermons; after much reading and re-reading of them that remains the most vivid impression. There can be few more strongly personal documents in the whole literature of the pulpit. . . . When all is said, there is something here that defies analysis—something titanic, something colossal, which makes ordinary preaching seem to lie a long way below such heights as gave the vision in these words, such forces as shaped their appeal. We are driven back on the mystery of a great soul, dealt with in God's secret ways and given more than the ordinary measure of endowment and grace. His hearers have often wondered at his sustained intensity; as Dr. Joseph Parker once wrote of him: "many would have announced the chaining of Satan for a thousand years with less expenditure of vital force" than Dr. Whyte gave to the mere announcing of a hymn. —*From the Preface*

Buy online at our website: **www.KingsleyPress.com**
Also available as an eBook for Kindle, Nook and iBooks.

# The Way of the Cross
## by J. Gregory Mantle

"DYING to self is the *one only way* to life in God," writes Dr. Mantle in this classic work on the cross. "The end of self is the one condition of the promised blessing, and he that is not willing to die to things sinful, *yea, and to things lawful,* if they come between the spirit and God, cannot enter that world of light and joy and peace, provided on this side of heaven's gates, where thoughts and wishes, words and works, delivered from the perverting power of self—revolve round Jesus Christ, as the planets revolve around the central sun...

"It is a law of dynamics that two objects cannot occupy the same space at the same time, and if we are ignorant of the crucifixion of the self-life as an experimental experience, we cannot be filled with the Holy Spirit. 'If thy heart,' says Arndt in his *True Christianity,* 'be full of the world, there will be no room for the Spirit of God to enter; for where the one is the other cannot be.' If, on the contrary, we have endorsed our Saviour's work as the destroyer of the works of the devil, and have claimed to the full the benefits of His death and risen life, what hinders the complete and abiding possession of our being by the Holy Spirit but our unbelief?"

**Rev. J. Gregory Mantle (1853 - 1925)** *had a wide and varied ministry in Great Britain, America, and around the world. For many years he was the well-loved Superintendent of the flourishing Central Hall in Deptford, England, as well as a popular speaker at Keswick and other large conventions for the deepening of spiritual life. He spent the last twelve years of his life in America, where he was associated with Dr. A. B. Simpson and the Christian and Missionary Alliance. He traveled extensively, holding missions and conventions all over the States. He was an avid supporter of foreign missions throughout his entire career. He also edited a missionary paper, and wrote several books.*

# GIPSY SMITH
## HIS LIFE AND WORK

This autobiography of Gipsy Smith (1860-1947) tells the fascinating story of how God's amazing grace reached down into the life of a poor, uneducated gipsy boy and sent him singing and preaching all over Britain and America until he became a household name in many parts and influenced the lives of millions for Christ. He was born and raised in a gipsy tent to parents who made a living selling baskets, tinware and clothes pegs. His father was in and out of jail for various offences, but was gloriously converted during an evangelistic meeting. His mother died when he was only five years old.

Converted at the age of sixteen, Gipsy taught himself to read and write and began to practice preaching. His beautiful singing voice earned him the nickname "the singing gipsy boy," as he sang hymns to the people he met. At age seventeen he became an evangelist with the Christian Mission (which became the Salvation Army) and began to attract large crowds. Leaving the Salvation Army in 1882, he became an itinerant evangelist working with a variety of organizations. It is said that he never had a meeting without conversions. He was a born orator. One of the Boston papers described him as "the greatest of his kind on earth, a spiritual phenomenon, an intellectual prodigy and a musical and oratorical paragon."

His autobiography is full of anedotes and stories from his preaching experiences in many different places. It's a book you won't want to put down until you're finished!

Buy online at our website: **www.KingsleyPress.com**
Also available as an eBook for Kindle, Nook and iBooks.

# THE AWAKENING
## By Marie Monsen

REVIVAL! It was a long time coming. For twenty long years Marie Monsen prayed for revival in China. She had heard reports of how God's Spirit was being poured out in abundance in other countries, particularly in nearby Korea; so she began praying for funds to be able to travel there in order to bring back some of the glowing coals to her own mission field. But that was not God's way. The still, small voice of God seemed to whisper, "What is happening in Korea can happen in China if you will pay the price in prayer." Marie Monsen took up the challenge and gave her solemn promise: "Then I will pray until I receive."

*The Awakening* is Miss Monsen's own vivid account of the revival that came in answer to prayer. Leslie Lyall calls her the "pioneer" of the revival movement—the handmaiden upon whom the Spirit was first poured out. He writes: "Her surgical skill in exposing the sins hidden within the Church and lurking behind the smiling exterior of many a trusted Christian—even many a trusted Christian leader—and her quiet insistence on a clear-cut experience of the new birth set the pattern for others to follow."

The emphasis in these pages is on the place given to prayer both before and during the revival, as well as on the necessity of self-emptying, confession, and repentance in order to make way for the infilling of the Spirit.

One of the best ways to stir ourselves up to pray for revival in our own generation is to read the accounts of past awakenings, such as those found in the pages of this book. Surely God is looking for those in every generation who will solemnly take up the challenge and say, with Marie Monsen, "I will pray until I receive."

Buy online at our website: **www.KingsleyPress.com**
Also available as an eBook for Kindle, Nook and iBooks.

# A Present Help
## By Marie Monsen

Does your faith in the God of the impossible need reviving? Do you think that stories of walls of fire and hosts of guardian angels protecting God's children are only for Bible times? Then you should read the amazing accounts in this book of how God and His unseen armies protected and guided Marie Monsen, a Norwegian missionary to China, as she traveled through bandit-ridden territory spreading the Gospel of Jesus Christ and standing on the prom-ises of God. You will be amazed as she tells of an invading army of looters who ravaged a whole city, yet were not allowed to come near her mission compound because of angels standing sentry over it. Your heart will thrill as she tells of being held captive on a ship for twenty-three days by pirates whom God did not allow to harm her, but instead were compelled to listen to her message of a loving Savior who died for their sin. As you read the many stories in this small volume your faith will be strengthened by the realization that our God is a living God who can still bring protection and peace in the midst of the storms of distress, confusion and terror—a very present help in trouble.

Buy online at our website: **www.KingsleyPress.com**
Also available as an eBook for Kindle, Nook and iBooks.

www.ingramcontent.com/pod-product-compliance
Lightning Source LLC
Chambersburg PA
CBHW070638050426
42451CB00008B/215